Transcending Conquest

Transcending Conquest
Nahua Views of Spanish Colonial Mexico

STEPHANIE WOOD

University of Oklahoma Press : Norman

Also by Stephanie Wood
(ed., with Susan Schroeder and Robert Haskett)
Indian Women of Early Mexico (Norman, 1997)

Library of Congress Cataloging-in-Publication Data

Wood, Stephanie Gail, 1954–
Transcending conquest : Nahua views of Spanish colonial Mexico / Stephanie
Wood.
p. cm.
Includes bibliographical references and index.
ISBN 0-8061-3486-0 (alk. paper)
1. Nahuas—History—Sources. 2. Mexico—History—Spanish colony,
1540–1810—Sources. 3. Nahuas—Attitudes—History. I. Title.
F1221.N3 W66 2003
972'.02–dc21   2002069589

1 2 3 4 5 6 7 8 9 10

Contents

Illustrations

Preface

I grew up picking fruit in the summers to help buy my school clothes, toiling under the hot sun in the agricultural fields of Alta California, formerly an extension of New Spain. It was in the fields that I first started learning Spanish from my co-workers, and it was there that I occasionally heard Mexican indigenous languages spoken to little ones waiting in the shade of a blueberry bush or an apple tree for their parents to finish work.

Seeking an authentic connection to the former Mexican territory, my grandparents, of Scottish and English heritage, proudly built and lived in an adobe house down the road from the blueberry farm. These same grandparents, enamored of California's heritage, named my mother "Ramona." It was ironic that shortly after I gave my daughter the middle name Ramona and one of my old Mexican boyfriends teased me that it was "antiguo y ranchero," a brave Maya rebel leader emerged under this name in Chiapas, alongside the more famous Subcomandante Marcos, giving the name a whole new currency. My little one, Alexis Ramona, is not Maya but is very proud to tell people she is part Cherokee.

Are these the kinds of qualifications that might permit me to write a book about indigenous points of view in early Mexico? Or are these sources of self-identification simply cultural constructions that enable me to justify a passion for a kind of work that some observers might contest as lacking sufficient authority? Are these—in the view of a traditional social scientist—clues to a dearth of objectivity that I might otherwise bring to my research? Is it wishful thinking that a person born on the periphery of a certain culture and historical context can still bring insights to its interpretation that might complement those offered by its direct descendants?

Impressed as I am by my elders and teachers, whose own work testifies to the advances in understanding one might hope to make, I follow with some trepidation on their heels. I hope to improve my skills at native-language document translation and interpretation, to emulate their rigorous attention to detail and their search for patterns, and to learn to better comb the archives for key contextual materials. More than anything, I want to produce a body of work that resonates with people of native and European heritage alike, recapturing in a convincing way vital voices and perspectives overlooked for centuries.

Some might fear that a book about how indigenous people "transcended conquest" will fail to stress sufficiently the disruptiveness of military invasion and colonial rule, will fail to focus on Spanish imperial policy and action as the most important subjects for tracing the evolution of the colonial state—subjects that might provide us with the greatest lessons about imperialism as we face the new millennium. Certainly, we can extract lessons from those kinds of studies. We can use them to forge a new determination to alter hegemonic international relations in the future. Even if this is not precisely one of those books, there are elements of such approaches embedded here.

Some might also object that *Transcending Conquest* will encourage those who believe that one culture may be justified in conquering another and ease their consciences regarding the fate of the conquered. That is definitely not my intention, and if one reads the book carefully, one should find sufficient material to be persuaded that colonialism includes a dialectic of terror and injustice. But my greater intention in this work is not to focus on victimization. It is to foreground views that have been dismissed or denied in Eurocentric histories, to bring greater balance, and to allow readers to derive empowerment from identifying the humanity and creativity of the people who endured the hardships. I hope readers will find inspiration in their stories (or those of their leaders, at least, which the people as a whole seem to have embraced over time), will better appreciate their strategies, struggles, and survivals, and will be able to imagine them as the protagonists of their historical experiences. I hope to highlight the diversity in native responses to the invasion and occupation of American territory. *Transcending Conquest* honors the indigenous people of New Spain as individuals and groups who negotiated, mediated, and exchanged with the invading cultures in complex and sometimes subtle ways, but always as equally important actors on the stage.

In *Transcending Conquest* I hope to stimulate a rethinking of the "conquest" framework that has dominated the historiography and open a new dialogue that incorporates greater consideration for the neglected but striking presence of indigenous identities and memories in Mexican history.

Many thanks are due to various individuals for their contributions, direct or indirect, to this project. Above all, I want to acknowledge James Lockhart for his unselfish Nahuatl (not to mention musical) instruction at his dining-room table, for his impeccable modeling of research methodology and analysis, for his feedback on my scholarship, and for his continuing support as friend and mentor. Reaching even farther back, I also want to mention my undergraduate adviser, David Sweet, for his passionate "people's history" approach that so captured my attention and for his particular formulation of a "struggle and survival" perspective on the history of indigenous peoples of the Americas. To the various referees of my journal articles, commentators on panels where I have given drafts of some of these chapters, and the careful readers of this book manuscript, I extend my sincere gratitude for their thoughtful comments. They are certainly not responsible if I have inadequately followed their advice, but I feel fortunate to have had their learned input.

Let me also tip my hat to the Mexican colleagues I have come to know in the evolution of this project, thanking them for welcoming me into their esteemed circles, especially the periodic symposia on codices where I continue to learn from the expertise of anthropologists and art historians. Among these scholars, Xavier Noguez and Enrique Florescano are foremost in my thoughts. To William B. Taylor I would like to say thanks for introducing me to the indigenous communities of the Toluca Valley when, as an undergraduate, I went off to the archives to study uprisings for my thesis and he so generously provided me with some initial citations and general encouragement. I also wish Woodrow Borah were still with us to see this project come to fruition, because he graciously read and offered advice on some of its contents.

Several institutions showed me generosity, a few of which I wish to recognize here. The staff of the Archivo General de la Nación, Mexico, have graciously and unquestioningly allowed me crucial access over nearly a quarter of a century. The Hispanic Division at the Library of Congress, especially Georgette Dorn and the former director of the *Handbook of Latin*

American Studies, Dolores Martin, and the special people at Dumbarton Oaks, especially the former director of pre-Columbian studies, Elizabeth Hill Boone, kindly provided facilities and services and invited my participation in a way that was beyond the norm. The American Council of Learned Societies also crucially underwrote a year of writing.

The architect Gabriela Quiñones made careful tracings of many of the images analyzed in this study. I wish to thank her for that and for being such a wonderful member of our extended Latin American family.

Finally, I wish to mention my immediate family, including my partner, Bob Haskett, who shares the responsibilities of home, discussions around teaching, and the intensive labor of research and writing. He has shown unwavering support and thoughtful suggestions. I cannot thank him enough. I am particularly indebted to him for our precious gems, our precious green stones, Jeffrey Hugh and Alexis Ramona Haskett-Wood, who keep us from becoming completely and permanently glued to keyboard and monitor. To them I say thanks for your forbearance in allowing us to divide our time between family and work. We treasure you!

S. W.
Eugene, Ore.

Transcending Conquest

I

Rereading the Invasion
UNCOVERING INDIGENOUS VOICES

The subversion of a great empire by a handful of adventurers, taken with all its strange and picturesque accompaniments, has the air of romance rather than of sober history.

So wrote William H. Prescott, celebrated mid-nineteenth-century author of *The History of the Conquest of Mexico*, one of the first seemingly comprehensive treatments of the Spanish invasion of Mexico (Prescott 1964 [1843], 17). His thrilling account of Spanish bravery, luck, and skill in the face of indigenous "barbarity" and, ultimately, military incapacity fired the imaginations of generations of readers. Later historians of what is still commonly called the "conquest" of Mexico produced translations of many Spanish accounts of the events of the first half of the sixteenth century and wrote synthetic studies that perpetuated this image of Spanish ingenuity and prowess. Other Europeans may have "settled" what is now the United States, but Spaniards "conquered" Latin America. In their regularly retranslated and republished letters and memoirs, Spaniards bragged to the king and other European audiences about the fortitude of a small band of astute strategists with phenomenal technology who wrestled power away from the vast and mighty Aztec empire.[1] Armchair adventurers ate it up.

The voices of the new power holders and their latter-day biographers prevailed for centuries. Hernando Cortés, Bernal Díaz del Castillo, Francisco López de Gómara, and their champions confidently drew upon belief in their own racial and cultural superiority and enjoyed recalling how easily the "daring adventurers" had convinced the hapless, superstitious *nat-*

urales, or natives, that they were gods, then quickly seized the advantage.[2] In the wake of Prescott's gritty re-creation of the deeds of the conquistadores,[3] most synthetic studies of the invasion continued to emphasize the invincibility of Spanish arms. The mighty Aztecs were regularly reduced to the status of incapacitated victims unable to cope with the exceptional wits of the Europeans and the fearsome innovations of deadly firearms, snorting, armored horses with lethally pounding hooves, and ferocious dogs of war.

Alternative views won little tolerance. Under Spanish rule, counternarratives could be seized, burned, or stashed away in archives to collect dust. Spanish authorities suppressed, for example, the work of the Franciscan friar Bernardino de Sahagún (Lockhart 1993).[4] Sahagún had the admirable audacity to work with indigenous scholars and their informants in the mid-sixteenth century to record for posterity—in Nahuatl as well as Spanish—native survivors' oral histories of the Spanish invasion. Other accounts, pictorial or textual, were likely hidden away voluntarily for their preservation as people witnessed the destruction of indigenous records at the hands of less open-minded ecclesiastics and civil officials. Fortunately, the need for internal record-keeping thrived. Manuscripts continued to be produced in relative secrecy as the years of colonization wore on, and some have survived to the present day. But it was centuries before such documents began to come to light.

Sympathetic European defenders of the indigenous cause periodically tried to speak on native peoples' behalf but, ironically, may have ended up perpetuating the dominance of the conquistador's voice and image of power. The zealous Dominican friar (and reformed participant) Bartolomé de Las Casas, in his *Brevísima relación de la destruición de las Indias* (1999 [1552]; Montiel 1992, 31), condemned the Spanish invasion and excoriated his fellow Europeans for their brutality, for the unthinkable yet starkly real destruction of millions of indigenous lives through violence and epidemic disease.[5] In the process, his work spawned a thoroughly negative memory of the Spaniards, a narrative of excessive and deliberate cruelty known as the "black legend."[6] Yet while black legend accounts sympathize with or even take the side of the "downtrodden," they give true agency only to the Spanish invaders. In the very success of the Spaniards' allegedly horrific deeds, the image of invincibility remained and perhaps even became enhanced; the hapless victims remained just that, faceless objects of Spanish greed, cruelty, and aggression, incapable of meeting either the physical or the intellectual challenges of the supposedly definitive "conquest."

Some historians of recent times have approached the question of the Spanish colonial enterprise and its extreme consequences more dispassionately. Recognition is growing that if the population of Mexico dropped from more than 25 million to perhaps just over 1 million persons by 1580 (Borah and Cook 1963, 4, 88),[7] it was in large part owing to what we technically call "virgin soil epidemics," in which diseases spread like wildfire among local populations previously unexposed to such imported germs. Sharpening the virulence of this unintentional catastrophe were battles for power, excessive labor demands, and intolerance for certain indigenous ways; yet some scholars have also demonstrated how, at least in the central areas of Mesoamerica and Peru, Spanish colonists wanted the indigenous people to live. Only then—in the most mercenary view—could they become laborers and tribute payers, and so the custom was to preserve and build upon indigenous cultural, social, economic, and political structures (Lockhart 1992).[8]

ELEVATING INDIGENOUS PERSPECTIVES

Recent years have witnessed a strong desire in some academic quarters to elevate indigenous perspectives while simultaneously questioning imperialism. Notable contributions in this vein are a book by Guillermo Bonfil Batalla (1987) and an essay by Michael Kearney and Stefano Varese (1995). Bonfil Batalla's spirited manifesto, *México profundo* (1987, xv–xviii), challenges people to tap the enormous cultural potential of the social sectors, largely indigenous, that make up the bulk of Mexican society. He points to the fallacy behind the supposed mestizo nation, of mixed heritage yet culturally unified, which disavows its predominantly "Indian face" (1987, 15, 61, 165). He calls for a new consciousness that draws lessons from the ways in which this social sector made its own survival possible over the past five hundred years, despite the European invasion and the tenacious and wrongheaded efforts of the elite, power-wielding, and outward-oriented "imaginary Mexico" to "Westernize" it.

Unfortunately, Bonfil Batalla's study of the colonial experience focuses on policies and programs that were determined to alter indigenous communities—policies that wreaked havoc but in significant ways failed, given the evidence he provides for the continuing Mesoamerican stamp on Mexican life today. He rightfully asks us to understand better how these citizens "fought to continue being themselves, not to give up being the protagonists of their own history" (1987, xix), but in his chapter about the first centuries of an enduring colonialism, he relies, ironically, on European sources and actions, perpetuating a view of indigenous people as objects and not actors, their voices from the period in question still stifled.

In "Latin America's Indigenous Peoples: Changing Identities and Forms of Resistance," Michael Kearney and Stefano Varese remind us of the tension between identities formed by "othering" and by "self-attribution" (1995, 208). Yet in their very next paragraph they emphasize that "the identity of *indígenas* was shaped by their subordinate position as colonized subjects." Except for noting a few rebellions during the Spanish era, the authors again state that "the identity of the *indígenas* during the Conquest and colonial periods was shaped mainly by Spanish, Portuguese, French and English policies" (1995, 209). As sympathetic as they are toward indigenous peoples' struggles for autonomy and self-determination in the neoliberal world, for earlier periods they reduce such people to "passive subjects of history made by Europeans and other non-*indígenas*" (1995, 216). One wonders whether the people who occupied indigenous communities under Spanish rule would recognize themselves in these descriptions. Would they have embraced such identities? Or do these identities, grievously lacking in crucial elements, tell us more about the perspectives of the nonindigenous?

A great deal more remains to be said today about the first centuries of the colonial experience. In order to paint a new picture of the roles of indigenous peoples in the transformation of their societies as a result of invasion and colonization, we absolutely must draw from their internal historical sources and discourse. Major advances have been made in bringing to light material that will help correct some of the distortions. Sahagún's vital work has been rediscovered, translated, and published, providing us with unsuspected new ingredients in the drama behind the Spanish seizure of power. Sahagún only partly sought to "extract some truths," as he put it (Lockhart 1993, 49), about the battle for power and nature of the colony. He was at least publicly more concerned with scientifically recording the Nahuas' vocabulary of war. Yet in spite of itself, his compilation of testimonials shows how the Nahua warriors were not stupefied but quickly learned to dodge cannonballs and set up effective ambushes, even if such tactics availed little in the long run. The account provides a heartbreakingly hard-edged description of the painful and disorienting world of epidemic disease: "The pustules that covered people caused great desolation; very many died of them, and many just starved to death; starvation reigned, and no one took care of others any longer" (translation from Lockhart 1993, 182).[9]

Scholars in our own era have begun to give deserved attention, particularly in the form of Spanish and English translations, to the many surviving native-language texts that were produced either with the friars' guidance or thanks to the friars' teaching the surviving elite indigenous males to write in their own languages but with the Roman alphabet.[10] Miguel León-Portilla advanced this pursuit considerably with his anthology *Visión de los vencidos* (1959; in English translation, *The Broken Spears*, 1962), which countless undergraduates have devoured in the intervening years.[11] It is no coincidence that an expanded and updated English version of León-Portilla's work rolled off the presses in 1992, the year of the five-hundredth anniversary of Columbus's landfall, when intellectuals on both sides of the Atlantic engaged in heated debates over the nature, consequences, and morality of the European invasion of the Western Hemisphere.[12] Although very popular, this volume might mistakenly be received as representative of communities outside the Mexican capital and beyond the sixteenth century. It also leaves a lingering impression of weak indigenous leadership, with a focus on Moctezuma, and of gullible people immobilized by the Spaniards-as-gods notion. The title of Nathan Wachtel's *Vision of the Vanquished* (1977) strikes a similar tone, as does the more recent *Los conquistados* (Bonilla 1992). One would hardly imagine that "the conquered" or "the vanquished" were participants in a contentious scene in which rioting and "indefatigable litigiousness" (Van Young 1996, 144) were regular features of daily life (see Taylor 1972, 1979, 1993).

We People Here: Nahuatl Accounts of the Conquest of Mexico, with translations and analysis by James Lockhart (1993), emerged in the same period as the second edition of *The Broken Spears*. This book offers side-by-side, multilingual versions of key texts with added attention to context, forms of expression, and ways of thinking. Together, through such publications, León-Portilla and Lockhart have introduced a broad audience to a different kind of colonial discourse, "the Nahuas' version and vision of things" (Lockhart 1993, 2).[13]

As such ground-breaking English translations and analyses show,[14] native-language accounts of the Spanish invasion are shot through with conceptual complexity and encompass a variety of genres and multiple viewpoints. Among the hundreds of indigenous ethnicities, one finds strong feelings of micropatriotism that kept people loyal to their own sociopolitical unit. There was little or no "pan-Indianism," no unified response, no united front to the Spanish invasion.[15] Some groups, such as the Tlaxcalans, who allied themselves with the invaders, risked everything when they gambled that the Spaniards would turn out to be the "winners." The Aztecs ended up "losers" after they lost their own wager by at first trying persuasion and then more aggressively resisting the Spaniards and their indigenous allies to the bitter end (Lockhart 1993, 6).

The major texts of the invasion, thought to have been produced closest in time to the actual events being described, have logically preoccupied the majority of scholars seeking indigenous voices. Getting as near as possible to initial encounters, responses, and reactions is obviously desirable. The corrosive impact of fading memory is only one concern. Obtaining indigenous views that were least influenced by the culture changes set in motion by the new foreign authority figures—especially the Catholic friars—is another part of this goal, although identifying such influences and their effects continues to be another significant challenge and an illuminating endeavor.

COMPLEXITIES OF INDIGENOUS IDENTITY

The deceptively "eyewitness" accounts of the invasion turn out to deliver their own brand of challenges to investigators. Lockhart (1993, 3) believes that what has been regarded as the earliest indigenous-language text on the Spanish invasion, the *Anales de Tlatelolco*, dates not from 1528, as previously thought, but from the 1540s or later—unfortunately, two decades or more after Spain captured power in the capital. In fact, the majority of significant early indigenous accounts date from the mid-sixteenth century or later, a time when *mestizaje*, or cultural and biological mixing, was already proliferating and possibly influencing the thinking of many of the chroniclers and annalists writing in Nahuatl, inadvertently breaking down

8

the sometimes convenient but perhaps too facile Spanish-Indian binary. Were these authors truly "indigenous"? Or should we think of them as "half-caste" in their outlook (Todorov 1987, 201), or as "hybrid"? These are questions of considerable import for understanding issues of ethnic identity and their impact on constructions of historical memory.

It becomes complicated to conceive of a "pure" indigenous view of the European invasion after Spain took power in 1521. Cultural exchange and the rise of a mixed-heritage generation with divided loyalties cloud the clear delineation of an unaltered native view. Yet to split the binary into a triad and speak of three categorical perspectives—Spanish, mestizo, and indigenous—also causes discomfort, for there was considerable internal diversity in each ethnic grouping, and positions were rarely static over time.[16] Mestizos tended to try to locate themselves within either the largely Spanish world or the largely indigenous world, depending upon their parentage, means, and predilection. Some indigenous people and mestizos naturally crossed the boundaries or dwelt in the intersecting zone between the two worlds, taking sometimes one side, sometimes the other, depending upon how they might better be served, but such negotiations did not erase the general distinctions between the two worlds. Still, we must resist the temptation to discount the mixed-heritage perspectives as primarily Spanish.[17] Many of the earliest mestizos, despite contact with Spaniards, were raised by indigenous parents (often mothers) inside the indigenous milieu and continued to hold outlooks that were essentially indigenous—not in the sense of pre-Columbian or culturally and biologically "pure," but in the evolving, negotiated, political senses of the term.

Because identities were so permeable and changing, making their clear definition elusive, perhaps we can obtain greater profit from examining the process behind an identity's construction and the relationships between different cultural and social groups. As Dana Leibsohn (1994, 161) has written recently, "To speak of 'identity' is to evoke a constantly shifting set of positions, a series of inter-linked negotiations between self and world." Because indigenous people far outnumbered both Spaniards and mestizos in New Spain for quite a while, and despite ethnic variation, some circumstances provided for the possibility of an indigenous common ground, even if such unity rarely coalesced.

It is likely that what Wachtel (1977, 202) found for sixteenth-century Peru was true for Mexico as well: "Although the [indigenous] imperial

9

edifice as a whole crumbled away, here and there local or partial versions of the old order remained and in some cases were strengthened." Given the demographic losses, such an image surprises us. But in the central highlands of New Spain, as in Peru, population density was such that a critical mass of people endured the waves of epidemic disease and was able to preserve a way of life that was undoubtedly changed yet still more indigenous than anything else. Large numbers of the survivors continued to live in predominantly indigenous communities and neighborhoods, speaking and writing in their own languages, dressing distinctively, farming and eating maize, beans, and other mostly local foods, living in housing with ancient architectural styles, choosing their own local leaders, and thinking about or worshiping the spiritual world in some traditional ways.[18] A battle for self-determination and autonomy within the foreign political framework persisted and thrived, particularly in the central-area pueblos, contributing to the longevity of their identification by outsiders as "pueblos de indios" composed of "naturales."[19]

People involved in this dynamic process of adaptation and survival developed their own unique ways of looking at and explaining the Spanish presence in their lives. Individual survivors of lower social rank, whose voices were less likely to be recorded, surely held additional, unelaborated class and gender perspectives that we may never recover and about which we may only speculate. We are fortunate, though, that some people lived to draw, paint, and write their ideas down on paper. We can and should try to hear and at least begin to understand their voices.

LOCATING AND INTERPRETING NEW VOICES

One might travel down a number of different roads in search of these voices. If we must look for "responses" to Spanish pretensions of overlordship, then revolts speak loudly about oppressive conditions and hint at dreams of liberation in its varying degrees. Passive acts of resistance provide testimony not only to constraints but to ingenuity and creativity. Even modern indigenous theater can recall the era of the Spanish invasion and imperial takeover. Wachtel (1977, 159) wrote of these and other phenomena for sixteenth-century Peru, and Max Harris (1990, 1992, 1993, 1994) more recently has done the same for central Mexico. A notable study of rebellion in central New Spain and Oaxaca is that of William B. Taylor's

(1979). Following another fork in the road, Serge Gruzinski (1989) has brought us fascinating life stories of unusual individuals' responses to colonialism and Catholic evangelization in Mexico, which landed such people in front of ecclesiastic tribunals, accused of idolatry and witchcraft.

Other investigative avenues are being explored today, but we have yet to exhaust the analytical potential of many kinds of sources, particularly the large volume of those produced in the central Mexican highlands. An excellent and incompletely explored path lies sketched out in paintbrush and pen in the many indigenous manuscripts, pictorial and textual, that give us concrete expressions and statements with which to grapple. Although Michel Foucault (1972, 227) cautioned us against a complacent certainty in our pursuit of the thoughts or ideas behind words, we can still probe the gap and search for reliable links. One strength of the New Philology movement in Nahua studies (see Lockhart 1991, ch. 11), which has influenced some parts of the study at hand, is its documentation and contextual analysis of multiple attestations of certain indigenous terms (and their sometimes elusive underlying concepts) as they appear in native-language texts. Indigenous written expression now two or more centuries old can seem inscrutable, but patient and continuous study, comparison, and recovery of historical context can lead to new revelations and understandings.

Even more challenging than words are graphic images. Depending on the observer, one image can elicit myriad interpretations, none of which may have anything to do with the artist's original intent.[20] But specialists in the study of codices are sharpening their skills, becoming ever more confident in their ability to approximate the intended meanings of gestures, poses, encoded details, and compositions, fully aware that the loss inherent in not trying makes the risk of failure worthwhile. Truth and meaning—however multiple, relative, tentative, or illusive they may be—are still highly worthwhile objects of pursuit, whether they hide behind words or behind images. In the quest to distinguish realities, we strive to find greater sensitivity and awareness and to cultivate dialogue and improved, multilateral comprehension.

Luckily for us, tucked away in dusty boxes of litigation records and other old documents in the national, state, parish, municipal, and private archives of Mexico, or scattered like leaves to repositories in all corners of the earth, are manuscripts written and painted by individuals literate in native languages such as Nahuatl, who lived the Spanish colonial experience and reflected on it. To examine a representative sampling of these little-known testimonials is my driving purpose in this book. I closely study two contrasting discourses (pro- and anticolonial) and undertake surveys of two groups of manuscripts—one pictorial and relatively early in the chronology of New Spain, the other textual and relatively late.

The indigenous views of the Spanish invasion and occupation of Mexico contained in the lesser-known manuscripts I analyze were directed, in large part, to an internal audience. Many of the documents appear to have been made away from the watchful eyes of ecclesiastics. Often, their artists or authors were less skilled than the notaries and painters who received more concentrated coaching from the friars. Sometimes these manuscripts do not conform neatly to the more formal genres preferred by the trained elites. None of this undercuts their essential importance. Indeed, it is one of their assets. In turning our attention to these less orthodox sources we discover more keys for unlocking the mystery of how the indigenous legacy and living presence can be so evident in Mexico today in the face of so much loss and destruction over the past five centuries.[21]

We historians can be overdependent upon the written word, rooted as we are in the analysis of textual documents, often preferably of European genres. This may be why colonial Mexican pictorials of humbler origins, such as *lienzos* and *mapas*—canvases and manuscripts that might describe landholdings in a certain territory, record the genealogies of a region, or depict images of local history—seemingly made by untrained painter-scribes, have yet to be utilized in any significant way by anyone other than art historians, and only relatively recently by them. In this book I hope to tap such pictorial records for insights possibly overlooked in the more usual textual sources. These kinds of "writings without words" (Boone and Mignolo 1994; Mignolo 1995) were not only abundant but also enjoyed longevity, eventually merging with a text-based tradition in native communities as time passed.

By the same token, it is still rare, though becoming less so (see Lockhart 1991, 39–64; Gruzinski 1993, 98–141; Pohl 1994b, 1–17; Restall 1998), to find scholars analyzing material from locally focused, indigenous alphabetic histories such as annals and the later colonial *títulos primordiales*, "primordial titles," accretive community histories written by nonprofessionals and often emphasizing land tenure and provincial authority. Those of us trained to place importance on texts with precise dates and "original" copies find it difficult to cope with manuscripts whose foundations are oral, whose chronologies are not always lineal, and whose written forms have been recopied and amended over generations or centuries. But such writings not only record indigenous perspectives on the history of the euphemistically labeled "encounter"; they are also records in and of themselves of the agency indigenous people exerted in the emerging colony.[22]

The study of these kinds of unorthodox and overlooked manuscripts can both broaden and deepen insights that have already been developed in recent scholarship. They can add to the repertoires of investigators who, whether consciously or not, entertain postmodernist or postcolonialist perspectives that "challenge the grand march of western historicism" (Barker, Hulme, and Iversen 1994, 22, quoting McClintock), a historicism that centered on, explained, and justified European colonization of other parts of the world.[23] Attention to localized indigenous worldviews will certainly support the reconstruction of history by giving increased attention to "local geographies and histories . . . [in order] to allow them to count in a way previously denied," as part of a "counterhegemonic" strategy (Barker, Hulme, and Iversen 1994, 22).[24] It will also help as we strive to reconceive of the "colonized subject" as an "author or agent of discourses" (Adorno 1988, 20; my translations) and transform the history of people some have called "subalterns" (e.g., Beverley 1992, 7) until they are no longer envisioned as either subjugated or othered. In the process we will seek insights into the evolution of cultural constructions of domination, both as exercised and as imagined.

Many scholars are finding that when indigenous people incorporated the foreign, they often did so by reinterpreting it to fit existing structures. In Yucatán, argues Inga Clendinnen (1987, 158), when "some adjustment and some innovation in those traditional forms" took place, the meaning and the purpose "remained obdurately Mayan." In *The Nahuas*, Lockhart (1992, 243) notes, "A general principle of Spanish-Nahua interaction is that wherever the two cultures ran parallel, the Nahuas would soon adopt the relevant Spanish form without abandoning the essence of their own form." Frances Berdan's (1993:190–92) analysis of the cultural meaning of the Spanish invasion of Mexico concludes with an emphasis on "considerable continuity of native forms." Louise Burkhart (1989) has also demonstrated the endurance and strength of indigenous religious modes of thought

13

among the Nahuas, showing us convincingly how we need to rethink the concept of syncretism. What appears to some as a hodgepodge of fused traditions was for Burkhart the product of a selective adoption and remodeling of Christian ways, resulting in a Nahua Christianity.

It is true that ecclesiastics did their best to reshape such thinking and behavior through a concerted program of doctrinal instruction, which did obtain some results. The clergy's impact was surely greatest on the more educated native writers. Franciscan friars, especially, launched Nahuatl literacy in highland Mexican cities in the first half of the sixteenth century, leading to the production of Nahuatl documents in increasing abundance and variety from about the 1540s forward (Lockhart 1992, 33).[25] Those produced in the schools and under close ecclesiastical inspection would have differed from the more independent or mundane records. Sahagún's immense oral history project, begun around 1547 and spanning perhaps half a century, involved individuals who had received Spanish tutelage of various kinds, included questions molded by the friar, and went through multiple drafts and reshapings under his guidance or by his very hand (Lockhart 1993, 27).[26] The *Relación de Michoacán*, which contains Uacúsecha accounts of the Spanish invasion and seizure of power in that central-western state,[27] was similarly compiled by a Franciscan friar, probably Jerónimo de Alcalá, whom James Krippner-Martínez describes as one of the account's "authorial voices." This friar's influence "as translator, transcriber and editor hangs over the entire compilation" (Krippner-Martínez 1990, 177, 181). Of Toribio Motolinia's *Historia de los indios de la Nueva España*, Tzvetan Todorov (1987, 225) writes, "The content comes from informants, the point of view from Motolinía; but how are we to know where one stops and the other begins?" Sometimes these ecclesiastics concealed information they deemed too "idolatrous." Alternatively, in some clergy's zeal to criticize the behavior of the colonists, they may have encouraged native people to reveal their considerable woes.[28]

Thus, any texts produced at some distance from ecclesiastical interference (whether expurgatory or promotional) and kept isolated in indigenous community archives for extended periods might contain more candid expressions of native views on the power struggle. One feature that increases this likelihood is a text's intended audience. When the audience was someone like the local friar, the judge of the *audiencia* (high court), or the Spanish monarch, we assume that authors slanted the manuscript to appeal to that person. An example is a letter from the pueblo of Hue-jotzingo (fig. 1.1) to the king in 1560, which contains "transparent self-interest" and offers a "public perspective on the conquest and its aftermath" in an effort to obtain rewards for services rendered in support of the European invaders (Lockhart 1993, 46). "Public" is the operative term for describing the tone of this supplicatory document. In striking contrast is the *Historia Tolteca-Chichimeca*, whose authors "were working on their own, for their own factional and corporate purposes, thereby showing us how they spontaneously expressed themselves and what their most urgent concerns were" (Lockhart 1993, 45). Writing for an internal, native audience would not have lessened self-interest, but it would have captured indigenous versions of history that possibly were influenced by the colonizers but were not tailored to meet their scrutiny. It would have established interpretations of the past that future generations within the native communities were expected to embrace. Being inadvertently or intentionally released now for wider consumption, such accounts bring equilibrium to scales that have long tipped in favor of Europeans' own self-interested narratives.

With the recent desire to elevate suppressed indigenous perspectives, and with more investigators digging through archives, our repertoire of native texts and pictorials has been growing and will certainly continue to do so. Expanding our documentary base of indigenous accounts of the Spanish invasion and the solidifying occupation of what became New Spain and later Mexico will enrich our appreciation for the complexities and subtleties of evolving native experiences and responses. In turn, this may help to reconcile the sometimes widely diverging interpretations we have had from scholars to date.

TRANSCENDING DIVERGENT INTERPRETATIONS

With equal access to the already recognized source base, modern interpreters of the Spanish invasion and occupation of Mexico reach remarkably different conclusions about those events. Todorov (1987, 14), for instance, emphasizes a "radical difference" between peoples from either side of the Atlantic and calls the "discovery of the Americans" the "most astonishing encounter" known to history. He continues: "The radical difference between Spaniards and Indians, and the relative ignorance of other

FIGURE I.I. Central Mexico. By Eugene Carpentier.

Acatlan
Acaxochitlan
Tulancingo
1000
2000
3000
3000
3000
3000
Otumba
Acolman
Tepetlaoztoc
Tetzcoco
Huexotia
Coatlichan
3000
Tlaxcala
Humantla
alco/
enco
ula
Tlalmanalco
3000
Amaquemecan
(Amecameca)
Huejotzingo
ngo
tzingo
Calpan
Cholula
Atlauhtlan
Puebla
pan
Chimalhuacan
Cuauhtinchan
4000
3000
ecapixtla
2000

civilizations on the part of the Aztecs, led, as we have seen, to the notion that the Spaniards were gods" (1987, 117).[29] Many other modern observers have joined Todorov in perceiving the Aztecs as immobilized in a way manifested, for instance, in the Aztec emperor's hesitant response, his reluctance to take up a stronger defense and prevent the invaders' march into the capital. Enrique Dussel (1995, 43) writes: "Moctezuma . . . was absolutely determined by the auguries, sorceries, astrological definitions, myths, theories, and other sources that revealed the designs of the [Aztec] gods." Dussel gives to the European player, in contrast, all the agency: "The conquistador exerted his power by denying the Other his dignity, by reducing the Indian to the Same, and by compelling the Indian to become his docile, oppressed instrument" (1995, 44). The image of a world turned "upside down"—the *mundo al revés* that Felipe Guamán Poma de Ayala legitimately decried in his seventeenth-century chronicle—appeals to the imagination more than stories of successful adjustments.[30] One hesitates to speak of adaptation for fear of justifying or rationalizing imperialism. Some well-meaning and sympathetic interpretations, however, reduce the indigenous person to a pathetic pawn.

Diverging considerably from many other scholars, James Lockhart (1993, 5) rejects the common image of Nahua survivors of the Spanish takeover as "a people shocked out of its senses, amazed, bewildered, overwhelmed, benumbed by the intruders, paralyzed, fate-ridden, prepared for imminent doom and disappearance." He believes they probably went "about their business, seeking the advantage of their local entities, interpreting everything about the newcomers as some familiar aspect of their own culture, showing concern with the Spaniards only insofar as they impinged on local life" (1993, 5)—an interpretation supported by indigenous accounts of a later period.

Because we currently have few records, if any, made at the time of the first arrival of the Spanish invaders, we may never be certain of local people's original impressions. It may be that some people were initially stunned but quickly strove to incorporate the invaders into their understanding of the world. According to Marvin Lunenfeld (1991, 268), for instance, the indigenous account of the campaign in Michoacán "demonstrates the natives' effort to locate parallels within their own lives that would help them make sense of the behavior of the newcomers." Such an effort might have been a widespread phenomenon; it corresponds to Lockhart's findings for the Nahuas and even reverberates in the work of James Axtell on North America and the Caribbean.[31] It is likely that indigenous people living under colonialism experienced moments of both pride in successful adjustment and despair due to lost equilibrium—when they contemplated oppressive conditions at all.[32] But we have yet to explore more fully which feelings prevailed most of the time and for which social groups.

The "flashpoint of contact" (Axtell 1992, 297) holds unparalleled drama as we look back today, but the multifaceted indigenous responses and their evolution over the succeeding centuries may better illuminate the lasting essence of foreign colonization in native lives. How thorough and penetrating—or limited—was the so-called conquest? Did native people interpret the events of the early sixteenth century as a "conquest"? How was power negotiated by the stricken population under a colonial regime? Did indigenous people surrender their cultures to an unconscious dependency through gradual integration (Zapata 1992, 203)? Or did they accommodate the new ways and allow change while also defending and protecting (again, sometimes unconsciously) their cultural integrity? To what extent was the Spanish invasion even a lasting preoccupation in their lives? The modern reader cannot assume, just because indigenous writers of the Americas today have imperialism in the forefront of their consciousness, that it was central in the minds of native authors and painters of the seventeenth and eighteenth centuries. A long period of oral tradition intervenes, and ideas and perspectives may have shifted. Certainly, the Spanish colonial presence loomed large and affected many aspects of native people's lives, but the records that embody indigenous memory and identity perhaps selectively emphasize pride in their own leadership and ancestry, their own creation stories, and the moments in history that strengthened their communities and autonomy, that pointed to their own heroism and even their own conquests.

The chapters that follow provide a closer examination of many of these distinct yet fundamentally related issues by intellectually dissecting the images and texts of some of the less familiar manuscripts from the colonial indigenous world. In chapter 2 I survey portraits of Spaniards in the codices.[33] Here we begin our search for a possible *other* other, analyzing native views of Europeans as possibly "different" kinds of beings, the flip side of more standard inquiries. What kinds of Spaniards appear? How are they portrayed? Are there recurring themes, and if so, what accounts for them? How do the pictorial or graphic traditions compare to the emerging textual traditions?

In chapter 3 I approach the same issues in a different way by examining a radically different kind of historical medium.[34] I dissect an anguished report on the Spanish invasion from a small town called Santo Tomás Ajusco. This text represents an extreme viewpoint, conveying sadness, fear, anger, and pragmatism, seemingly expressed in the early years of the Spanish occupation, seemingly with more than a kernel of oral tradition dating from 1531, although some view it as an invented narrative of 1710 (León-Portilla 1992, 159). In an effort to understand how perspectives might have evolved over time, I explore the content of the Ajusco manuscript, searching for temporal clues and comparing it with documents that share themes and a similar tone. Does this obscure manuscript contain a rare memory of the height of the struggle for power between indigenous peoples and Spaniards? Members of the Ajusco community today certainly do not believe this manuscript was invented, and they regularly reaffirm it as part of their official record in public celebrations such as one I was able to witness in 1994.

Next I consider a counterpoint to the Ajusco document in the form of the little-studied, later colonial *Mapa de Cuauhtlantzinco,* from the Tlaxcala region.[35] This vivid manuscript combines pictorial images with brief texts to offer a rare, possibly internal view of an alliance or partnership with the intruders. This one touts the indigenous community's role in aiding—and sometimes taking the lead from—Hernando Cortés and other Spaniards in their Christianization of reluctant converts in nearby communities. The theme is not especially unusual, but the way in which it is framed, as an internal record rather than one aimed at gaining favors from the Crown, makes the manuscript's perspective intriguing for its possible frankness about the famous alliances.[36] No uniform agreement exists about the Tlaxcalan sentiments underlying the public stance of alliance; at least one scholar suggests that "disguised transcripts of dissent" penetrated the dramatic scripts performed in the area in the sixteenth century (Harris 1993). Does the *Mapa de Cuauhtlantzinco* provide a script for a local play about the indigenous-Spanish military and religious front? How does it compare with the *Mapa de Chalchihuapan* (Castro Morales 1969), a similar record from another town in this area? Does the positive portrayal of the Spaniards in both reveal cunning or candor? In chapter 4, regional traditions on the invasion and their complexities come to light.

In chapter 5 I explore texts that raise the issue of perceptions of the "*other* other," of colonialism, of community, and of the past from more moderated positions.[37] These visions are expressed in the illustrated but predominantly textual, Nahuatl-language "primordial titles" of the seventeenth and eighteenth centuries. The titles look back on early colonial events to remember some fear and resistance as well as to celebrate accommodation and change, yet they also exhibit distrust and caution regarding the nonindigenous settlers increasingly in their midst. Against a core of central Mexican *títulos* (Lockhart 1991; Wood 1991; Haskett 1992; Gruzinski 1993) I compare findings from studies of similar manuscripts from Michoacan, Oaxaca, and the Maya zone (Restall 1991, 1998; Terraciano and Sousa 1992; Roskamp 1998), in order to add breadth and probe regional variations. In these records, is the pattern still one in which we find some fear and resistance but ultimately a celebration of accommodation and change? Do titles originating across great distances show a general reverence for Spanish officials yet again exhibit distrust and caution regarding nonindigenous settlers? Might these sentiments represent a mounting groundswell of anti-Spanish sentiment that would pave the way for popular participation in the struggles for independence?

By way of conclusion, I reweave the many separate skeins of this riotously colored intellectual tapestry. I look for general indicators across Mesoamerican cultures and for change over time as indigenous people of central Mexico beheld Europeans' increasing penetration and growing influence in the realm. I revisit the question of a possible radical difference and divinity accorded the Spaniards and the applicability of the European concept of "other" in indigenous people's consciousness as they observed the ever-firmer foothold of the foreigners' presence. After examining a possible other, I shift to a consideration of the indigenous self, especially the self as a possible "conqueror," and ask whether the indigenous self was really a hybrid. Ultimately I examine again the emergence of a spreading anti-Spanish attitude.

My aim in this study, which is in a certain way a collection of thematically related essays, is to substantiate that the Spanish invasion and its aftermath were not monochromatic. They were pastiches of cultural experience enveloping those who were defeated and lost power, their neighbors who helped the European invaders, some who experienced the heat of battle, others who never raised a weapon, citizens of cities and members of small rural communities who survived the epidemics, some who felt early and intense evangelization, others who saw a generation pass before the first priests came to visit regularly, and then the descendants of all of the above, who learned myriad techniques for coping with the emerging colonialism, its economic, social, and cultural diversity, and its exacting demands. I hope to demonstrate how native records transcend the traditional historiographer's fixation on the transfer of power as cataclysmic (surprisingly, often underrepresenting the demographic disaster) and render inaccurate the old assumptions of immediate and thorough domination and destruction in the surviving communities. Indigenous historians constructed identities for their communities and memories to preserve for future generations a heritage of active participation and a native orchestration of crucial events.

2

Pictorial Images of Spaniards
THE *OTHER* OTHER?

They write and –picture the achievement of victory and the conduct of wars, the succession of principal lords, bad weather conditions, noteworthy signs in the sky, and pestilences—at what time and under which lord these things occurred.

THE FRANCISCAN FRIAR MOTOLINIA, DESCRIBING THE NAHUAS' YEAR-COUNT ANNALS, AS QUOTED IN ELIZABETH HILL BOONE, "AZTEC PICTORIAL HISTORIES"

Drawing and painting were already the media of choice for indigenous author-artists alive at the time of the Spanish invasion, including native historians who kept the annals Motolinia described. It is logical, then, that they employed images to record some of their first impressions of the foreigners who invaded their lands in the second decade of the sixteenth century.[1] These invaders were visually remarkable, too, with their fair skin and often lighter hair color, far more body hair, distinctive clothing, hats, and other striking objects of material culture.[2] They consumed unusual foods and beverages, things that members of one North American group described as wood and blood, probably referring to hardtack and wine (Axtell 1991, 8).[3] They traveled in unusually large vessels when on the sea, and some of them rode oversized, deerlike beasts when on land.[4] Giant, salivating dogs accompanied them.

The first figure for this chapter (fig. 2.1) is the small, glyphlike image from the entry for 1518 in the atlas portion of the mid-sixteenth-century *Codex en Cruz* (1981, 21; Robertson 1959, 144–46), enlarged here in order to highlight the details.[5] It shows two profile busts of Spaniards with thick short beards,[6] metal helmets, lances, the Christian cross, and banners, all tucked neatly inside a minimalist, stylized ship sailing west. The sea appears at the bottom in the form of pre-Columbian imagery for water. This glyph-like symbol encodes considerable information about the invaders in the space of about two centimeters and would surely have caught the native eye as something unprecedented, even though it received no extra attention in its size.

In these kinds of records, graphic images actually serve as texts, although sometimes glosses or other written explanations accompany them.[7] Like alphabetic texts, some of these pictorials sought to meet internal, indigenous needs, and others were made at the prompting of ecclesiastical or judicial Spanish colonial authorities.[8] The challenge is to interpret the images as they were intended by the artists who painted them and as they might have been read by indigenous audiences, bearing in mind whenever possible the context that produced each pictorial. With hundreds of extant pictorials produced in as

FIGURE 2.1. Spanish arrival in 1518. Hand drawn by Gabriela Quiñones from the reproduction or "Dibble Copy" of the *Codex en Cruz: Atlas* (1981). Reproduced with permission of the University of Utah Press.

many contexts, the challenge is daunting. The modest goal here is to survey a fairly broad range of graphic images and begin to identify recurring types of figures, contexts, activities, and themes, as well as their general presentation and treatment. A principal question to keep in mind as we survey pictorial material for basic elements is, what can we learn from these images about the way indigenous people viewed the historically unprecedented landing of the European strangers, their seizure of power, and their introduction of a new faith, polity, society, and economy? How did they incorporate all of this into their mind-set and express it in their most familiar medium of nonverbal communication?

It would be ideal to have a chronological catalog of pictorial images, in order to determine how they evolved over time and to see how they interfaced with or were supplanted by textual descriptions. Unfortunately, many or most pictorial manuscripts are difficult to date with precision, as are colonial native texts. Yet we can still think of the pictorial tradition as the older of the two, even if friars gave the production of texts a large boost in certain population centers in the first generation of contact, so that some texts are older than many pictorials. For about a century the two forms continued side by side and overlapped. By the late sixteenth century, however, alphabetic literacy had spread to most central-area indigenous communities, making alphabetic writing the primary medium for native notaries and historians at that time (Glass 1975a, 15; and see Lockhart 1992, 330–31). Still, author-artists, whether notaries or other educated members of these communities, continued to produce pictorials and illustrated texts even into the nineteenth century.[9]

The survey of pictorial manuscripts in the *Handbook of Middle American Indians* includes 434 examples of such documents (Glass 1975a, 15), and many more have been identified in the decades since that census was compiled (see, for example, *Catálogo de Ilustraciones* 1979; Reyes García 1993). Fortunately, a large number of colonial pictorials have been published in whole or in part, some in wonderful facsimile editions. The extensive collection in the library of Pre-Columbian Studies at Dumbarton Oaks in Washington, D.C., gave me an excellent starting point for surveying indigenous pictorial images of Spaniards, with various other repositories and interlibrary loan helping to broaden this base.[10]

The Spanish colonists referred to these pictorial records—usually made on European paper, sometimes on native bark paper or fabric, and less often on animal skin—nearly indiscriminately as *pinturas* or *mapas,* among other names that we continue to use today. But in Spanish the preferred generic term for pictorials is now *códices*—in English, "codex" in the singular, "codices" in the plural.[11] Although we recognize only about a dozen as genuinely pre-Columbian today, large numbers of codices (loosely defined) survive from the post-invasion period. A majority of them record historical information of some kind. Among the more obvious pictorial histories are the genealogical histories, cartographic histories, and year-count annals (see Boone 1994b), but indigenous documents of all types can have historical references. A great many pictorial manuscripts include images of Spaniards, marking first the invasion and then their activities during the establishment and evolution of the colony. Any search for indigenous Mexican views of the Spanish invaders and settlers should therefore start with native colonial pictorial records.

THE INVADER

After scanning only a few codices, one quickly realizes that these manuscripts contain abundant images of assorted Spaniards involved in varied activities. Perhaps least surprising from our modern historical perspective, with its overemphasis on the European landing as the defining moment, is the presence of the Spanish combatant, dressed for war or participating in scenes of battle. In some cases he—Spaniards are nearly always pictured as male[12]—appears counterpoised against an indigenous warrior, usually also male,[13] almost as if the Spaniard and the indigenous man are equally powerful, even though they are outfitted somewhat differently. This is the case, for example, in figure 2.2, from the *Azcatitlan Codex* (Smith 1968, 162, 166), which shows two figures of equal size face-to-face, gripping shields and swords beneath a European-style banner. In European symbolism, the banner would suggest a contest over dominion, which may be how the indigenous artist also saw it. Interestingly, the Spaniard's shield seems to be adorned with the sun's face, possibly a graphic representation of the appellation Children of the Sun, which at least one Nahuatl text from Oaxaca employs to refer to Spaniards (Terraciano and Sousa 1992, 45, 73, and n. 86, 87). The *Relación de Itztepexic,* from Oaxaca, also refers to the "new people who came dressed in iron . . . who were said to be sons of God or the Sun" (Acuña 1984, 2:249; my translation).[14] Still, the image

FIGURE 2.2. Battle scene. Hand drawn by Gabriela Quiñones from a leaf of the *Códice de Azcatitlan,* Bibliotheque Nationale de France, Mexican Manuscript 59-64. Reproduced with permission.

from the *Azcatitlan Codex* paints the Spaniard no more godlike than his native opponent.

There are images, in contrast to this image of parity, in which indigenous warriors appear to have the advantage. In a depiction of a Mexica counterattack that followed a massacre, the native warriors occupy more space, are painted in color, and advance with strength and bravery, having cornered the Spanish opposition, which appears only in black and white (Gruzinski 1992, 46–67).

In other manuscripts, such as the *Códice Telleriano-Remensis,* from the Valley of Mexico in the 1560s, the foreign invader can appear more powerful and better prepared for war than the native warrior. In the scene associated with the year 1541 (*Codex Telleriano-Remensis* 1995, 95), the indigenous warrior is completely nude and therefore seems more vulnerable, at least according to a European reading.[15] In the battle scene of 1521 depicted in the *Histoire Mexicaine,* or Mexican Manuscript number 40 in the Bibliothèque Nationale de France (hereafter, BNF-MM40), a sixteenth-century chronicle from Mexico City, the figures of the Spaniards are a little larger and their armor is more detailed in comparison with the indigenous figures (fig. 2.3). The author-painter gave greater attention, at least, to the European invaders. But those interlopers were the fascinating creatures of an unknown culture, whose every detail could be remarkable, especially while it was something new and different. It is instructive that the Spanish fighters do not appear so disproportionately large as to be superhuman and are neither monsterlike nor godlike. The firearm is probably the most formidable element, yet in this scene it does not appear especially large or destructive.

FIGURE 2.3. Battle scene. Hand drawn by Gabriela Quiñones from a leaf of the *Histoire Mexicaine,* Bibliotheque Nationale de France, Mexican Manuscript 40. Reproduced with permission.

The invaders' attire and weaponry, however, could sometimes have lent an impression of ferocity. Their metallic garb attracted considerable attention in native texts such as the *Florentine Codex* (Lockhart 1993, 96), which states, "Some of them came wearing iron all over, turned into iron beings, gleaming. So that they aroused great fear and were generally seen with fear and dread." The *Título C'oyoi* of Guatemala lists the impressive weapons of the newly arriving foreigners: "lances, battle axes, rifles, shields, and swords; all the chiefs were finished, killed by the metal weapons they used against them" (Carmack 1973, 302). In the pictorials they also carry deadly weapons, including firearms, swords, and lances. Yet while European arms could be daunting, so could the indigenous *macana*, a club with imbedded obsidian blades (fig. 2.3), described by the Spanish chronicler Bernal Díaz del Castillo (1963, 145) as having nearly completely severed a horse's head. Perhaps, in the indigenous view, the sword and the macana were complementary. In the *Florentine Codex,* furthermore, descriptions of the foreigners' weapons make them sound like works of art and beauty, possibly even coveted objects: "Their iron lances and halberds seemed to sparkle, and their iron swords were curved like a stream of water" (Lockhart 1993, 96).

Although there is some variation in the size and presentation of Spanish warriors from one manuscript to another, possibly indicating who had the alternating upper hand, for the most part the combatants appear to be men squaring off against other men, not humble humans fighting an impossible battle against all-powerful deities. The battles appear to be deadly serious, but a sense of abnormally heightened fear is difficult to find. The drama behind the Europeans' victory—proverbially achieved despite being vastly outnumbered, though in reality supported by thousands of indigenous allies—is appropriately absent.

The portrayal of Spaniards in the *Codex en Cruz* (fig. 2.1), which captures a memory of the expedition of Juan de Grijalva (Díaz 1963, 27–43), one of the voyages launched from Cuba that explored Yucatán and the Gulf of Mexico in 1518, prior to the Cortés expedition, intentionally or incidentally conveys the militarized nature of their "exploration" while reminding viewers of the central presence of the cross. It is an ominous marker to those of us today who know of the considerable and lasting consequences of transatlantic contact. Yet what is especially noteworthy is the ease with which this tiny image enters into the record, quietly and even inadvertently marking the transition from the so-called pre-Columbian epoch to the Spanish colonial, making scarcely a splash across the page. Of course, if the original version of this record was not made in the same year as the sighting, but rather in retrospect, then the impact of the first appearance of those unusual boats with strange men would have been diminished somewhat.

Still, the memory of a similar sighting does hold some prominence in written texts. The *Florentine Codex* (quoted in Gruzinski 1992, 38) recalls at mid-century how a scout witnessed a Spanish vessel for the first time: "There was a terrible thing in the bay, it was big and round, in the middle of the water, and went back and forth on the waves." Serge Gruzinski (1992, 38–39) reproduces a comparable event, attributed to 1517, from the *Codex Durán*, possibly the expedition of Francisco Hernández (Díaz 1963, 15–26), in which we can see an indigenous scout looking down upon the water from a treetop. But again, this picture conveys no fear; it is even less ominous than the quiet image of the *Codex en Cruz*. Here, one unarmed Spaniard sits alone in a small launch near a larger ship, pulling a fish out of the water with a pole while three other Spaniards, also unarmed, watch from the decks above. None of the Spaniards wears armor; all seem most concerned with getting their meal.

In some codices we do find scenes of the period of most intense conflict, which today can appear tragic and stir anti-imperialist sentiment. Bodies of indigenous people, cut up in pieces, lie strewn over the steps of pyramids or spread out over the ground, as we see in the *Durán Codex* from the sixteenth-century Valley of Mexico (Gruzinski 1992, 42), the *Lienzo de Analco* from the sixteenth-century Villa Alta, Oaxaca (Blom 1945, fig. 5), Book 12 of the *Florentine Codex* (Lockhart 1993, 50), the BNF-MM40 (fig. 2.3; Lehmann 1981, 345), and many scenes from the *Lienzo de Tlax-cala* (*Antigüedades mexicanas* 1892, lám. 9, 14, etc.). But was this portrayal of carnage a desensitized formula for conquest that the native painters had long employed? A reading of terror behind segmented body parts is more European than indigenous.[16] Further, for the Nahuas, the spilling of blood was viewed as an important means of feeding the earth and sustaining the heavens, keeping the cosmos in balance. This is not to say that survivors of the battle for power were not traumatized by their losses, as texts such as the *Cantares Mexicanos* (Bierhorst 1985, 151) attest: "Only sad flowers, sad songs, lie here in Mexico . . . it's misery, yes, it is felt . . . Tears are pouring, teardrops are raining there in Tlatelolco . . . The smoke is rising, the haze is spreading."

Illustrations of executions by hanging or burning at the stake indigenous people who resisted Christian evangelization or fell back on former ways, such as that in the *Descripción de Tlaxcala* (fig. 2.4), present another dimension of the human drama of this colonization project. Here, Spanish officials and friars coldly point their fingers in authority and admonition as people with manacled hands helplessly burn or hang. Today the hanging cadavers, with their drooping heads, provoke sympathy as well as indignation for the extreme religious intolerance they represent.[17] Shock-

FIGURE 2.4. Executions for religious reasons, directed by Cortés and two friars. Tracing by Gabriela Quiñones from the *Descripción de Tlaxcala* (MS Hunter 242), folio 242r. Reproduced with permission of Glasgow University Library, Department of Special Collections.

ing also is the image in the *Codex Coyoacán*—also known as the *Manuscrito del Aperreamiento,* or "Manuscript of the Dogging"—of a group of indigenous people in chains with a Spaniard allowing (or encouraging) his gigantic dog to attack one of them (fig. 2.5).[18] The Nahuatl version of Book 12 of the *Florentine Codex* (Lockhart 1993, 80) completes the horror of such images in its description of the previously unknown dogs brought by the Spaniards, with their yellow eyes burning like fire, their tongues emerging from their fangs, and their coats spotted like the jaguar. Native dogs were nowhere near the size of the mastiffs, greyhounds, and wolfhounds that crossed the Atlantic (Varner and Varner 1983, xiv). The *Florentine Codex's* description of horses, neighing, sweating, and thunderously pounding the ground (Lockhart 1993, 8), gives the same impression of fright, at least in depictions of the earliest encounters.

Although we have texts that help us interpret some images, in many of these scenes that are so disturbing from a modern perspective we do not know the full intention of the author-painter or whether an indigenous observer of that period would have seen in them a sad, an angry, or a cautionary portrait. An indignant artist, for instance, might have wanted to preserve a memory of an injustice in the loss of life. Another artist might have wanted to show his indigenous audience images of Inquisition-like executions as a somber warning about what could happen to those who did not comply with new laws and regulations. Still other painters, recalling their

FIGURE 2.5. A dogging. Tracing by Gabriela Quiñones from the *Manuscrito del Aperreamiento,* Bibliotheque Nationale de France. Reproduced with permission.

community's warriors who fought alongside the Spaniards, could conceivably have taken pride in presenting an enemy indigenous group in a weak or defeated position as their own people gloated from behind the scenes.

In codices from the region of Tlaxcala, among a few other regions,[19] the European invaders turn up forming alliances with indigenous communities and fighting with these allies at their side. Or rather, the Spaniards are the allies of the indigenous warriors. This relationship, accordingly, demonstrates a positive attitude toward the Spaniards and, by extension, their plan for colonizing Mexico—an attitude often formed after some period of resistance and perhaps regretted by some indigenous groups or individuals as time went by. Gordon Brotherston (1995, 36) reminds us that bloody battles took place on the eastern frontier of Tlaxcala, as we see in the *Códice de Huamantla*, which is reproduced in his book. Charles Gibson (1952, 18–20) also speaks of the initial resistance in Tlaxcala. Some leaders, such as Axayacatl Xicotencatl, wanted to break the alliance with the invaders, and in modern Tlaxcala people still celebrate the memory of the young Xicotencatl, who was executed in 1521 for his opposition to the Spaniards.[20] But in the majority of codices from all over Mexico, a certain amount of respect seems to be accorded the ally or the worthy opponent, embodied in the European victor.

Just as Western histories dwell on the movers and shakers, the omnipresent individual European combatant in the codices is none other than the *capitán*, the captain of the *entrada*, or expedition, later the Marqués del Valle, a title attached to his dominion—Hernando Cortés. He appears nothing like the hunchback with inflamed knees and weak chin of Diego Rivera's mural on the balcony of the National Palace in Mexico City today, a portrait that makes Rivera's disdain for the interloper obvious (see Pellicer and Carillo Azpeitia 1985, 228). The Cortés of the codices has no physical defects. He is a central figure of authority. He frequently meets with the most eminent indigenous lords. It may be that for the author-painters, the presence of the historical figure of Cortés lent importance to documents in which he appeared.[21] He commonly sits on a curule chair, which indigenous painters quickly recognized as the Europeans' seat of authority. He rides a horse, walks with a staff of authority in his hand, or stands pointing his finger (fig. 2.6).[22] The pictorial tradition reserves many of these same actions and iconographs for indigenous dignitaries, indirectly conveying to Cortés the authority or status they typically enjoyed.

FIGURE 2.6. The arrival of Cortés in 1519. Tracing by Gabriela Quiñones from the photograph of the *Tira de Tepechpan* (LC-USZ9-317) in the photographic collection of Mexican Indian Pictorial Documents, Archive of Hispanic Culture, Division of Prints and Photographs, Library of Congress, Washington, D.C., and the photograph published in Boban 1891, 243–73.

Many times the expedition leader appears in the company of the indigenous woman baptized as "doña Marina." Their relationship may provide clues to the way the indigenous author-artists meant to portray Cortés. In figure 2.7 we see her quite close to the *marqués,* speaking and gesticulating with authority. As her title of nobility indicates, doña Marina (here, typically called "Malintzin," the Nahuatlized and reverential form of Marina)[23] enjoyed some status among both indigenous groups and the members of the Cortés expedition, even though she had been victimized by her own family and then lived for a time as a slave in an indigenous community (Karttunen 1994; 1997). Once the Spaniards recognized her unusual linguistic abilities, she served as one of the expedition's principal interpreters and informants. She also bore a child by Cortés, taking a prominent if unfair place in subsequent nationalistic histories of the nineteenth and twentieth centuries as Mexico's Benedict Arnold and a whore—but also as one of the mothers of mestizaje.

The codices completely ignore Malintzin's motherhood and focus on her interpreting. Interpreting involves two-way communication, of course, yet because of her presence in the Spanish camp—originally, at least, not a fate of her own choosing—her principal job was to obtain and disseminate information for the invaders. More specifically, she had to work for Cortés. She was always at his side and, intentionally or not, may have strate-

FIGURE 2.7. Cortés and Malintzin, or doña Marina. Tracing by Gabriela Quiñones from the *Mapa de San Antonio Tepetlan* in the American Museum of Natural History. Reproduced with permission.

gically advanced his effort to seize power. She made his speeches intelligible to indigenous observers and audiences while secondarily conveying their messages back to him.

That she was more his voice than their voice becomes evident when we find that some indigenous people called both Marina and Cortés by the same name—hers. Bernal Díaz del Castillo (1963, 172) wrote that the indigenous people who were just getting to know Cortés originally called him "Marina's Captain" (which would have been *Malintzin ycapitan*), but this got shortened to just Malintzin, or "Malinche" as Díaz wrote it. He also noted how another Spaniard, who went everywhere with Marina trying to learn Nahuatl, also came to be called Malinche. It is interesting that she was the referent in both these cases; in the indigenous perspective, she lent her identity to or shared it with these men.

Pictorial images of Malintzin place her in close proximity to Cortés (fig. 2.7).[24] Sometimes one of the two figures stands in front, more prominent than the other; it is not always clear who is the auxiliary.[25] Perhaps there is a certain pairing and complementarity of the two figures in the indigenous reading. The alliance Cortés forged with this woman (whether or not with her consent) gave him entree into the indigenous world and probably diminished his difference or strangeness in the indigenous viewpoint. She also helped him overcome the considerable barrier that language differences can create between peoples, a barrier that plays a part in the "othering" process.

ECCLESIASTICS

Spanish combatants turn up in the codices not just in battle scenes but also in religious settings, helping to spread the Christian faith. The late colonial *Mapa de Cuauhtlantzinco* (Starr 1898, nos. 12, 13, 12a, 13a; Ojeda Díaz 1985, Fragment 8) provides numerous examples. In one scene (fig. 2.8), Spaniards dressed in armor assist a friar who is administering the sacrament of baptism to some indigenous people in a small community near Cholula. One armored figure stands behind the friar, holding the cross, while the other kneels in front, extending the baptismal font to pros-

FIGURE 2.8. Baptism scene. Sketch by Gabriela Quiñones, based on the copy of the *Mapa de Cuauhtlantzinco* held in the Latin American Library, Tulane University. Reproduced with permission.

trate neophytes. The artist or artists who made these paintings were well versed in European stylistics and Christian ideals. They had also embraced the elevated evangelical motive some Spanish chroniclers accorded the entrada in their own narratives, as we will see in chapter 3.

Ecclesiastics, whether regular or secular, appear with frequency in the pictorials, a frequency that suggests importance and possibly respect. Only rarely do the manuscripts attach an obvious negative connotation to the portrait of an ecclesiastic.[26] In some cases we find a preference for a certain order, such as the Franciscans. They were the first of the three most prominent orders to arrive in the 1520s and 1530s, and together with the Dominicans and Augustinians, they dominated the Christian presence in indigenous communities for many decades (Sell 1992, 159, 170). Georges Baudot (1995, 450) sees the Franciscans as also having taken an especially prominent stance in support of certain "institutions of pre-Hispanic native society." In the *Códice de San Juan Teotihuacán* (*Los códices de México* 1979, 46–47), from about 1557, indigenous people show their resistance to the establishment of the Augustinians. Sometimes, however, what appeared to be a preference for or against a particular order was actually more an attempt to gain local control over changes imposed from outside the community.

The highest clergy generally enjoy an exalted position in the pictorials. Annals announce the arrivals (and later, deaths) of bishops or archbishops in the capital, their representations filed under the appropriate pre-Columbian year signs. Their comings and goings, heralded as occasions for important observations or celebrations in the Spanish community, take precedence over their activities; perhaps the daily routines of high ecclesiastics were not significant or remained something of a mystery in the native view.[27] Similarly, these portraits rarely convey individual identity in a precise manner (unless the images are glossed), but ever present are emblematic accouterments such as the scepter, miter, and vestment that clarify the figures' legitimacy and presiding role (fig. 2.9).[28]

Annals of a more textual nature similarly pay notable attention to representatives of the church. When the arrival of a bishop represents the only event worth mentioning for a certain year, we can get the impression that this was viewed as noteworthy—and more important than any event taking place solely in the indigenous world. (Entries can read "nothing happened" in a given year, or they might mention two to three events.) The

FIGURE 2.9. Bishops and archbishops. Hand drawn by Gabriela Quiñones from small portions of leaves in (1) the *Histoire Mexicaine,* Bibliothèque Nationale de France, Mexican Manuscript 40, folio 17v; (2) the *Códice Telleriano-Remensis,* Bibliothèque Nationale de France, Mexican Manuscript 385; and (3) the *Codex Aubin,* Add. MSS. 31219, folio 49r, British Museum. Reproduced with permission.

Anales de Tlaxcala, 1519–1720, for instance, have this entry for 1529: "11 House year. This is when the bishop of Mexico City, don fray Juan de Zumárraga, arrived."[29] He has a name and a geographic association, and he graced the land with his presence; either nothing more was known about him or nothing more seemed worth recording in the typically economical prose of many of these manuscripts.[30]

In contrast, the friars and secular priests mentioned in the annals enjoy greater agency. They actually visited the indigenous communities and penetrated local life in an increasingly concerted manner. The Tlaxcalan annals state: "1523. 5 Reed year. This was when the friars arrived, and the houses of the devils were torn down" (obviously the author had already been instructed in the new Christian vocabulary for describing indigenous divinities).[31] In the pictorials, too, priests are busy in evangelical activities, setting up crosses, baptizing local people, and leading prayer (fig. 2.10).[32] In the *Codex Yanhuitlán*, from Nochistlán, Oaxaca, in the 1550s, the largest figure is a Dominican friar (fig. 2.11; see also Prem 1974, 731v). Here we see him engaged in another popular exercise, sitting at a desk with quill in hand, possibly holding an audience with or writing on behalf of the much smaller indigenous lords standing to the side of and behind him. The civil authorities from Spain who appear elsewhere in this document are not quite as diminutive as the indigenous lords, but neither are they as prominent as the friar (*Códice de Yanhuitlán* 1940, lám. 8, 19).

CIVIL AND ECONOMIC FIGURES

In general, however, Spanish civil authorities do hold conspicuous places in the codices. For the authors of these documents, the most illustrious king of Spain was Charles V, who governed when the Europeans arrived in Mexico and continued in power until the middle

FIGURE 2.10. Friar with a cross. Hand drawn by Gabriela Quiñones from part of the MATRÍCULA DE HUEJOTZINCO, 731v, Bibliothèque Nationale de France, Mexican Manuscript 387. Reproduced with permission.

FIGURE 2.11. Dominican friar. Hand drawn by Gabriela Quiñones from part of the *Códice de Yanhuitlan*, Academia de las Bellas Artes, Puebla. Reproduced with permission.

of the sixteenth century. In at least three scenes, Charles V—someone who never visited the Americas—is shown receiving various caciques, recognizing their local authority and the territory of their pueblos.[33]

Those who indeed arrived in Mexico were the viceroys, highest colonial representatives of the king. Indigenous annals announce their appearances and departures just as they announce those of bishops and archbishops. Annals also highlight some of the viceroys' major pronouncements. In the text of the *Codex Aubin* we learn of the viceroy's dispatching an expedition to Florida; a small figure of the viceroy or perhaps the expedition leader appears at the right of the text (fig. 2.12). The two first viceroys of Mexico, don Antonio de Mendoza (1535–49) and don Luis

FIGURE 2.12. Viceroy don
Luis de Velasco (the elder).
Hand drawn by Gabriela
Quiñones from the *Códice
Aubin*, Add. MSS. 31219, folio
51v, British Museum. Repro-
duced with permission.

de Velasco, who arrived in
1550 and governed until his
death in 1564, play a notable
role in various activities represented in the codices (fig. 2.13).[34] Often they
participate personally in meetings with members of the indigenous nobility in the pueblos (figs. 2.14, 2.15). We know from the *Tlaxcalan Actas*
(Lockhart, Berdan, and Anderson 1986, 16), for instance, that such visits
were not outside their purview and occurred on various occasions. The

town prepared special feasts for
these official visits. Pueblo dele-
gations also made calls upon the

FIGURE 2.13. Viceroy don Antonio
de Mendoza. Hand drawn by
Gabriela Quiñones from the *Códice
Telleriano-Remensis*, Bibliothèque
Nationale de France, Mexican Manuscript 385, folio 44v. Reproduced
with permission.

FIGURE 2.14. Viceroy with indigenous nobles and interpreter. Hand drawn by Gabriela Quiñones from folio 471v of the *Códice Osuna*, Biblioteca Nacional de España. Reproduced with permission.

FIGURE 2.15. Viceroy Velasco (the elder) with the indigenous judge don Esteban de Guzmán. Tracing by Gabriela Quiñones from the *Códice Osuna*, Biblioteca Nacional de España. Reproduced with permission.

viceroys in Mexico City. In the primordial titles of the later viceregal period—including the Techialoyan codices—Mendoza and Velasco are also "favorites," as we will see in chapter 5 (Lockhart 1991, 59–60; and see Robertson and Robertson 1975, passim).[35]

The regularity of Mendoza's and Velasco's presence in pictorials and texts alike indicates some favoritism for their memory, giving the impression that these viceroys, in contrast to others, better served the interests of the indigenous communities. But these men held office at a crucial time and devised policies that necessarily affected the native population, which was dwindling rapidly. A mercenary view would be that such demographic losses robbed the royal treasury of tribute and colonists of laborers. At any rate, in response, these viceroys pronounced edicts that helped shore up indigenous communities' territorial holdings and semiautonomous municipal governments. The result is that their exalted signatures appear liberally sprinkled throughout whatever early sixteenth-century Spanish-sponsored documents towns could obtain and preserve. From there, the early viceroys' names became legendary in oral tradition, and their portraits regularly made their way into local pictorial and indigenous-language histories.

Provincial authorities known as *corregidores* and *alcaldes mayores,* along with judges of the high court, also surface in the pueblos, acting in a variety of capacities (figs. 2.16–2.18). Corregidores and alcaldes mayores became the intermediaries between indigenous communities and the Spanish royal government by the second generation. They received tribute and managed labor arrangements, passed down pronouncements from higher governmental

FIGURE 2.16. *Corregidor* with indigenous nobles. Tracing by Gabriela Quiñones from the reproduction of the *Códice de Xicotepec* (1995, 153). Reproduced with permission of the Fondo de Cultura Económica, Mexico.

FIGURE 2.17. *Alcalde mayor,* notary, and interpreter. Hand drawn by Gabriela Quiñones from the *Códice Sierra* (1933, appendix facsimile 15). Reproduced with permission of the Instituto Nacional de Antropología e Historia.

FIGURE 2.18. *Oidor* of the *audiencia* (seated). Hand drawn by Gabriela Quiñones from the *Histoire Mexicaine,* Bibliothèque Nationale de France, Mexican Manuscript 40, folio 18v. Reproduced with permission.

authorities, and acted in a judicial capacity. After originally teaching indigenous *cabildos* (town councils) some of the functions of European councils,
by mid-century corregidores usually attended meetings only during annual
council elections, and cabildos became increasingly independent (Lockhart, Berdan, and Anderson 1986, 15–16).[36]

The corregidor in the *Códice de Xicotepec* (fig. 2.16) sits with three
indigenous lords, he in his curule chair and they on their indigenous seats
of authority, all facing the same direction and displaying serious counte-
nances. But the figure of the corregidor is the more commanding of the
four, not only because he is higher off the ground but also because the
artist gave him a somewhat larger scale, elevating his consequence. Nothing in his image necessarily implies tyranny, in contrast with an image from
the *Códice Azoyú I,* from the late sixteenth century in what is now the state
of Guerrero. There we find an example of a corregidor or alcalde mayor
"who has the staff of authority and orders torture by the stocks, boiling
water, hangings, and chains for the indigenous people who have opposed
his mandates," according to Constanza Vega (1991, 87), who identifies in
his actions the image of an oppressor.[37]

Encomenderos appear in some pictorial manuscripts. These holders of
grants enabling access to tribute and labor from a set group of indigenous
persons were competitors of the provincial authorities and clergy in the
pursuit of local influence, and indigenous author-painters apparently felt
little affection for them. According to Charles Gibson (1964, 78), the
encomenderos of the first generation greatly abused their power, demand-
ing excessive labor and exacting heavy taxes. It follows that we find startling images of them in the *Codex Kingsborough,* from the sixteenth-century
region of Tetzcoco (see *Memorial de los Indios de Tepetlaóztoc* 1992, 137),
including a portrait of the encomendero Gonzalo de Salazar holding the
decapitated head of an indigenous person and a portrayal of a man named
"Antón" burning people at the stake (figs. 2.19, 2.20).[38] The *Codex Osuna,*
from the basin of Mexico and Tula, Hidalgo, in the year 1565 (see Robertson 1994, pl. 35), seems to describe either encomenderos or their assis-
tants. It shows them demarcating a reduced plot of land for an indigenous
family and directing the work of indigenous people in agriculture and in
textile sweatshops (figs. 2.21, 2.22), actions that would have been unpop-
ular with most indigenous audiences. This codex represents other complaints, as well, against the obligations of tribute and labor for a judge and

for the viceroy.[39] In the *Códice de Yanhuitlán* (1940, lám. 9), some encomenderos or colonial officials oversee the extraction and delivery of gold dust by indigenous laborers. The painters make no obvious commentaries against these Spaniards, but they portray them wearing armor and standing over the workers, seemingly impatient for the gold.

SPANISH MATERIAL CULTURE

Many times, if their portraits are not glossed, we find it necessary to identify colonial authorities or other Spaniards by their dress or other items of material culture that make up parts of the scenes in which they appear. In the beginning, unknown objects caught the author-artists' attention, probably entering into the pictorials in delightful detail almost as curiosities. Quickly, however, animals and effects such as tables, ships, flags, weapons, and clothing the Spaniards wore came to represent the identity of the new power holders in the colonial system. The props formed integral parts of the portraits and gradually took on lives of their own, becoming potential indicators of indigenous attitudes toward at least certain aspects of the intruding culture.

As in so many other examples of transatlantic encounters, European goods

FIGURE 2.19. The *encomendero* Gonzalo de Salazar holding a decapitated head. Tracing by Gabriela Quiñones from the *Codex Kingsborough* (1912).

FIGURE 2.20. "Antón" burning four indigenous men. Tracing by Gabriela Quiñones from the *Codex Kingsborough* (1912).

FIGURE 2.21. Enclosing indigenous lands. Hand drawn by Gabriela Quiñones from folio 469v of the *Códice Osuna*, Biblioteca Nacional de España. Reproduced with permission.

FIGURE 2.22. Directing agricultural and textile labor. Tracing by Gabriela Quiñones from folio 500v of the *Códice Osuna*, Biblioteca Nacional de España. Reproduced with permission.

formed the basis of relationships between the intruders and native groups (Pendergast 1993, 116, 117). Spaniards typically bore gifts or goods to exchange with indigenous people they would meet on their expeditions, anticipating from earlier experiences that the locals would attach value to such things as necklaces and metal tools. The *Annals of Quauhtitlan* (Lockhart 1993, 281) pay special attention to the gifts Moctezuma received in greeting "the Christians": "a green frock; two capes, one black and one red; two pairs of footwear, shoes; a knife; a hat; a cap; a woolen cloth; a cup; and some beads." If local people resented some things about the intruding culture, they still could look favorably upon the acquisition of certain new items of material culture. In short order their preferences for specific objects became clear. The rationale behind these preferences, however, requires some interpretation. For example, one indigenous noble, a don Gabriel Curi, received a license in 1592 to carry a sword, wear Spanish clothing, and ride a horse (Colín 1968, 78). Textual and pictorial sources alike provide evidence that caciques were acquiring and using these effects of the European colonists, apparently wishing to emulate their behavior and enjoy some of the corresponding status.[40]

The native author-artists showed particular interest in the horse, an animal that is omnipresent in the codices, especially those of the sixteenth century (fig. 2.23).[41] This creature, which originated in the Western Hemisphere but died out long before Europeans reintroduced it, quickly found a comfortable niche in its former habitat. Not that it was welcomed right off the boats with open arms. For some central Mexicans in the flashpoint of contact, it was a startling beast whose hooves made a thunderous sound—"As they went they made a beating, throbbing, and hoof-pounding like throwing stones"—and which made battling its riders a special challenge (*Florentine Codex*, Lockhart 1993, 110, 192). Searching to incorporate horses into their own mental catalog of fauna, the Nahuas called them "people-bearing deer" (Lockhart 1993, 160, 170). Whereas the *Codex en Cruz* depicts the first Spaniards as arriving by ship (fig. 2.1), the *Anales de Tula* (LC/MIPD photograph LC-USZ9-369-20) capture their momentous arrival with an ideographic representation of two horses and their riders. In the graphic images of the *Florentine Codex* (Lockhart 1993, 48–49), horses are numerous.

Pictorial artists and other indigenous observers soon became better acquainted with the horse, observing the way it carried important people

FIGURE 2.23. Horses and a saddle. Hand drawn by Gabriela Quiñones from (1) the *Códice Telleriano-Remensis,* Bibliothèque Nationale de France, Mexican Manuscript 385, folio 44r; (2) the tracing of the *Lienzo de Coixtlahuaca no. 1* in the Latin American Library, Tulane University; (3) the photograph of the *Códice de Huamantla* (LC-USZ9-135-5) in the photographic collection of Mexican Indian Pictorial Documents, Archive of Hispanic Culture, Division of Prints and Photographs, Library of Congress, Washington, D.C.; and (4, 5) the *Códice Sierra,* Instituto Nacional de Antropología e Historia. Reproduced with permission.

on its back, could help make light of labor, demanded a sizable price, required stables and large amounts of fodder, sometimes trampled cornfields, and required a whole array of leather and metal gear. Horses' considerable appetites sometimes placed a serious burden on the indigenous community. The *Codex Aubin* (Lockhart 1993, 276–77) contains an example of concern over fodder for "the deer of the gods" (*inmaçavan yn teteo*) following the massacre in Mexico City during the fiesta of Toxcatl; with supplies being scarce, horses were eating reed mats. The *Tlaxcalan Actas* (Lockhart, Berdan, and Anderson 1986, 39) show the town council conferring on the need to build a corral to house the recalcitrant "cattle, sheep, and horses caught eating the Tlaxcalans' crops." The *Actas* (16) also tell of plans to prepare stables and hay well in advance of the viceroy's visit in 1559.

It was not long before indigenous communities were making efforts to procure these animals for their own uses. At least some of the time, they encountered restrictions. When the town council of Tlaxcala wanted to purchase horses in 1550, one of its members had to go before the viceroy to obtain permission (Lockhart, Berdan, and Anderson 1986, 141). The community of Santa Catarina Texupan, of the Mixteca Baja in the modern state of Oaxaca, entered the purchase of two horses and two saddles in its beautifully illustrated records, which make up the *Códice Sierra* and span the years between 1550 and 1564 (1933, Facsimiles 19, 20, 38). We do not know whether they had to obtain a license for these purchases.

Individuals wanted to have horses, too, as we saw earlier in the case of don Gabriel Curi, who obtained the desired license. The 1579 testament of an indigenous leader of Cuernavaca provides another example with its impressive list of possessions, including a horse, a set of tackle, and eight saddles (Haskett 1988, 44).[42] This man obviously had had considerable experience with horses and possibly mules, given the large number of saddles. Mule teams carried most of the freight around New Spain. Thus, as beasts of burden, horses had an attractive practical side in addition to their association with rank.

Riding a horse may have been one of the most coveted privileges for which caciques applied, but it was also the most expensive and therefore somewhat rare. It was less costly to purchase European garments. The acquisition of clothing perhaps offers a stronger indication of the desirability of emulating the power holders. Pre-Columbian Mesoamerican apparel presumably met the needs of the various societies prior to the arrival of Europeans, and so aesthetic value and status association more than practicality probably drove the market in imported fashions.

The construction of European clothing, however, did offer some differences that might have had a practical side. It was more form-fitting, and upper-body garments had sleeves (Anawalt 1981, 214). It may be that form-fitted apparel, if not too tight or binding, provided more rapid mobility than the draped fabrics of pre-Columbian Mesoamerican garments, which could cause people to trip. Tlatelolca women who entered into battle, for example, had to raise their indigenous skirts in order to give pursuit, according to the *Anales de Tlatelolco* (Lockhart 1993, 267).[43] It may also be that form-fitted apparel offered some comfort in the cooler seasons in the highlands. Certain imported fabrics or those made in the colony under

European direction, such as wool cloth for the highlands or silk for the lowlands, could have had a similar practical appeal for some individuals. In the fifteenth chapter of most sixteenth-century *relaciones geográficas*, or detailed descriptions of towns of New Spain, there are numerous references to the switch from native apparel (often simply loincloths plus woven garments and skins attached at the shoulder, neck, or chest) to Spanish garments (shirts, crude trousers, loose coats, and sometimes shoes and hats).[44]

Priests may have encouraged people to cover their bodies more extensively, teaching them to associate nudity with demonic or shameful behavior. Shocked by indigenous people's tendency to wear fewer garments, Spaniards seem to have developed an exaggerated stereotype of the native American of ancient times as preferring to go about entirely or partially nude. The relaciones geográficas give away the colonial administrators' own discomfort with nudity in their frequent references to the way loincloths covered the "shameful" parts. The *Relación de Tezcoco* (Acuña 1985–86, 3:97) refers, for example, to a covering of the men's "shameful members" ("miembros vergonzosos"). The women of Tetzcoco, according to the same *Relación* (98), were dressing almost as they had in pre-Columbian times, but "for modesty, they have added a white shawl" ("por honestidad, han añadido una cobija blanca"). Many Tetzcocans had also shed their ancient *cutaras* (sandals?) for shoes.[45]

Leather shoes offered more protection for the feet than, say, the henequen sandals that workers once wore in the mines of Taxco (see the *Relación de Minas de Tasco* of 1581, Acuña 1985–86, 2:127). Extracting ore was an extremely hazardous activity, and workers might have welcomed the new form of foot covering. But moving well beyond the concern for protection, one late colonial indigenous family of Cuernavaca, a town that provided laborers to Taxco, boasted the possession of "leather shoes with shiny buckles" (Haskett 1988, 45).

The shine on the buckles returns us to the importance of status. Clothing, as Tom Cummins (1991, 226 n. 13) has noted, was "a critical ethnic and social signifier" for the indigenous peoples of the Americas. One could argue this for other cultural contexts around the globe and throughout history, but it was especially true in the Western Hemisphere. The Nahuas, for instance, had a tradition in which they could put on the ceremonial garb of a deity and imbue themselves with "the power and agency of the god impersonated" (Frank 1989, 201). Whether or not they saw divinity in the Spanish invaders, Nahuas may have considered the donning of European attire in this light. Their enthusiasm for wearing imported clothing was already apparent by 1528, only seven years after the Spaniards seized power, when the intruders legally forbade the practice except by licensed individuals (López Sarrelangue 1965, 119). Despite this edict, the practice continued and flourished. Obtaining a license was not difficult, especially for native elites. As Robert Haskett (1988, 45) suggests, officials may have seen in this situation a chance to "co-opt influential local Indian nobility and cement their loyalty as intermediaries in the colonial system." Spaniards may have largely left it to such intermediaries to prevent the lower strata of indigenous society from wearing such clothes and watering down the privilege it entailed.[46]

Like clothing, headgear was always meaningful in pre-Columbian times and formed part of the finery that distinguished the higher social echelon. The turquoise diadem, or *xiuhuitzolli*, of the Aztecs was not only part of the essential garb of the emperors, but in the *Codex Mendoza* it serves as "an ideograph for *tecuhtli* (noble)" (Berdan and Anawalt 1997, 187). Fray Alonso de Molina's excellent sixteenth-century vocabulary translates *xiuhuitzolli* as a "corona real con piedras preciosas" (royal crown with precious stones) (Berdan and Anawalt 1997, 191 n. 70). Other circular head ornaments made from various substances were worn by indigenous authority figures across the hemisphere, and Europeans equated such items with their own crowns (see Axtell 1991, 18–19). The Maya captain Tecum, according to indigenous sources, wore "three crowns of gold, silver, diamonds and emeralds and of pearls" in his battle with Pedro de Alvarado (Bricker 1981, 40). It is no wonder that Europeans' hats and crowns captured the interest of indigenous people. They were ubiquitous, too; notice the way Spaniards wear something on their heads in virtually every one of our sample portraits. Many Spaniards in the *Florentine Codex* (Lockhart 1993, passim) have plumage coming out of their helmets and hats in a fashion not too distant from that of indigenous headdresses.[47]

The native elites apparently understood the higher significance of crowns and concurred with their use being restricted to kings. The Nahuas saw their own highest nobles as deserving of this special privilege. Accordingly, we find caciques wearing crowns in the *Mapa de Chalchihuapan* (Castro Morales 1969, fig. 3), the *Mapa de Cuauhtlantzinco* (Starr 1898, nos. 30,

31, 33), and the *Manta de Salamanca* (Reyes García 1993, 282). From these crowns plumes emerge, representing perhaps a slight indigenous innovation on the European form or an original combination.[48] These crowns would have had the double power of the feathered headdress, with its incumbent honors, and the metallic colonial wreath symbolizing sovereignty and distinction. The coincidence of forms may have been accidental, but the association was not lost on indigenous observers.[49] In Michoacán, P'urhépecha speakers gave the name *curitiecha* to the European friars who wore crowns of thorns. This was the same name they accorded their own priests, who also wore fiber wreaths on their heads (Craine and Reindorp 1970, 87–89).

Hats may strike us today as a far cry from crowns, being made from less valuable materials and enjoying far fewer social restrictions. Native American observers probably also recognized the broader distribution of hats in comparison with crowns, yet they could have held both in special regard, putting crowns and hats into the general category of circular headgear to be donned by people of significance. In Michoacán, one name for the Spaniards was *acacecha*, meaning "people who wear caps and hats" (Lunenfeld 1991, 270), revealing the strong, early association between the newcomers and their headgear.[50] As with crowns, caciques were eager to wear hats. Some proudly sport hats in the *Códice Huapeán* (LC/MIPD photograph LC-USZ9-430-2), for example. In the sixteenth-century relaciones geográficas we also find references to *sombreros* (felt or straw hats?) as part of the new apparel adopted by individuals in indigenous communities (see the *Relación de Tuzantla* of 1579; Acuña 1985–86, 2:157).

Just as clothing and headgear carried powerful connotations of status for both Europeans and indigenous people, so, too, did furniture. For Spanish colonial officials the seat of choice was the wooden curule chair with heavy, curved legs (figs. 2.16, 2.18, 2.24). Once a throne mounted on a chariot and later a chair reserved only for the top echelon of officials in ancient Rome, in sixteenth-century New Spain the curule chair still enjoyed a privileged association with the elite members of the colonial world. For their part, indigenous lords had special mats, short stools, and the like, upon which to rest and from which to make pronouncements.[51] Figure 2.15 depicts an interesting pairing of a native governor and a viceroy, sitting face-to-face in a complementary fashion on their respective seats of authority. Figure 2.16, although less balanced, does give each of the figures of

FIGURE 2.24. Notary, friar, and *corregidor* (left to right). Tracing by Gabriela Quiñones from the *Códice de Cuetlaxcohuapan,* Instituto Nacional de Antropología e Historia. Reproduced with permission.

importance his corresponding seat. Any omission of such crucial status indicators would have been a considerable oversight.

As with other symbols of power, caciques felt it appropriate for them to adopt the curule chair, substituting it for their own thrones. The Nahuas' *icpalli,* or reed seat with backrest, was a clear symbol of power and authority.[52] Sometimes it was adorned with revered animal skins and feathers (Berdan and Anawalt 1997, 205). In the genealogical *Codex Valeriano,* from central Mexico in 1574 (LC/MIPD photograph LC-USZ9-383-1), we have a clear example of how the curule chair had taken the place of the icpalli over the generations. Some additional examples of caciques sitting on curule chairs include those in the *Títulos de Tocuaro,* Michoacán, from the same collection of photographs (LC-USZ9-357-1), the *Tira de Tepechpan* (notice also don Diego Yoloxochitl with his crown; LC-USZ9-317), the *Códice de Tlatelolco* (1948), the *Lienzo de Tlaxcala* (Reyes García 1993, 279), the *Códice Azoyú I* (1991, 88, lám. 20, and folio 38 of the facsimile), and the Sochitepec maps of 1579 (Mundy 1996, 163).[53] In the *Códice Sierra* (1933, facsimile 20), the indigenous community purchases a curule chair.

As it appears in the codices, the curule seat seems to have been very portable. It may have been possible in some examples to collapse the intersecting wooden legs for easy transport. Perhaps this increased the chair's visibility for indigenous artists and other observers as it was carried from town to town so that officials such as corregidores did not have to sit on the ground. At any rate, in the codices it typically stands in an open space, often in an outdoor setting, and not necessarily paired with a table.

But the wooden table, so useful for making and displaying large manuscripts—whether canvases, strips, screenfolds, or other popular forms—became another object of Spanish material culture one often finds at the center of an indigenous pictorial history. Like the curule seat, it could be set up in the open air, in the midst of a sizable gathering of people. Typically, men are pictured standing around it, whereas women sit on the ground with their legs tucked under them.[54] The table with documents spread out on top materializes in a scene in the *Codex Cuetlaxcohuapan* from sixteenth-century Puebla (*Los códices de México* 1979, 53), opposite a friar in the Techialoyan codex from Atlapolco, central Mexico, in the late viceregal period (*Handbook of Middle American Indians* 1975, vol. 14, fig. 90), and solely with indigenous people in the eighteenth-century *Pintura de San Lucas Tecopilco* from the region of Tlaxcala (Reyes García 1993, 255).[55]

European and Mesoamerican cultures alike placed enormous value on writing. Manuscripts and documents regularly grace the tables or appear in the hands of Spanish ecclesiastics (fig. 2.11), officials (fig. 2.18), or notaries (figs. 2.17, 2.24) and those of indigenous nobles. A vicar of the late viceregal period once remarked cynically about the Nahuas, "They think that, with a piece of writing, a point is won" (AGN T, vol. 1530, file 5, 13v). He apparently did not see this as a borrowed trait, probably knowing of the ancient written traditions of Mesoamerica. But it was a remark that could have been made of the Spaniards, too, who documented everything.

Spanish culture also had its vitally important pictorial imagery, which could be seen all over the colony. One notable example is the coats of arms the colonists carried on banners or with which they adorned their architecture (fig. 2.25). Such imagery permeates the portraits of Spaniards and records of their activities made by indigenous artists. It appears in scenes of battles and baptisms alike. It is no wonder. Besides carrying their crests around with them, Spaniards carved them in stone in prominent places where native people could regularly observe them. Hacienda workers from indigenous communities might gaze upon Spanish family crests every day as they entered the estate compounds (see Romero de Terreros 1956, 281); trips to the cities similarly brought them face-to-face with escutcheons emblazoned on urban architecture. Members of the native elite who had a Spanish education would also have observed books bearing images of

FIGURE 2.25. Coat of arms displayed on architecture, Puebla, Mexico. Photograph by Stephanie Wood.

heraldry. Commoners and nobles alike were surely familiar with colonial Spanish coins decorated with castles such as those from the royal coat of arms of Castile (see Mundy 1996, 49).

Coats of arms represent one of the most interesting and instructive symbols of power that indigenous people adopted and modified (fig. 2.26; Haskett 1996). Modifications included the infusion of the armorial structure with encoded indigenous images, as we will see in chapter 4. By the late viceregal period, the coat of arms had, ironically, become a shield used to protect the indigenous community from the intruders,[56] as the following passage from the "Municipal Codex" of Cuernavaca suggests (Wood 1991, 176; and see Haskett 1996): "The King, our lord, granted us [the right] to make this [coat of] arms; it is our strength and our assistance. It will be made so we can free ourselves of the Spaniards, so they will not dishonor us or take something from us, nor will our priests afflict us."

Some modern observers will see in all these examples of acquired material culture a process of gradual Hispanicization of the indigenous people. Portraits of the exotic beings who came ashore unexpectedly in the first years of the sixteenth century never made them stand out like sore

FIGURE 2.26. Coats of arms. Tracings made by Gabriela Quiñones from the *Título de Totonicapán* (left), Universidad Nacional Autónoma de México, and folio 4r of the *Códice Techialoyan de Xonacatlan*, Latin American Library, Tulane University. Reproduced with permission.

thumbs but did show them as identifiably different from the indigenous elites, in part because of the trappings that came with them—the armor, the horses, the hats, and the banners. Gradually, however, the native author-artists reveal the transfer of such symbolic attributes to the indigenous nobility. The question remains whether these individual nobles would have interpreted their own identity as having become increasingly Spanish. At least two considerations come into play: whether they desired such an identity and whether they could have gotten away with it if they had. Spanish officials and colonists living in that period would have been quick to point out the remaining, crucial differences, anxious to distinguish themselves from the indigenous other. One colonial administrator noted critically that indigenous people in Taxco were wearing the dress of the Spaniard, "although imperfectly" ("aunque imperfectamente") (Acuña 1985–86, 2:127). According to Sahagún, Spanish colonists of the late sixteenth century mocked indigenous people who imitated them. In 1579 he therefore urged the Nahuas "not to wear shirts . . . knee pants . . . hats . . . shoes" (cited in Sell 1992, 167).

The enthusiasm for such articles among indigenous commoners and nobles alike attests to their general disregard for Spanish ridicule and their relentless pursuit of avenues to power or status. Of course, it was only the nobles who might try to pass as Spanish on the rare occasions when this was possible or when it behooved them to do so, and usually they were more than content to flaunt their position at the pinnacle of native society. After all, indigenous nobles could enjoy higher status in some respects than commoner Spaniards, in that they could attach *don* and *doña* to their names and enjoy access to tribute and labor, among other privileges.

The transfer of material culture from the intruders to the locals is testimony to the latter's ability to make the foreign comprehensible, finding parallels in the different cultures. Our survey of portraits of Spaniards in the codices also suggests that the author-artists wove the newcomers into their tapestry of the world fairly seamlessly. Although portraits are about exteriors and are not very revealing of interiors—whether the thought processes or feelings of either Spaniards or indigenous painters—a picture can still convey a great deal. These European men, though different, were not obviously hideous, weird, or despised. They were portrayed not as deities or monsters but as humans.

Not all were necessarily appreciated, however, or viewed equally. Monarchs, viceroys, the highest colonial authorities, and ecclesiastics appear either neutrally portrayed or respected. The most negative portrayals may prove to be those of encomenderos and the Spanish officials who gradually took their places as labor managers and tribute collectors, making economic demands on the communities or interfering in local decision making. It may be that priests' portraits, if surveyed more comprehensively, would prove to contain a certain percentage of negative images, too. In pueblos' numerous complaints against priests in the eighteenth century, according to William Taylor (1996, 246), "the common terms of opprobrium were cheerless and blunt: 'avarice,' 'servitude,' and 'tyranny.'" Although the "tagwords usually employed in modern descriptions" of the Spanish colonizers, "'cruel' and the like," (Lockhart 1993, 15), do not enter into the corpus of early texts we have surveyed and only rarely might be attached to the pictorial images, such terms would apply to the anti-Spanish narrative that forms the subject of the next chapter.

3

A Cry from the Mountains

THE AJUSCO NARRATIVE

They want to make themselves owners of our lands and all that is our wealth.

FUNDACIÓN DE SANTO
TOMÁS AXUCHCO, 1531;
AGN, T, VOL. 2676, FILE 4

From Santo Tomás Ajusco, a small community in the mountains south of Mexico City, formerly of the jurisdiction of Coyoacan, comes a fascinating manuscript with some anguished descriptions of the heat of battle and the early years after the Spanish invasion. Marcelo Díaz de Salas and Luis Reyes García (1970, 194–95) poetically describe the document as "a beautiful, although no less heartrending, complaint in the face of the plunder suffered," and as "a cry, profound and impotent, from someone who now only wishes to save his life." Its voice appears to be that of a local elder authority figure who is not at all happy with the Spanish invasion and emerging colonial domination. It speaks directly to a local, indigenous audience. Seemingly embraced over many generations, the Ajusco narrative certainly falls on sympathetic ears in the community today. Owing to all these features and more, it deserves serious attention.

The original, or oldest, version of this story has either vanished or is kept well hidden, away from public view.[1] Considering its early content, one would expect that the Ajusco narrative originally had a pictorial form that served as a prompt for the oral tradition. At any rate, someone in the community eventually wrote down that oral tradition in a Nahuatl-language alphabetic text of four leaves, and this was translated into Spanish in 1710 when a program of title verification (*composición*) swept the region.[2]

The Ajusco conquest account reads like a speech given by a *tlatoani* (Nahuatl for indigenous noble) or *teuctli* (indigenous lord), in this case a

Señor Tecpanecatl. His harrowing tale of the Spanish invasion still echoes through the community during public ceremonies. In the transfer of land documents during such a ceremony in 1994, one of the principal speakers quoted the Spanish translation of Tecpanecatl's narrative at length (figs. 3.1, 3.2). Showing further pride in the community's indigenous heritage and consciously linking it to the early nineteenth-century defeat of Spanish rule, the festival's queen, the "Señorita Independencia," sang the national hymn in Nahuatl.

Tecpanecatl's first-person account opens with an indigenous calendrical date (the second day of the fourth month of *Toxcatl*) as well as a reference to the Christian year, 1531. He relates how at this time the indigenous lords are very upset because of what the Spaniards have done and are still doing, persecuting them for not coming forth with sufficient gold or gems, even killing some of them, shedding a great deal of blood. The Castilians are also abusing the lords' wives and daughters. In addi-

FIGURE 3.1. Señor Tecpanecatl's speech read to the community of Ajusco, May 22, 1994. Photograph by Stephanie Wood.

FIGURE 3.2. Transfer of guardianship of Ajusco's *títulos*, May 22, 1994. Photograph by Stephanie Wood.

tion, the intruders want land; Cortés will come to distribute parcels for the community yet will also take land for Spaniards. Meanwhile, Tecpanecatl will found the new town and construct a temple for the worship of the new god and for baptism. In the process, he voluntarily reduces the community's territorial base, knowing how the Spaniards are coveting land. He hopes to avoid more deaths.

The expanded edition of *The Broken Spears: The Aztec Account of the Conquest of Mexico* includes some of this narrative. But the editor, Miguel León-Portilla (1992, 159), describes the Ajusco document as an "invented narrative." He suggests that it is an "eighteenth-century Nahua testimony" on the conquest, presuming it was fabricated just before its translation by colonial officials into Spanish in 1710. He associates it with the strain of colonial records called Techialoyan codices (fig. 3.3), probably because of his interpretations of the timing of its appearance and its questionable

FIGURE 3.3. Typical Techialoyan scenes. *Códice Techialoyan de Chalco*. Photograph by Stephanie Wood, reproduced with permission of the British Museum.

antiquity.[3] It also contains some elements typical of the *tlalamatl*, or "land-book," a translation popular with some scholars, such as Gordon Brotherston (1995, 185–88), for the Techialoyan genre.

An opportunity to see the hand, check the orthography, and analyze any pictorial matter in the "original" Nahuatl (or a pueblo-generated copy) would aid substantially in settling questions about the dating of the document and its intended purpose.[4] Is this indeed a late colonial creation trying to pass as something originating two hundred years earlier? Such a practice certainly existed across New Spain.[5] Or could it be that the Ajusco document truly preserves more than the usual amount of sixteenth-century oral tradition or (re)written accounts? If it is indeed early, then it provides us with a rare, small-town cry of distress in response to European colonization. On the basis of my own familiarity with late colonial Nahuatl manuscripts, the Ajusco record strikes me as only somewhat characteristic of these later records and in some ways notably different. Several elements do appear to have an identifiably early origin.[6] Establishing a clearer picture of the timing of this outcry would help us chart the evolution of indigenous perspectives over time and provide a key to referencing additional manuscripts that might be discovered. Exploring some of the central features of this manuscript for their temporal dimensions also simultaneously brings to light what at least this community embraces as critical elements of the Spanish invasion and its legacy.

INVASION-ERA FIGURES

One starting place for analyzing these elements is with the principal speaker, "Señor Tecpanecatl."[7] This may be a title or a name derived from the title. Indigenous men of high social rank sometimes bore the prestigious title "Tecpanecatl teuctli" ("Palace-inhabitant lord"), even well after the Spanish invasion.[8] "Señor" is a typical translation for *teuctli* (lord); it was common practice in the sixteenth century for Spaniards to recognize the highest local lords and their natural right of rulership, *señorío*, calling them *señores*. If "Tecpanecatl" refers to a name rather than a title, or if the title was so important that it became absorbed into the local nomenclature, then these are other plausible scenarios in the Ajusco area. Ajusco was situated in the broader jurisdiction of Coyoacan in the sixteenth century, and records from there show, for example, a Juan Tecpanecatl alive in Iczotitlan in 1573.[9] The Ajusco Tecpanecatl's lack of a Christian given name suggests an early temporal frame, within the generation of the first baptisms.[10] Perhaps with further research more information will turn up about this lord's activities. We might also locate information about his nine co-signatories, who similarly lack Christian names.[11]

Large portions of the manuscript not only contain sixteenth-century perspectives but consist of detailed descriptions of events in the heat of the struggle for power with Europeans. One statement, though somewhat retrospective, gives the impression that the conflicts initiated by the invaders were still under way, describing "what the whites, people of Castile, did and still are doing."[12] The use of the racial description "whites" (*iztaque* in the Nahuatl version) has an early ring to it, although a few examples have been found in late colonial community manuscripts of central New Spain. Kevin Terraciano and Lisa Sousa (1992, 55, 78–79, n. 38) located a similar racial remark in the Mixtec *título primordial* of San Juan Chapultepec, apparently from the late seventeenth century: "Then we lived together in peace with the white people and the great ones and we gave them a place to build the big church." In 1696 a cacique translated the Mixtec term *chee cuisi* ("white people") as "Spaniards." Terraciano and Sousa say that this racial perception of Spaniards "is almost unprecedented in both the Nahuatl- and Mixtec-language documentary record." Another of the rare occurrences they cite involves the use (in 1611?) of *iztaque*, "whites," and *chipahuacatlaca*, "light [skinned] people," in seeming reference to Spaniards. James Lockhart (1991, 59) also includes in his study of the Sula primordial title its use of the phrase "white hides" to refer to the skins of the Europeans. These may be memories preserved from sixteenth-century oral or written traditions.[13]

Whiteness of skin would seem to have been something more noticeable in the early years of contact, when awareness of differences might have been at its peak. Initial impressions of Europeans described in the *Florentine Codex* include the simple remark, "They were very white" (Anderson and Dibble 1975, 19).[14] In Guatemala the *Título C'oyoi*, with seemingly sixteenth-century roots, recalls "the people with white skin, the soldiers of Don Pedro de Alvarado, the great captain" (Carmack 1973, 301).[15] Similarly, the Andean chronicle of 1551 by Juan Diez de Betanzos recalls "some people, white and bearded" having recently arrived (quoted in Pease 1989, 183; my translation). James Axtell (1991, 8, 9, 23–24) cites several examples of the indigenous recognition of Europeans' white skin in the contact period of what is now the United States. According to one European, "the natives 'wondred mervelously when we were amongst them, at the whiteness of our skinnes, ever coveting to touch our breastes, and to view the same'" (Axtell 1991, 23).[16]

A further indicator of the timing of composition of the Ajusco narrative emerges in the reference to the leader of the Spanish effort, don Hernando Cortés, as the "recently named Marqués del Valle."[17] He obtained that title in 1529, which would be consistent with the statement's supposed origin in 1531.[18] Most late colonial pueblo records show no indication of knowing when Cortés became the marqués. The Soyatzingo primordial titles fuse the expedition leader and his title with a later viceroy: "Cortés don Luis de Velasco Marqués" (Lockhart 1992, 412). These kinds of later records typically handle names and titles of invading Spaniards with some confusion, as they were usually written down after the fact and then were recopied and amended over time, with later copyists making mistakes.

GOLD HUNGER

Also in contrast to later colonial primordial titles, the Ajusco document makes several references to the Europeans' demands for gold, a characteristically early pursuit that gave way to endeavors attuned to other, more abundant natural and human resources of the colony. "Never are they contented, only with gold and sparkling crystals [i.e., gems]," states the Ajusco manuscript.[19] Gold hunger is more typically remembered in sixteenth-century indigenous records, such as the *Relación de Michoacán*, which has a chapter titled "Plundering the Gold," and the *Florentine Codex*. Lockhart's vivid translation of the latter (1993, 16) reads, "Like monkeys they grabbed the gold. It was as though their hearts were put to rest, brightened, freshened. For gold was what they greatly thirsted for; they were gluttonous for it, starved for it, piggishly wanting it."[20] Felipe Guamán Poma de Ayala's Peruvian chronicle similarly contains an illustration (fig. 3.4) of an indigenous lord asking a Spaniard, "Do you eat the gold?" He replies, "Yes, we eat the gold." Guamán Poma wrote: "All day long all they did was think of the gold, silver, and riches of Peruvian Indians. Because of their greed, they seemed desperate, stupid, crazy, and deprived of all judgment."[21]

FIGURE 3.4. Guamán Poma de Ayala's commentary on Spaniards' gold hunger in Peru. One leaf of *El primer nueva corónica y buen gobierno* (GkS 2232 4to), Department of Manuscripts and Rare Books, The Royal Library, Copenhagen. Reproduced with permission.

That the theme of excessive gold hunger appears in these sources may reflect Spanish ecclesiastical influences. It was a cause of concern to some sixteenth-century clergy that the invaders seemed to worship mammon rather than Christ, an old biblical issue. Bartolomé de Las Casas commented frequently about the deadly mining of gold and asserted that gold was indeed the conquistador's god (see Rivera 1992, 259). Nevertheless, it is easily conceivable that the exaggerated lust for gold caught indigenous people's attention independently. Again, it was an early phenomenon, as first-generation Spaniards in the central areas frantically sought out pre-Columbian golden objects to melt down for coin or for ingots to send to Spain. Beyond that, the theme would not have persisted in indigenous histories much after gold mining ceased to be a significant practice in the central areas, which was around the 1540s (Hennessy 1993, 28). Silver mining quickly eclipsed gold mining in these regions.[22]

RAPE

Contemporaneous with the literal lusting after gold, and similarly short-lived, was European men's lusting after indigenous women during the expeditions. The rape account by Michele de Cuneo, an Italian "noble" who joined Columbus on his second voyage, comes to mind, as does the account of the Taíno destruction of La Navidad in retaliation for the abuse of women (see Wood 1998c). Presumably, in the central areas, along with full Spanish immigration and the re-creation of Hispanic society in the colonies came social mores and penal codes that reduced the frequency of such blatant displays of abuse, except on the frontiers. Certainly, eighteenth-century histories from pueblos of central New Spain do not regularly speak of Spaniards ravaging native women. But the Ajusco document reminds us of the tone of earlier records as it recalls, "It is known how [the Spaniards] take away [the indigenous rulers'] revered women and also girls." Two other remarks additionally remember insults inflicted upon the community's noblewomen and, by extension, its elite men.[23] Bernal Díaz del Castillo's memoirs (completed in 1568) of the Spanish invasion of Mexico relate how the men's primary concern after breaking enemy ranks "was to look for a pretty woman or find some spoil."[24] Similarly, the *Florentine Codex* (Lockhart 1993, 248) recalls how, after the fall of Tenochtitlan, the invaders seized the indigenous women, "and [the Spaniards] took, picked out the beautiful women, with yellow bodies."[25]

EXECUTIONS

In the Ajusco narrative, reflecting the concerns of its principal speaker, Tecpanecatl, abuses in the form of executions are really aimed as much or more at the local men in authority, the "superiores gobernantes patronos de los pueblos," than at the lower-ranking audience he was addressing.[26] Native lords are still being burned at the stake (*quinmotlatilia,* "los queman") when they fail to deliver sufficient goods to the invaders. On this subject the manuscript reveals surprising breadth of worldview. The lords of which it speaks include the *cazonci,* a lord of Michoacán, and unnamed men as far away as Jalapa, Tlaxcala, Tehuantepec, and Oaxaca. Additionally, its speaker remembers how numerous rulers were killed in the company of the Aztec king, Moctezuma, in Mexico City.[27] (Incidentally and tellingly, Mexico City appears as "Anahuac," the place next to the water, the older Nahua way of naming the city by those who lived outside of it.) The author demonstrates a substantially broader familiarity with some of the geographical dimensions of the battles and with the fates of distant rulers than we have yet seen in later colonial primordial titles, which are considerably more locally centered and which often only vaguely remember violent conflict (as we will see in chapter 5).

Tecpanecatl appears to hold particular sympathy for his more illustrious Uacúsecha counterpart, the "really admirable ruler of Michoacan, the truly great Caltzontzi" (the cazonci Tzintzicha Tangaxoan II in Michoacán records).[28] If indeed he was recalling the cazonci's memory in 1531, it would have been only one year after that leader's execution by the Spaniards for his supposed practice of "idolatry," among other acts of resistance. Again, as with Cortés's becoming marqués, the time frame is consistent. Hernando Cortés personally pursued the court case against Nuño de Guzmán, the expeditionary leader in Michoacán, in 1531, bringing to light the plunder of gold and silver, the torture of indigenous elites, and the demand that the cazonci provide Guzmán with indigenous women (Baudot 1995, 414). Such abuses probably stirred up a maelstrom of discussion, anger, and anxiety among indigenous people across the heart of the colony and even beyond.

If the memory of the cazonci's execution by burning was more distant, or if the Ajusco record was drawing upon written sources, then there
are a number of possible origins for the information about the cazonci's
death. Two sources—one left by García del Pilar, advisor to Nuño de
Guzmán, and the other the "Fourth Anonymous Relation"—share this simple version of the leader's execution by fire. Other accounts relate that he
died either from torture before being burned (according to the seventeenth-century chronicler Fray Antonio Tello) or from strangulation
(according to the trial records of 1531), in a gesture of supposed humanity that had him pulled from the fire once he showed sufficient repentance
(Warren 1985, 234–35).[29]

The Ajusco record also leans toward an almost sympathetic rendering
of Moctezuma's fate, recalling "all the many insults" the Spaniards inflicted
on him.[30] But what brought all this on? Tecpanecatl heaps blame on the
lords of Azcapotzalco, Mexico, Tetzcoco, and Chalco themselves for being
too proud and warlike, spilling each other's blood.[31] He also censures
indigenous ancestors (*huecau tlaca,* "la gente antigua") in general for the
suffering of these lords while the Spanish struggled for power.[32] Does Tecpanecatl exhibit here a typical micropatriotism and ethnic rivalry, or has
he internalized Spanish justifications for the invasion and seizure of power,
reflecting the passage of time and ecclesiastical influence on his way of
thinking? If the latter, this would argue against the early date of 1531 for
all such statements; perhaps the narrative is a compilation of various
speeches, including some he uttered somewhat later in life and possibly
others invented by his descendants.

It is intriguing that Tlaxcala is one of the sites Tecpanecatl mentions
in association with the Spaniards' execution of indigenous lords. One of
the rulers executed there shares the Ajusco ruler's name or title, Tecpanecatl, although the latter does not consciously make the connection.
Did he know any of the details of those early executions? Might he have
heard of them by word of mouth or read about them in indigenous
sources? Some native annals from Tlaxcala memorialized that region's
executions (see Gibson 1952, 35, 254–55).[33] Annals from Cuauhtinchan,
southeast of Puebla, known as the *Historia Tolteca-Chichimeca* and believed
to have been written about 1547–60, recall how in the year Thirteen Reed,
"don Tomás, the Tecpanecatl [lord], was hanged at that point" (Lockhart
1993, 283). As a rule, títulos authors were not conversant with the annals

historical genre (Lockhart 1992, 413), but a few suggestive relationships have emerged.[34]

Whatever the source of Tecpanecatl's information about the execution of other indigenous lords, its effect was sobering. In several places the fear of further reprisals for resistance leads the speaker to recommend that "it would be best for us to turn ourselves in to the Castilian men," and "let's not get involved in anything, so they won't kill us."[35] The tone evokes a climate of fear and caution; the contest for imperial dominion is still under way.

PROPHECY

Another seemingly early feature of the Ajusco manuscript is its inclusion of two references to prehispanic prophecies forecasting the Spanish invasion. These read, "Our grandfathers . . . said that others would come from distant lands to make us sad, would come to take from us and make themselves owners of . . . our land." And, "Now, already we saw the ancient word fulfilled."[36] According to Werner Stenzel (1991, 102), the earliest mention of a prediction about the Spanish invasion was made in 1536, in the case against Martín Ocelotl. If the Ajusco prediction was first verbalized in 1531, and if this date is not an error or relevant only to some other portions of the narrative, then it would predate that trial.

The sixteenth-century *Florentine Codex* contains some of the better-known expressions of prophesying about the European invasion of Mexico, recorded in the mid-sixteenth century. It includes well-known omens that began unfolding ten years before the Cortés expedition landed in Veracruz in 1519. Part of the "seventh omen" has Moctezuma envisioning "people coming massed, coming as conquerors, coming girt in war array" (Anderson and Dibble 1975, 3).

According to Hans Roskamp (n.d.), the *Codex Plancarte* from Michoacán also contains a kind of prophesy of the European incursion. This manuscript, rich in sixteenth-century material, claims local gods knew that strange people wearing iron hats and riding horses were coming to the region.[37] Its authors foresaw—with some hindsight, perhaps—that the strangers would visit all the villages and kill the people, adults and children, using knives and whips and sometimes by poking out people's eyes. Horses, which seemed so formidable at first, were expected to assist in the killing, using their feet and teeth. This foretelling brought despair upon the entire community. Like the Ajusco manuscript, this one speaks bluntly of violent themes and captures negative indigenous sentiment about the Spanish invasion.

Such divination was not limited to predictions of the Europeans' arrival, for, as Tzvetan Todorov (1987, 66) has observed, "the whole history of the Aztecs, as it is narrated in their own chronicles, consists of realizations of anterior prophecies." Some of this prophecy, he suggests, "is all the more accurate in that it will be formulated only in a retrospective fashion, after the event has taken place." This type of foretelling, when used to explain a loss of imperial control to foreigners, might have offered some minimal comfort to those who formulated historical memories of their leaders' loss of power by reducing their responsibility for that loss. It might have offered some measure of dignity by preempting the victors in ascertaining knowledge of the end result before it happened. At the very least, it "provided a mode for the interpretation and the management of Spanish actions," as Inga Clendinnen (1987, 162) has suggested in analyzing the histories of the *Chilam Balam*. A singular invasion and defeat that is "perceived" in advance allows indigenous people to "mentally overcome it by inscribing it within a history conceived according to their requirements," proposes Todorov (1987, 74).[38]

Prophecy has also been interpreted as having weakened native resistance to the Spaniards in Mexico. Thus, if in the Ajusco narrative the power struggle is still in progress, and if the leaders announce that the ancient word has already been fulfilled, this could have had the effect of instilling a sense of futility in the people. Resignation echoes in the manuscript's treatment of the Europeans' determination to introduce Christianity, already nearly accomplished. The narrator refers to "the new God that the Castilians brought us,"[39] speaking of it in the past tense but directly recognizing Spanish agency, showing an awareness that is rare in post-1650 primordial titles. Usually, as we will see later, they simply report that "the faith arrived." The Ajusco document ponders whether to accept this new God and decides, "Let's become baptized."[40] The manuscript acknowledges the Christian God as the "really true God." Still, this deity is portrayed not just as occupying but as traversing the heavens ("corre sobre los cielos"), a Nahua interpretation that makes Christ into something of a solar deity.[41] In fact, Tecpanecatl says, "I have determined that he has to be the same

[god] as ours."[42] This ability to distinguish pre- and posthispanic deities, even if equating them, suggests an awareness that people might have had in the early sixteenth century or one they might have developed in the modern day. It does not echo in late viceregal-era indigenous histories, which often blur the distinction between religious beliefs and practices from before and after the arrival of the Spaniards, as we will see in chapter 5.[43] Finally, this newly introduced God will favor the people of Ajusco only "through the Castilians,"[44] another argument for surrendering.

PUEBLO TERRITORIAL ISSUES

A border survey was an integral feature of every primordial title. In the Ajusco border survey, an unusual element recalls the submissive but calculated statements just quoted: it self-consciously encompasses less territory than the town originally claimed, out of fear of retaliation from the foreign invaders if the local community's land base were too large.[45] "In order that they don't kill us, it is fitting that we do not recognize all our lands," recommends Tecpanecatl.[46] None of the known late colonial primordial titles willingly reduces the corporate land base, and none raises the possibility of being killed for the land. More commonly, community boundaries are idealized in those manuscripts.[47] Nevertheless, the Ajusco record's inordinate emphasis (for 1531) on the land issue hints at a later composition, at least for this part of the manuscript—a departure from much of its content, examined earlier. It is certainly possible that concern over territorial dimensions was felt in the early sixteenth century, but this is usually a feature of the post-1650 era, when the indigenous population began its gradual recuperation, Spanish estates were being formed or expanded, and competition over resources reached unprecedented heights. In fact, agricultural land, particularly in such places as the mountainous terrain of Ajusco, was much less an object of desire to Spaniards for several generations after their seizure of power than were grants of labor (*encomiendas*), to put to use in mining or in various enterprises on the valley floor.

Treating another possibly late theme, the Ajusco document speaks of the intention "to form here a pueblo" (*formar aquí un pueblo*). This could be a reference to a program of population concentration (*congregación*) of the mid-sixteenth century or—an even remoter possibility—to an earlier act

of recognition of the town of Santo Tomás Ajusco by some Spanish officials theoretically visiting in the 1530s.[48] More likely, this part of the manuscript has a late origin, reflecting the late seventeenth- and early
eighteenth-century consciousness that focused intently upon pueblo formation and encompassed any number of measures that might strengthen
the *altepetl,* the indigenous provincial unit, town, or city. One such measure involved invoking the decrees requiring a minimum territorial base for
indigenous communities of, by 1695, "six hundred *varas,*" or colonial Spanish yards.[49] Called the *fundo legal* only from the 1790s onward, this allotment was the centerpiece of the supposed *merced* (grant) of 1609 from
nearby San Andrés Totoltepec that Nicole Percheron (1983) published with
her transcription of the 1710 translation of the Ajusco document. The
Totoltepec manuscript speaks specifically of the "600" varas "de fondo
legal," unaware that the allotment was measured in 500-vara lengths until
1687 and that the term *fundo* (or *fondo*) *legal* was not coined until even
later.[50]

This tainted context for the Ajusco document again casts doubt on its
authenticity. The mixed impression one gets of the timing of its composition also raises questions about the manuscript's origins. Like most primordial titles of colonial derivation, however, it was probably "accretive,"
or a composite of written fragments and oral traditions put together, then
altered and augmented over time.[51] Certainly, components of the manuscript have strong connections to the early sixteenth century; when they
were put to paper we may never know, but they could have been recast
two or more centuries later as new concerns over resources arose.

OFFICIAL APPROVAL

That colonial Spanish judges were willing to legitimate the manuscript's
message is apparent in the magistrate's statement of 1710 that the "document that has been translated allows room for no doubt that the pueblo
was founded in the year 1531," and "it is clear that the foundation was made
in lands that they call patrimonial."[52] Sometimes such pronouncements were
pragmatic responses intended to bring order to documentary chaos uncovered in the composición proceedings (land title verification programs) that
produced the original 1710 translation. Even if a manuscript presented by
an indigenous community was neither accurate in every detail nor actu-

ally first written down at the time of the earliest event contained in it, magistrates accepted the thrust of its arguments, probably especially so when there were no counterclaims.[53] Towns were also paying fees for the supposed privilege of having colonial judges rubber-stamp their primordial titles.

The composición agent who handled the Ajusco case was certainly not stringent about obtaining an expert translation of the document. The 1710 translation is the work of a don Juan de los Santos, an interpreter of the court but surely an indigenous person who was not completely fluent in Spanish, if we can trust the 1741 transcription for every detail. For *allá* (there), for example, he gives "haya," and "llo" for *yo* (I), and he regularly omits or misuses the preposition *a*. Nonagreement of number results in phrases such as "los mismo." As with the coveted "original" (accretive) Nahuatl version, one longs to see even the original 1710 translation.

The colonial magistrate who approved the Ajusco document must have had either a particularly thick skin or a rare sensitivity to the plight and perspective of the indigenous people who witnessed the Spanish invasion or their descendants of the early eighteenth century, still struggling to survive in the face of foreign domination. An unusually strong anti-Spanish sentiment permeates the entire Ajusco piece, perhaps more than any other native account.[54] Where other accounts call the Spaniards "Christians," without reflecting on the meaning of the term, Tecpanecatl angrily labels them "those covetous ones, greedy ones who are called Christians" and "those who strike terror, Castilians."[55] Speaking with confidence to his internal audience, he points in rare form to the Spaniards' goal of sole power, an abhorrent prospect for him.[56] These are not words written to please a composición official (unless he were known to be another Bartolomé de Las Casas). Tecpanecatl adds that the foreigners want to "have us under their heels"—as we might say, "under their thumb.[57] Finally, "they want to make themselves owners of our lands and all that is our wealth."[58]

There can be little doubt that by 1710 the Ajusco community had taken a considerable risk to legalize its territorial standing before the colonial magistrates, sharing this acerbic denunciation of greedy, rapacious invaders with the heirs of those power holders. Possibly calculating the psychological payoff that would come from suggesting that their territorial claims had already been reduced by their own town founder, they nevertheless were making public a possibly injurious record of devious manipulation.

They not only hit pay dirt with the approval of the composición in 1710, but they also took a second risk, returning to the courts in 1741 to obtain another copy of this unflattering portrait of "shameless invasion."[59]

Whether the Ajusco document recalls the alarm that reverberated through central-area indigenous communities within a decade after the fall of the Aztec capital, Tenochtitlan, or imagines it two hundred years later, the human drama it captures is moving. This rare transcript of dissent is not embedded in "songs, gestures, jokes, and theater," whereby subordinate people can "insinuate a critique of power while hiding behind anonymity or behind innocuous understandings of their conduct," as, according to James Scott (1990, xiii), may often be the case.[60] Rather, it is a blatant and caustic expression of fear, pain, and disapproval. It does not, however, go so far as to call for insurrection to throw out the hated tyrants, nor does it raise the banner of messianic revitalization and rejection of the Christian god. Whereas the millenarian leader Antonio Pérez of Yautepec might in 1761 call bravely for *gachupines* (a slur meaning Iberian-born Spaniards) to burn and the archbishop to be carried off in chains by devils (Gruzinski 1989, 65),[61] Tecpanecatl of Ajusco counsels caution and pragmatism to pull his people back from the brink of disaster. Not all indigenous voices from the viceregal era resonate with a revolutionary spirit gratifying to anti-imperialists five hundred years after Columbus's landing—the manuscript under inspection in the next chapter definitely does not—but they nevertheless provide a moving articulation of indigenous difference and distinction throughout the centuries.

4

A Proud Alliance

THE *MAPA DE CUAUHTLANTZINCO*

This most pure virgin . . . is she whom Señor Don Fernando Cortés, Marquis of the Valley, brought, and who condescended to illuminate with the light of the gospel us, who were in the darkness of idolatry.

Tepoztecatl's speech in
the Mapa de Cuauhtlantzinco

Indigenous memories of the Spanish incursion and presence can swing from radically different perspectives. The Ajusco manuscript, as we have seen, makes a scathing attack on the men of Castile, who "want to impose themselves upon us, because they are utterly gold hungry, voracious of what belongs to others: our chiefdoms, our revered women and daughters, and our lands" (León-Portilla 1992, 160). In startling contrast, a letter from indigenous citizens of Huejotzingo to the Spanish king in 1560 proudly proclaims, "We took you as our king, to belong to you and become your people and your subjects; not a single town here in New Spain surpassed us, in that first and earliest we cast ourselves toward you" (Lockhart and Otte 1976, 167). Such public discourse might have belied individuals' private sentiments, but it was pronounced loudly and regularly, becoming internalized over time.

The name Huejotzingo will not ring a bell with historians of Latin America the way the name Tlaxcala might. Although other groups like the Huejotzincans, including the Cholulans, Cempoalans, Chalcans, and Tetzcocans, cast their lot with the Spanish invaders, the Tlaxcalans achieved greater fame for their alliance with the Europeans against the Aztecs, their traditional enemies. Tlaxcalans went in greater numbers than any other indigenous group and participated in continuing expeditions, even settling distant frontiers for—ostensibly, at least—European monarchs and their colonial viceroys. To some extent the Spaniards singled out the Tlaxcalans in granting them rewards and making an example of their coop- eration, which the foreigners hoped other indigenous groups would imi- tate. But the Tlaxcalans also campaigned long and hard for their privileges and often felt that the honors they received were no match for the sacri- fices they had made (see Gibson 1952, ch. 6). Their legal maneuverings, combined with the chronicles of Spanish, mestizo, and indigenous writ- ers, with less formal histories, both oral and written, and with murals and dramatic plays, contributed to the enduring fame of the Tlaxcalan-Span- ish alliance.

One of several lesser-known manuscripts that share in this cultural tra- dition is the *Mapa de Cuauhtlantzinco,* associated with a town called San Juan Cuauhtlantzinco, which lies between Puebla and Cholula and there- fore not far from Tlaxcala (see fig. 1.1). Multiple copies of the *Mapa de Cuauhtlantzinco* exist today (Glass 1975b, 121–22). For this study, I con- sulted two of these, both probably dating from the nineteenth century, one held at Tulane University's Latin American Library and the other an uncatalogued copy owned by the University of Oregon's Museum of Nat- ural History. Photographs of two manuscripts held in the pueblo, pre- sumably the original and a later copy that is remarkably similar to the two copies I consulted, were published by the anthropologist Frederick Starr in 1898. His photographs attest to the quality of the reproductions in the Tulane and Oregon copies.

The *Mapa*'s principal theme is the warm welcome and subsequent cooperation locals extended to the Spaniards in spreading the Christian faith as the Europeans headed for Mexico-Tenochtitlan from Xalapa, pre- sumably in 1519. Although this pictorial, consisting originally of thirty-three oil paintings on European paper and probably dating from the seventeenth century, came to serve as evidence of the community's antiquity and illus- trious heritage, its focus is the activities of four indigenous leaders (fig. 4.1) who have a somewhat shadowy connection to this particular town, as I discuss later. A preliminary inspection of this ethnohistorical record not only highlights the dispersion of Tlaxcalan lore but also reveals the influ- ence individual *caciques* (indigenous leaders) could have over local, sup- posedly community history.[1]

FIGURE 4.1. Scenes 30–33 from the *Mapa de Cuauhtlantzinco*, depicting the four caciques who supposedly met Cortés: Tepoztecatl, Cacalotl, Cencamatl, and "Sarmiento." Reproduced from Starr 1898.

DATE OF ORIGIN

Adolph Bandelier, who visited Cuauhtlantzinco in 1881, wrote about how the people of the community believed that the original paintings dated from the sixteenth century and were composed by the cacique Tepoztecatl, one of the major figures in the manuscript's storyline and illustrations (Starr 1898, 3). The earliest known observation of the original paintings by an outsider took place in 1836, providing a *terminus ante quem* for their origin. This observer was a Spanish priest, resident in Cholula, who visited Cuauhtlantzinco again nearly two decades later and worked with the local people to translate the Nahuatl glosses and brief texts. At that time, 1855, he noted that the Nahuatl was "more pure and old-fashioned than that now in use" (Starr 1898, 10).[2]

If the transcriptions of the glosses and texts are as careful as the copying of the paintings, I would posit that the "originals" Starr photographed could not have been written before about the mid-seventeenth century. The loanword particle *hasta* (Spanish for "as far as") appears, for example, in the gloss for the scene numbered 22 (fig. 4.2). James Lockhart, who is eminently familiar with Nahuatl manuscripts, has not seen this particle in documents dating any earlier than 1653 (Lockhart 1992, 309).[3] Also appearing in the *Mapa* is the post-1650 phenomenon in which *y* is written as *ll* (fig. 4.3; cf. Lockhart 1992, 336).[4] The *Handbook of Middle American Indians* (Glass 1975b, 121) suggests a seventeenth- or eighteenth-century origin for the earlier *Mapa* photographed by Starr, which would concur with this linguistic assessment drawn from the copies.

Another element in the *Mapa* that indicates something of its date of origin is the reference in scene 22 to the famous invaders "Señor Don Bernal Díaz del Castillo and Señor Don Pedro Alvarado," along with Hernando Cortés. Here Tepoztecatl describes one or more of them as recorders of the history of the cacique's deeds.[5] Díaz del Castillo's role as

FIGURE 4.2. Scene 22 from the *Mapa de Cuauhtlantzinco,* depicting the departure of Cortés. Photograph by Stephanie Wood, courtesy of the late Martha Barton Robertson at the Latin American Library, Tulane University. Reproduced with permission.

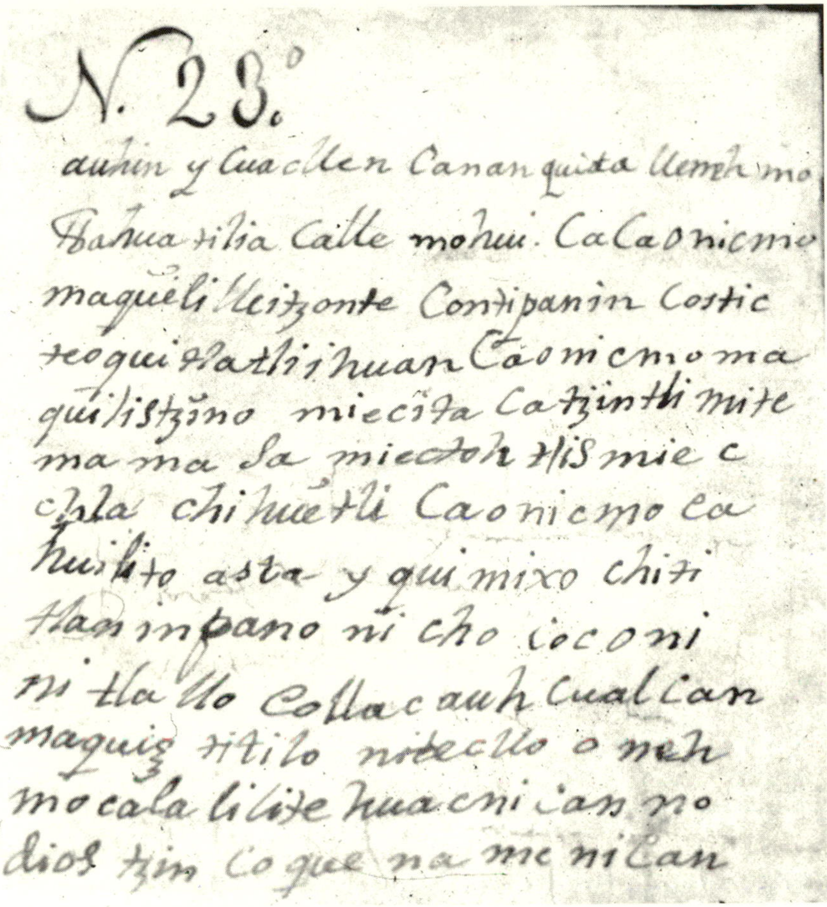

FIGURE 4.3. Text for scene 23 from the *Mapa de Cuauhtlantzinco*. Photograph by Stephanie Wood, courtesy of the late Martha Barton Robertson at the Latin American Library, Tulane University. Reproduced with permission.

a historian is even more clearly spelled out in the related *Mapa de Chalchi-huapan* (Castro Morales 1969, 18–20), to be discussed in more detail later. Although based partly on journals written at the time of the entrada, Díaz del Castillo's history book was not completed until 1568 and was not published until 1632 (Carmack 1973, 93–94). It may be that his fame as a historian did not emerge until the mid-seventeenth century or later, again supporting such a date for the compilation of both *Mapas*.[6]

AUTHORSHIP

A late viceregal origin for the oldest version of the *Mapa de Cuauhtlan-tzinco*, which might still be in the pueblo—although I did not uncover it during a visit in 1994—would mean that it could not have been made by the four caciques who figure so prominently in it and who allegedly met Hernando Cortés in person. More likely, the descendants of one or more of the caciques assembled this record of their illustrious heritage, possibly drawing upon oral tradition—perhaps including theatrical dialogue—and fragments of older written records and/or mural paintings.[7] The four men who supposedly met Cortés appear in the *Mapa* as Tepoztecatl (Tepoztecatzin in the reverential form), Cacalotl (Cacalotzin), Cencamatl (Cencamatzin), and "Sarmiento," a cacique who took a Spanish last name but apparently no first name.[8]

A legend of the coming of Christianity in Tepoztlan, Morelos, more logically features a Tepoztecatl (the name can substitute for "someone from Tepoztlan"), according to an informant who spoke to Oscar Lewis (1963, 255) in the mid-twentieth century. This Tepoztecatl, "king and cacique," accepted the new faith quickly and tried to convince other indigenous notables that they worshiped a false idol. Baptism and the erection of special crosses also figure in the legend. During the town's annual fiesta on September 8, at least at the time of Lewis's fieldwork, town officials were still reciting a dialogue in Nahuatl between Tepoztecatl and his indigenous enemies. Locals also believe that El Tepozteco, dressed as a Zapatista, made a miraculous apparition in Tepoztlan in 1920 (Lewis 1963, 260). The lore of Tepozteco has been powerful and widespread and may have influenced the content of the *Mapa de Cuauhtlantzinco* or, more generally, Tlaxcalan lore, a subject of more detailed discussion farther on.[9]

The Tepoztecatzin of the *Mapa* may also have truly local roots. The actual orthography of the *Mapa* substitutes an *s* for the first *z* in the name Tepoztecatzin, rendering it Tepostecatzin, which is not at all unusual. Over subsequent generations the name may have been shortened to "Tepos." Among the distinguished citizens bearing the honorific title "don" before their names in Cuauhtlantzinco as of 1855 were several individuals with the last name Tepos.[10] The name Sarmiento holds a prominent place in this list, too (Starr 1898, 10), suggesting that this clan was local and, like the Tepos family, had an interest in preserving this particular account of sixteenth-century events.[11]

A further hint that the authorship or compilation of the *Mapa* might have originated with people claiming descent from the four caciques comes from scene 21 (fig. 4.4), in which Tepoztecatzin's son ("Tepostecatzin ypiltzin") joins the group of leaders. Here is the continuation of a potentially significant postcontact lineage. An illustration of a grant of *cacicazgo*—the right of rulership and nobility, usually passed from father to son—given by Charles V to Tepoztecatzin appears in scene 27 (fig. 4.5); his heirs would certainly have coveted this precious award. Tepoztecatzin also asks the Spaniards in the text of scene 22 to "honor my descendants and do not oppress them in distributing and working my lands" (Starr 1898, 19). In the text to scene 29, Tepoztecatzin states: "Know you, oh my sons who are growing up, the portion of lands that belongs to you; these are my [coat of] arms which I merited together with the title of Cacique, which was given me and which was executed to me in the Pueblo of Santiago Xalitzintla" (Starr 1898, 21).[12]

FIGURE 4.4. Scene 21 from the *Mapa de Cuauhtlantzinco*. Photograph by Stephanie Wood, courtesy of the late Martha Barton Robertson at the Latin American Library, Tulane University. Reproduced with permission.

FIGURE 4.5. Scene 27 from the *Mapa de Cuauhtlantzinco*. Photograph by Stephanie Wood, courtesy of the late Martha Barton Robertson at the Latin American Library, Tulane University. Reproduced with permission.

SHADOWY *ALTEPETL* AFFILIATION

The reference to this *altepetl,* or town, of Xalitzintla(n) is somewhat puzzling. Santiago Xalitzintlan lies about twenty-six kilometers, as the crow flies, west of Cuauhtlantzinco (see Tichy 1979, map coordinates F3). Tepoztecatzin also mentions it earlier, in the text to scene 22, in which he refers to "this my *mapa,* wherein you are shown the grant which was made to me in the Pueblo of Xalitzintlan" (Starr 1898, 19). Why would these caciques have received their favors in Xalitzintlan if their home town was Cuauhtlantzinco, as the title of the *Mapa* indicates? In scene 27 (fig. 4.5) we do see the place-name San Juan Cuauhtlantzinco, but could it have been added to what was originally a manuscript associated with another town?[13] Or is there a Mapa de Xalitzintlan somewhere from which this one borrows?[14]

Whatever doubts it may raise about the originality of the *Mapa de Cuauhtlantzinco,* the possibility of borrowing is not remote, and for the sake of better understanding the situation that produced this document, the possibility should be explored.[15] The previously mentioned *Mapa de Chalchihuapan*, associated with a pueblo approximately fifteen kilometers southwest of Cuauhtlantzinco (Tichy 1979, map coordinates G5), has striking similarities to this one. Adolph Bandelier first described it as "analogous" to the *Mapa de Cuauhtlantzinco*. A more recent study, by Efraín Castro Morales, also mentions the strong affinities, and his photograph and tracings (fig. 4.6) made from the original remove all doubt about a shared style (Castro Morales 1969; also compare figs. 4.4 and 4.7). There are fewer Nahuatl glosses or texts on the *Mapa de Chalchihuapan*, but the orthography echoes the *Mapa de Cuauhtlantzinco*. Both employ the post-1650, yet still somewhat unusual, orthographic phenomenon of using *ll* in place of *y*.[16]

Castro Morales relates how two residents of Chalchihuapan told him about another, similar pictorial that disappeared from the town long ago. Was this another copy of the *Mapa de Chalchihuapan*, a copy of the *Mapa de Cuauhtlantzinco*, perhaps the source upon which both were based, such as the hypothetical Mapa de Xalitzintlan, or something even older? In various colonial manuscripts such as these, there is some evidence to support the existence of mass production, regionwide distribution, and sharing between communities, activities that do tend to raise questions about the authenticity of each manuscript and its identification with a single altepetl.[17] On the other hand, such activities alone do not negate the claims inserted into each document. Even the best-trained European historians of the period borrowed heavily from their sources. Research still remains if we are to verify or disprove the assertions the *Mapas* contain.

THE *LIENZO DE TLAXCALA* AND REGIONAL LORE

As much as these mapas lack strong anchors to particular towns, they do hold strong ties to the broader Tlaxcalan tradition. Two of the better-known narratives of proud alliances with Europeans are the *Lienzo de Tlaxcala*, a cloth bearing illustrations of historical events possibly first painted in the 1550s (extant copies are much later), and Diego Muñoz Camargo's *Historia* or *Descripción de Tlaxcala*, from the 1580s, a copy of which was recently found in Scotland accompanied by 156 previously unknown illustrations.[18] Among the many scenes in these pictorials are at least three that became the stuff of legend. One is a depiction of four Tlaxcalan lords greeting Cortés (fig. 4.8). Later, they are christened in allegedly the first act of

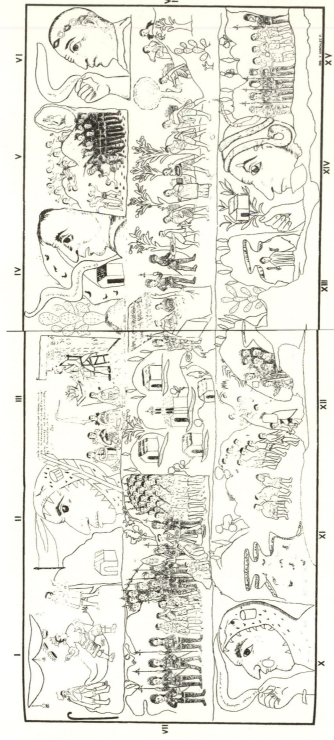

FIGURE 4.6. Tracings of the entire *Mapa de Chalchihuapan*. Reproduced from Castro Morales 1969, with permission of the Instituto Nacional de Antropología e Historia.

FIGURE 4.7. Tracing of a scene from the *Mapa de Chalchihuapan* (compare with scene 21 of the *Mapa de Cuauhtlantzinco*). Reproduced from Castro Morales 1969, with permission of the Instituto Nacional de Antropología e Historia.

FIGURE 4.8. *Lienzo de Tlaxcala,* caciques greeting Cortés. Photograph courtesy of the University of Texas, Austin. Reproduced with permission.

baptism carried out in Mexico, supposedly within the first twenty days after the Spaniards landed in 1519. The third legendary scene captures the erection of a miraculous cross at the site where the four lords were baptized. The historian Charles Gibson refutes the historicity of the last two legends, which came to be widely held as true in the Tlaxcala region by the late sixteenth century (Gibson 1952, 30).

Because of the popularity of the themes in the *Lienzo* and *Descripción*, the fact that multiple copies and versions circulated,[19] and the apparently extensive mural-painting tradition of the Tlaxcala-Cholula area, which may have antedated both documents,[20] we can surmise that the diffusion of this legendary material was widespread. Several communities soon claimed to be the site of the first baptism and the miraculous cross. The *Mapa de Cuauhtlantzinco* shares something of this material, emphasizing the acceptance of baptism by its featured caciques (fig. 4.9) and proudly displaying a special cross (fig. 4.10).

According to Gibson, the names of the four caciques of the original legend became distorted as the legend spread. He notes how the Tlaxcalan lord Xicoténcatl, the elder, came to bear the names "Lorenzo, Lorenzo de Vargas, Gonzalo, Vicente, and Bartolomé" in different sources (Gibson 1952, 31). Although the names change, four is the recurring number of caciques across a variety of manuscripts from this region. Besides the *Mapa de Cuauhtlantzinco*, with its emphasis on the activities primarily of four men, other Nahuatl-language records with the same number are the *Códice de Contlantzinco* and the *Códice de Santo Tomás Xochtlan* (Gibson 1952, 265, 266). The persons mentioned in the first codex are Pedro Maxixcatzin, Pablo Xicotencatl, Tepantetzin, and "Melendez." Appearing in the second are Juan de Guevara, Juan Maxixcatzin, "Leonardo," and "de Torres." In both cases, and echoing the *Mapa de Cuauhtlantzinco*, one of the four caciques bears only a Spanish surname. Note also the recurring name Maxixcatzin, a quintessential Tlaxcalan appellation, in these two codices.[21]

Although it makes sense for Tlaxcala, which was a composite state made up of four altepetl, to be represented by four lords in the legend of the baptism, it is less clear why this same number also enters into the regional lore picked up by other communities, such as Cuauhtlantzinco. Further research will be necessary to determine whether these towns had the same symmetrical sociopolitical arrangement as Tlaxcala or whether

FIGURE 4.9. Scene 13 from the *Mapa de Cuauhtlantzinco*. Photograph by Stephanie Wood, courtesy of the late Martha Barton Robertson at the Latin American Library, Tulane University. Reproduced with permission.

FIGURE 4.10. Scenes 16–17 from the *Mapa de Cuauhtlantzinco*. Photograph by Stephanie Wood, courtesy of the late Martha Barton Robertson at the Latin American Library, Tulane University. Reproduced with permission.

the number four simply represented a legendary ideal. A four-part organization may have been one of the more common in Nahua culture.[22] But Cholula, to which Cuauhtlantzinco was attached, had an ancient six-part organization, according to the Franciscan missionary and historian Juan de Torquemada (see Simons 1967, 281; 1968, 291).

The sixteenth-century invader-historian Bernal Díaz del Castillo may have unwittingly contributed in some way to the *Mapa*'s featuring four caciques. Bandelier suggested that a reference in Díaz del Castillo's account to four men from Cholula who invited Cortés there and, after the massacre that followed, had to go found another town involved the caciques of the *Mapa*. The new town they founded in exile, he suggested, might have been San Juan Cuauhtlantzinco (Starr 1898, 7). This is only speculation. Various towns might have tried to lay claim to this origin, hoping to bolster allegations of an early and firm allegiance to Cortés. At any rate, Díaz del Castillo's work does contribute this additional example of the recurring number of four caciques so prominent across the region.

Another element of Tlaxcalan-area lore that repeats itself across a few manuscripts, including the *Mapa de Cuauhtlantzinco*, is the indigenous adoption of Spanish heraldry. Setting a memorable example, the Spanish Crown granted special coats of arms to Tlaxcalan nobles and to the indigenous community itself (Gibson 1952, 163–65), concessions that were captured in the central picture of the *Lienzo de Tlaxcala* (fig. 4.11). Coats of arms open and close the *Descripción de Tlaxcala* (Brotherston and Gallegos 1990, 117). According to Torquemada, Tlaxcala's heraldic shields were a source of considerable pride and were displayed in indigenous community processions as early as 1536. Motolinia also remarked about the special privilege, noting that the Spanish monarch had never before rewarded an indigenous group in this way (Baumann 1987, 148).

Neighboring towns and caciques were envious, and they either petitioned and won shields of their own or perhaps fabricated them. In nearly every scene of the *Mapa* in which Spaniards appear, the foreigners hold banners bearing the arms of León and Castile. In scene 26 (fig. 4.12), the cacique Tepoztecatzin holds the same banner, and in scene 27 (fig. 4.5), he gazes upon a particularly elaborate representation of the same shield. The *Mapa* credits Charles V with endowing Jacinto Cortés, as the cacique was called following baptism, with a coat of arms. It is somewhat ambiguous in scenes 26 (fig. 4.12) and 28 (fig. 4.13) whether the cacique received

FIGURE 4.11. Coat of arms from the *Lienzo de Tlaxcala*. Reproduced with permission of the University of Texas, Austin.

the arms of León and Castile or his own unique shield composed of a variety of native and European elements, including possibly a crow, a nopal cactus, an arrow, a wooden version of the *macana*, the native club with obsidian blades, and a European trumpet.[23]

Creativity with shields was not unique to the *Mapa*. Four "hieroglyphic coats of arms," as Gibson (1952, 267) called them, including one with a smoking star for Citlalpopoca, can be found in the *Manta de Salamanca* (also known as the *Manta de Tlaxcala*), one of several indigenous manuscripts that recount the legend of the Tlaxcalan lords' baptism.[24] The *Manta* may have served as an inspiration for the *Mapa de Cuauhtlantzinco*. The *Relación de Cholula* exhibits a coat of arms with a thick tule bush and a hill with a trumpet on top (UDLA/RBC, File 53). The *García Manuscript 8* in the Benson Collection of the University of Texas, Austin, depicts what may also be a coat of arms with mixed elements, including, for example, both swords and macanas (fig. 4.14).[25]

FIGURE 4.12. Scene 26 from the *Mapa de Cuauhtlantzinco*. Photograph by Stephanie Wood, courtesy of the late Martha Barton Robertson at the Latin American Library, Tulane University. Reproduced with permission.

FIGURE 4.13. Scene 28 from the *Mapa de Cuauhtlantzinco*. Photograph by Stephanie Wood, courtesy of the late Martha Barton Robertson at the Latin American Library, Tulane University. Reproduced with permission.

FIGURE 4.14. Indigenous coat of arms in the *García Manuscript 8*. Photograph courtesy of Robert Stone and Yasmin Khan; reproduced with permission of the University of Texas, Austin.

Another theme that intersects both the *Mapa* and the *Manta* is the indigenous adoption of golden European crowns. The Tlaxcalan lords in the *Manta* wear gold crowns (Gibson 1952, 267), as do the caciques in the *Mapa de Cuauhtlantzinco* (fig. 4.1) and the *Mapa de Chalchihuapan* (upper left corner of fig. 4.6).

ELITE EMPHASIS

While fitting with Tlaxcalan-area lore, the prominence and importance given the indigenous leaders in the *Mapa de Cuauhtlantzinco*—ostensibly a document intended to support corporate concerns—is somewhat exaggerated compared with the emphasis given them in most informal community histories, or *títulos*, from central New Spain. This manuscript seems to straddle the genres of cacique records and town records. Certainly, most communities' títulos, or primordial titles, do feature town founders and subsequent indigenous notables in a variety of functions, but they usually give considerable space to territorial boundaries and group land claims. Still, the function of titles could evolve over time. In discussing títulos from the Maya zone, Robert Carmack has written, "I think a good case can be made that at an early time some of the documents were not written primarily as land titles, but later came to function as such, as contests over land became more critical." In the beginning, land "was not an issue at all" for some manuscripts, as Munro Edmonson has found (see Carmack 1973, 19).

The preservation of the town and land issues do come up in a few places in the glosses and texts of the *Mapa*. On the outside cover of the copy in Oregon, the caciques Sarmiento and Cencamatl admonish that the document be respected as the "*mapa* of the pueblo." It was probably in the eighteenth century, when competition over agricultural land heightened, that the *Mapa de Cuauhtlantzinco* became increasingly identified with the town and with agrarian concerns. At that time it might also have been used to defend the collective ownership of land, which often lacked written verification.[26]

Citizens of Chalchihuapan have shed light on the role and purpose of their *Mapa*, which may help us better understand the *Mapa de Cuauhtlantzinco* as well. One informant explained to Castro Morales (1969, 17) how the elders believed that individuals featured in their mapa represented the "'lords' of the hills surrounding the town" and "guardians of the lands" held by the local population. Castro Morales also found Nahuatl-language títulos for Chalchihuapan that "refer undoubtedly" to the contents of that mapa and underline its late viceregal-era importance in the defense of corporate landholding (1969, 18–20).

From before European contact until sometimes as late as the eighteenth century, commoners worked certain corporate town lands for the support of their indigenous rulers. Thus, the prominence of caciques in these mapas would not necessarily have undermined the paintings' use for the support of group (as opposed to individual) interests. Founding fathers and mothers, as depicted in títulos, even represented the "symbolic incarnation of the altepetl," in James Lockhart's words (see Haskett 1992, 3, who quotes Lockhart). Or, according to Robert Haskett, they were simultaneously "symbols of noble privilege and the altepetl's corporate integrity" (Haskett 1992, 19; also see Wood 1998a).

On the other hand, it is easy to imagine these paintings being used to sustain elite families' claims to what they had come to consider private, entailed properties, sometimes part of what remained of cacicazgos, interspersed among parcels held by the community.[27] The descendants of sixteenth-century indigenous nobles came to view the collectively owned parcels once worked for their families' support as tracts they could alienate from the community and sell at whim. Furthermore, by the last century or so of Spanish control, and across New Spain, caciques also regularly tried to enlarge their holdings at the expense of indigenous corporate lands and operated increasingly like Spanish hacienda owners.[28]

PROCOLONIAL SENTIMENT

Setting aside questions about ambiguous agrarian interests, to what extent did the elite group's memory of alliance with Spaniards diverge from the commoners' view, considering that the latter tended to bear the greater burden of labor and taxation in service to the new colonial power? Commoners might have also been leery of trusting the Spaniards after the famous massacre at Cholula in 1519.[29] Did caciques' own personal interests in pursuing rewards dominate and significantly color the corporate perspective on the history of the Europeans' seizure of power? The Guatemalan *Título Cajcoj*, for example, contains a description of the introduction of the Christian faith to the Verapaz area that portrays the citizens of Cajcoj as very cooperative toward the friars. Robert Carmack advises that we "must read with caution" this portrayal of the people's cooperation, because the account's compilers had an ulterior motive relating to political and jurisdictional issues (Carmack 1973, 56–57).

Some doubts have also been raised in recent research with regard to the pervasiveness of the Tlaxcalan people's pride in the famous European alliance. In a special Columbian quincentenary issue of *Radical History Review,* Max Harris (1992) summarizes and concurs with various modern analyses of the religious play *The Conquest of Jerusalem,* put on by indigenous Tlaxcalans in the sixteenth century, which detect in it a radical anti-Spanish perspective. Borrowing James Scott's language, Harris argues that this script contained "hidden transcripts of dissent," because the prominent expeditionary leaders Hernando Cortés and Pedro de Alvarado figured at the heads of armies of infidels that Christian Tlaxcalan Indian forces were able to defeat. In this way, Tlaxcalans could quietly ridicule the Spanish invaders and take satisfaction in symbolically routing the men who defeated their people in 1519. Harris argues that they could "celebrate past resistance" and possibly even "anticipate future liberation" (1992, 16–17).

It may be that the surprising roles given Cortés and Alvarado seemed subtler at the time or were inoffensive because they were exhibited "all in good fun," the way Latin American Carnival celebrants mock the rich and powerful. Harris's summary of the literature covers these kinds of rationalizations, which he finds insufficient. He also minimizes Roland Baumann's argument that this one example of anti-Spanish sentiment is far outweighed by the more widespread Tlaxcalan tradition of acceptance and alliance. Harris draws a distinction between official stories and the "disguised" messages from the "theater of the powerless" (a phrase also from Scott), believing that one does not preclude the other (Harris 1992, 15–17).

The *Mapa de Cuauhtlantzinco's* championing of the missionary effort of local caciques is certainly more in line with the official story, if we can call it that, imbedded in such sources as Muñoz Camargo's *Descripción* and the *Lienzo de Tlaxcala.* It also echoes a performance from 1585 and an early seventeenth-century play, *Colloquy of the Last Four Kings,* that Baumann has uncovered. The performance of 1585 features four old caciques who wear crowns on their heads and speak of privileges they had won through their brave support of Cortés in the Spanish takeover of the Aztec empire. The

Colloquy play has the four "kings" worshiping an idol and falling asleep. An angel awakens them with the Christian message, which they adopt and then celebrate by sending gifts to Cortés. Soon they receive baptism and are protected from their former idol by a special cross (Baumann 1987, 143–44). All four of the foregoing sources, as well as the *Mapa*, contain many of the same elements, such as four men, gold crowns, idols, infidels asleep, gifts for Cortés, baptism, and crosses, among others.[30]

Baumann believes this "Tlaxcalan vision of the 'conquest'" should really "be restricted to the nobles," which returns us to the question of whether the *Mapa* represents only an upper-class or a full corporate view of the past (Baumann 1987, 147). Unfortunately, we must speculate about its intended audience. Was it made primarily to serve as an internal record, a memory for the townspeople of their illustrious ancestors and history of Christian glory? Or was it compiled for presentation to the colonial viceroy or Spanish king, in order to strengthen the claims of elite individuals? Unlike some other títulos, this manuscript does not form part of a litigation record, which might have highlighted its intended audience.

Yet even though some titles ended up in the courts, there is growing agreement that their original and principal audience was an internal, indigenous one. They regularly warn future generations not to show the manuscripts to Spaniards, and they contain negative remarks about individual Europeans who had come to live in or near their indigenous communities, as we will explore in chapter 5 (see also Wood 1991, 187–88). Just as "Sarmiento" declares the *Mapa* to represent the pueblo and Tepoztecatzin calls on the community to "maintain yourselves in unity," so town elders in later títulos, speaking in the first person, typically exhort younger generations to protect the town and its boundaries.[31]

The reader of these manuscripts can almost hear the elders speaking as the strong oral tradition flows into the writing. Charles Gibson (1975, 321) likened the scene to the modern conciliar meeting where "one person arises and delivers a kind of village manifesto, with boundary points, patriotic exhortation, and historical narration all fused in an eloquent oral recital." Dialogue in Guatemalan títulos, suggests Robert Carmack, not only stems from oral tradition but "may ultimately derive from song and chant accompaniments to codices" (Carmack 1973, 40).[32] Aztec pictorial histories "were painted specifically to be the rough text of a performance," suggests Elizabeth Hill Boone (1994b, 71; and see Boone 1991). John M. D.

Pohl cites a reference in Francisco de Burgoa's *Geográfica descripción* about annual religious celebrations that included dramatizations of local histories in the Mixtec zone. A codex mounted on a wall would serve as a story board, prompting "artists, actors, and musicians" to "act out a story before hundreds" (Pohl 1994a, 141).[33]

These descriptions seem particularly apt for a reading of the *Mapa de Cuauhtlantzinco,* especially because it comes from the Tlaxcala region, where dramatic performances are so well documented for the viceregal era. As Harris (1994) has also shown, dramas of "conversion" not only commemorated the earliest evangelical activities but were parts of the very first religious demonstrations that accompanied the entradas, reaching even as far north as New Mexico. Many of these dramas show clear roots in the reconquest experience in Spain—mocking battles between Moors and Christians—or in even earlier medieval morality plays.

The *Mapa,* then, may capture in paintings live dramas anchored in the heritage of theater held dear by both Spaniards and indigenous peoples. These might have been dramas that were acted out within one or more communities in the vicinity of Cuauhtlantzinco, employing duplicated or slightly varying pictorial and textual scripts. If so, to what extent would such performances have incorporated the townspeople as actors or as approving, interactive audiences? It was not unusual to find interaction between performers and audiences in prehispanic drama (Ravicz 1970, 9), and commoners were presumably both in the cast and on the sidelines. In *The Conquest of Jerusalem,* mentioned earlier, Tlaxcalan nobles took what they deemed the best roles but apparently allowed commoners to play other parts (Baumann 1987, 143). Another author states specifically that *macehual* (commoner) boys were instructed in singing and dancing "so they could serve in ecclesiastical festivals."[34]

If colonial Nahua dramatic practices and other written and oral traditions can be compared to modern storytelling, we may find some insights there. Storytelling today among the Nahuat of the Sierra de Puebla, for example, involves usually older males who pass on narratives containing what James Taggart calls "collective images," or "the shared beliefs, concerns, and experiences of those in the audience." When individual storytellers "impose their private views," they meet with disapproval from the community and fail to achieve lasting success in their role (Taggart 1983, 1–2, 245). It is remotely possible that the *Mapa de Cuauhtlantzinco* represents a case of individuals imposing private views on the past that were incongruent with the view of majority, emphasizing an unduly favorable memory of the alliance with Spaniards.[35] But its version of history does coincide with a prominent strain of Tlaxcalan lore. If there was a tendency on the part of elites to deemphasize the history of resistance and disguise any brewing anti-Spanish sentiments, then large numbers of commoners might have been parties to it, whether consciously or unconsciously, considering how long-lived and widespread this tradition was. Furthermore, there is no hint in the *Mapa* that local people might have performed this story with a disguised, anti-Spanish twist such as the one Harris has read in other Tlaxcalan religious dramas.[36]

RESPONSE TO CHRISTIANITY

One *can* read in various surviving texts a storyline of strong initial resistance to Christianity on the part of indigenous people in the Tlaxcala area. Even Cortés recounted the mighty battles he fought against the Tlaxcalans before they capitulated (Cortés 1928, 41–48). Then, for some time after the formation of the military alliance, the Tlaxcalan chieftains remained bravely defiant about abandoning their gods, fearing an uprising of their own priests and citizens and divine retaliation in the form of "famine, pestilence, and war" (Díaz del Castillo 1976, 133).[37] Although the caciques finally relented, this attitude persisted among certain persons, such as the native priests who tried to preserve the worship of the gods Ometochtli and Tezcatlipoca in the province of Tlaxcala a number of years after the Spanish invasion. One warned that everyone who had forsaken their god for the Virgin Mary would die; the other counseled people not to accept Christian religious instruction or baptism. Both men were punished severely (León-Portilla 1974, 25).

The demise of the priest who promoted Ometochtli seems to have had a poignant significance for indigenous people of the region in the sixteenth century. It was not the colonial church that punished him; he was stoned to death by his own people, Tlaxcalan youths who were students of Franciscan friars and had been won over by Christianity. A crusade of sorts followed, managed by the Franciscans but conducted by their indigenous pupils (León-Portilla 1974, 25–26; Baumann 1987, 140). From 1525 to 1531, this religious campaign took on a decidedly violent character as youths burned temples and destroyed images (Gibson 1952, 33–35.) Muñoz Camargo related how various caciques and one *cacica* (noblewoman) were hanged or burned at the stake for falling back into idolatry (Moreno de los Arcos 1991, 23–36). The execution of four Tlaxcalan chiefs in 1527, part of the Franciscan Martín de Valencia's quest to extinguish lingering pre-hispanic practices and beliefs, says Charles Gibson (1952, 35), must have had an "extreme effect upon the religious life of the province." Gibson concludes that "idolatry" was considerably reduced in Tlaxcala by the 1530s.

The theme of indigenous agency in spreading Christianity, at times forcefully, is a prominent one in the *Mapa de Cuauhtlantzinco*. In scene 3 (fig. 4.15), Tepoztecatzin leads Spaniards in armor to some sleeping nobles, raises his sword, and demands that they accept baptism. As in the early seventeenth-century *Colloquy* play, sleeping seems to be associated with not yet having seen the light of the new faith.[38] In scene 5 (fig. 4.16), Tepoztecatzin, again followed by Spanish warriors, battles native resisters of baptism in Malacatepec.[39] The same cacique takes other nonbelievers before Cortés in scene 9 (fig. 4.17). In a similar vein, two other featured

FIGURE 4.15. Scene 3 from the *Mapa de Cuauhtlantzinco*. Photograph by Stephanie Wood, courtesy of the late Martha Barton Robertson at the Latin American Library, Tulane University. Reproduced with permission.

FIGURE 4.16. Scene 5 from the *Mapa de Cuauhtlantzinco*. Photograph by Stephanie Wood, courtesy of the late Martha Barton Robertson at the Latin American Library, Tulane University. Reproduced with permission.

FIGURE 4.17. Scene 9 from the *Mapa de Cuauhtlantzinco*. Photograph by Stephanie Wood, courtesy of the late Martha Barton Robertson at the Latin American Library, Tulane University. Reproduced with permission.

caciques, Sarmiento and Cencamatzin, demand in scene 6 (fig. 4.18) the acceptance of Christianity by a native lord seated on a serpent throne.[40] This quintessential symbol of Mesoamerican faith, the snake, literally separates indigenous figures dressed in skins and carrying bows and arrows from Spaniards with armor and muskets—and the appropriately hovering protector, the Virgen de los Remedios—in scene 7 (fig. 4.19). Representing a more passive form of agency, one noble agrees in scene 10 (fig. 4.20) to accept baptism and serve as an example to others.

Although there is plenty of resistance, violent conflict, and coercion in the *Mapa*'s account of the introduction of Catholicism in this province, if not specifically around Cuauhtlantzinco, this is nevertheless a record compiled by proud converts who rejoice in the Christian victory. Fully aware of the consequences of resistance and the possible benefits of alliance, such individuals probably saw little choice in the matter. If they gave in under duress in the beginning, some of them came around to a new posture over time. Cooperation and, especially, enthusiastic intermediary efforts ensured their survival and protected their elevated status. If leaders lost internal support from cooperating with the invaders, as Ross

FIGURE 4.18. Scene 6 from the *Mapa de Cuauhtlantzinco*. Photograph by Stephanie Wood, courtesy of the late Martha Barton Robertson at the Latin American Library, Tulane University. Reproduced with permission.

FIGURE 4.19. Scene 7 from the *Mapa de Cuauhtlantzinco*. Photograph by Stephanie Wood, courtesy of the late Martha Barton Robertson at the Latin American Library, Tulane University. Reproduced with permission.

FIGURE 4.20. Scene 10 from the *Mapa de Cuauhtlantzinco*. Photograph by Stephanie Wood, courtesy of the late Martha Barton Robertson at the Latin American Library, Tulane University. Reproduced with permission.

Hassig (1994, 145) has suggested, this "was offset by the power and political support gained from Spaniards." Furthermore, if they could prove that
they had accepted Christianity in the period prior to their military alliance
with Cortés, they could win the right to "consider themselves conquerors,"
as Gordon Brotherston and Ana Gallegos (1990, 131) posit to have been
the case with the *Lienzo* and the *Códice de Tlaxcala.* Participating caciques
of the era of the Spanish takeover, and their descendants in subsequent
generations, would then have shaped and maintained the official story that
it was prudent and wise to have accepted Catholicism, an attitude that
endured over the centuries.[41] Within the first century of the invasion, the
majority of the indigenous people would receive baptism and eventually
embrace (or reinterpret) the tenets of the new faith, becoming proud of
their *catolicidad.*[42]

Acceptance of the new faith was the most pervasive dimension of the
changes that came with the Spanish seizure of power commemorated by
indigenous people of early Mexico. As Charles Gibson noted, the alleged
first baptism and miraculous cross became legendary. Roland Baumann,
who has studied colonial plays performed in Tlaxcala, supports Gibson in
this, noting how the Tlaxcalan version of religious conversion was reported
by Juan de Torquemada in 1615, an indication that it "had gained major
acceptance." Baumann, citing Peñafiel, also finds that this version was "represented through paintings or sculptures" and was incorporated into history, appearing in the *Gaçeta de México* (Baumann 1987, 148). While
indigenous nobles facilitated the spread of Christianity and guided the
preservation of its memory in drama, paintings, and texts, leaders and average citizens alike seem to have absorbed the emerging tradition.

POLITICAL AGENDAS

The *Mapa de Cuauhtlantzinco,* with its pro-Spanish position, does not represent a popular political stance today. Nevertheless, it helps to reveal some
of the multiple dimensions of the "indigenous perspective" on colonial history, particularly in the region of Tlaxcala. Indigenous communities that
allied with the Spaniards won a certain collective fame and, occasionally,
corporate exemptions from taxes or other duties, but it was usually individual leaders who petitioned for rewards for services performed by themselves or their illustrious ancestors. They were quick to understand and

tap into the Hispanic compensation system for expeditions, having witnessed Spanish veterans pleading poverty and royal neglect despite endless efforts put forward and seeing them finally come away with various favors. Caciques took their place in line before the king or viceroy to claim that they, too, had served the crown and should be able to don Spanish clothing, wield a sword, mount a horse, or even bear a fancy coat of arms. Tlaxcalan nobles were regular participants in these pursuits, as the *Mapa* and other manuscripts illustrate.[43]

The tightrope that such individuals had to walk in trying to please both Spaniards and indigenous audiences is reminiscent of that reflected in the writings of Fernando del Alva Ixtlilxochitl, a mixed-heritage historian of colonial Mexico. As Rolena Adorno (1989, 209) points out, "his own political agenda consisted in presenting his case to the new, distant Spanish overlord and his local representatives in a way that would be persuasive to them and yet not alienate the native colleagues whose support he needed." Further, the case he was trying to make was similar to that of the *Mapa* caciques, "to pull Christian warrior culture over to his side." He put his own heroic actions center stage, much the way the *Mapa* caciques made themselves the key players, and recounted episodes from the struggles associated with power shifts that do not even appear in Spanish records (Adorno 1989, 210–11).

Alva Ixtlilxochitl's version of the supposedly Spanish victory over the Mexica, actually fought by far greater numbers of indigenous warriors, may have represented more an intellectual's conscious, pro-indigenous, revisionist history than we find in the *Mapa*, which was a less sophisticated, provincial memory of real or supposed events. Still, the *Mapa* caciques were, like Alva Ixtlilxochitl but perhaps less consciously, appropriating and refashioning the discourse of the official record, taking the lead for themselves. These men were redrawing the "divisions" and "boundaries limiting cultural fields" in the "dominant discourse," to paraphrase Michel de Certeau's discussion of the craft of history (Adorno 1989, 211). Ironically, the *Mapa* caciques sought to extract a measure of autonomy for their communities through their alliance with the Spanish invaders and by taking the initiative to push Christianity on their reluctant neighbors.[44]

Individuals have always been key players in the process of cultural change, as ethnohistorians have increasingly brought to light in recent years.[45] The ability of certain individuals, whether already privileged or poised in some way to take advantage of opportunities, to carve out a reasonable, even comfortable existence in the new world emerging around them led to numerous "success stories." En route, they accepted or promoted a degree of cultural change as a means to physical and ethnic survival and material gain. While some humanistic anti-imperialists will find solace in the survivals, others may see the ironies behind them, as Steve Stern (1982, 159) does when he observes the "tragedy of success" in the Andes: "The tragedy of Indian success lay in the way it recruited dynamic, powerful, or fortunate individuals to adopt Hispanic styles and relationships, thereby buttressing colonial domination."

In the Tlaxcala area, caciques found their greatest "success" in negotiating their identities as allies of the Spanish invaders. To be fair, this was one of the few realistic paths to survival, given the unfortunate fate of those who resisted, such as Tupac Amaru, to cite a Peruvian example. The indigenous population was too fragmented into separate states and ethnicities for an indigenism to emerge rapidly and help in the formation of a united opposition front. Besides, the solidification of cacique families' prominence in the postcontact era may have brought prominence to their communities, at least initially. Such families left a definite stamp on the local historical tradition, which came to serve both group and individual interests. Titles of individual honor merged with proclamations of corporate rights.

This said, there was still plenty of material in manuscripts such as the *Mapa* that could have been exaggerated in the late viceregal period's recording or recopying of paintings and texts, to the benefit of elite families, forsaking the common good.[46] Even if the townspeople fully embraced the memory of friendship offered to the invaders and proud acceptance of a new religion embodied in their "mapa del pueblo," it behooves the historian to read with caution the braggadocios' accounts of individual valor and reward.

5

The Growing Threat

LATE VICEREGAL-ERA VIEWS

The Spaniards are coming!

The Spaniards are coming!

Central Mexican indigenous community histories were pronouncing this alarm in the seventeenth and eighteenth centuries with an urgency one might have expected in 1519, when the Cortés expedition first landed. Meanwhile, any memory of a sixteenth-century panic associated with that landing–where it had ever existed–seems to have faded.

Among the best sources for examining the popular memory of New Spain's indigenous people about the Spanish invasion and colonization experience are the indigenous-language documents known as *títulos primordiales* (primordial titles) or, more simply, *títulos*. Recorded in many communities across New Spain, but not in the polished language of professional indigenous notaries and seemingly not under the direct supervision of Spanish officials or priests, they contain examples of the indigenous popular lore that can elude so many other types of ethnohistorical sources. Conforming to internal structures yet somewhat free in form and idiosyncratic, these local histories and assertions of political authority and territorial dominion made their appeals primarily to a local, indigenous audience. They concentrated on shoring up community autonomy while also cementing certain families' places of authority in those independent realms.[1]

Deciphering these cryptic documents, which reveal a unique sense of chronology and contain many orthographic and linguistic rarities, is a major challenge. As Robert M. Hill (1989, 285) discusses, títulos draw from prehispanic writing traditions. They also came to incorporate some European documentary genres in modified form (Hill 1989, 293; Lockhart 1991, 60; Wood 1997). We have no firm sense of the dates of composition, precise authorship, or original context of most of the known títulos, weakening the modern historian's ability to assess their full thrust and to grasp completely their spectacular indigenous voices.[2] What messages and attitudes do títulos convey about the colonial experience for the individual—whether of humble or comfortable means—and for the community? Is the notion that these documents represent the community exaggerated? How do these messages compare with the pictorial images we have already surveyed, with the Ajusco narrative, and with the nobles' pursuit of glory we saw in the *Mapa de Cuauhtlantzinco?* Do we find the same invasion-era descriptions of Spaniards lusting after gold? Do we find the same emphasis on the heroic assistance given Cortés by communities such as Tlaxcala and Huejotzingo? Or, many generations after Cortés's triumph, had the collective indigenous consciousness reframed the Spanish seizure of power and the changes it set in motion? How had the foreign invasion come to figure in indigenous people's sense of their own, local history? Did it play a major role? Was it viewed with some degree of acceptance, tolerance, or perhaps indignation? If so, what might account for these changing perspectives? Before addressing these themes and questions, it is necessary to sketch out the genre's major characteristics.

THE *TÍTULOS* GENRE

Although primordial titles are proving to be a significant source of information about indigenous views of the Spanish assumption of power and colonization of Mexico, including the evangelization project, they are best known for their descriptions of corporate and sometimes elite landholding. One of the principal components of each título is a detailed, allegedly sixteenth-century border survey of all territory claimed by a given community. The document typically relates how an early viceroy or other high Spanish official presided over the survey and granted the land to the town or to its leading citizens. For this reason, and despite the presence of many other kinds of information about the town's history from prehispanic times through the seventeenth or eighteenth century, many scholars have viewed the entire genre primarily as land tenure records—hence the denomination "titles," in the sense of "deeds." When translators in the nineteenth century reflected on the many centuries of tradition a set of títulos usually contained, they began adding the adjective "primordial." This label also gave a nod to their unorthodox chronologies and historicity.[3]

Charles Gibson (Gibson 1975, 321) has described the typical title as representing "an individual or collective memory of lands possessed or once possessed and endangered." That memory, he adds, "might be misguided or deliberately contrived to support a claim." James Lockhart (1991, 42), in his study of four títulos from the Chalco region, concurs with the assessment that, as proof of territorial claims, they are usually inaccurate and "in some sense deliberately falsified." But because these manuscripts were made primarily for indigenous people's consumption, deceiving the courts probably was not their original intent. They may have been reassembled or altered in later times by people other than their original authors. For example, the so-called Díaz Título of Cuernavaca conveniently surfaced in the midst of a land dispute by don Josef Gaspar Díaz, an alleged descendant of one of the speakers in the text (AGN HJ, legajo 447, exp. 7). Capturing some of the complexities behind the composition of such manuscripts, Matthew Restall (1991, 125) describes a título-like Maya land document from Yaxkukul as "an authentic eighteenth-century contrivance."

Spaniards commonly disputed primordial titles as records of land tenure in particular and as historical records in general, pointing to factual inaccuracies in their claims, such as incorrectly dated terms of office for well-known viceroys. Multiple copies of títulos often surfaced. Slight differences suggested to the non-native audience that copyists had not only made careless errors but also amended the various versions over the years, which further lessened the documents' legal value. Because sections of them spoke of sixteenth- or early seventeenth-century happenings in the first person and in the present tense, whereas the handwriting and the paper they were written on were late seventeenth or eighteenth century, they were likely to be denounced as fraudulent (see fig. 5.1 for a handwriting sample). The folkloric historical nature of primordial titles, based on centuries-old oral traditions, probably fragments of earlier written records, and fading memory, was misunderstood, belittled, or disregarded, particularly when outsiders viewed the land claims they contained as grandiose.

Even though all land was native land before the arrival of Europeans, the territories best defended in the courts were those still held after

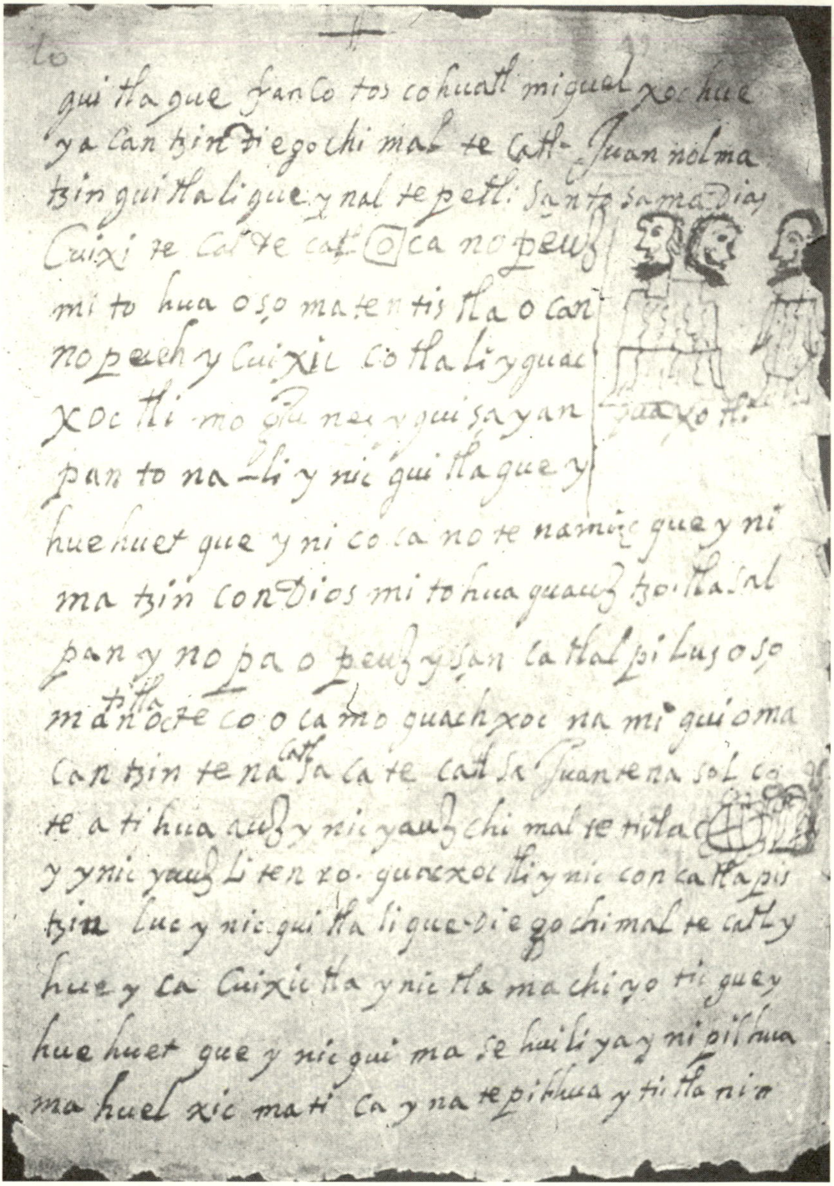

FIGURE 5.1. *Títulos* of San Matías Cuixingo. Photograph of sample page courtesy of the Archivo General de la Nación, Mexico. See also *Catálogo de ilustraciones* 1979, vol. 5, photograph 2232.

considerable indigenous population decline at the time of official Spanish recognition in the mid-sixteenth century. The need for formal colonial documents of such recognition—documents that rarely existed in the era of the more intense eighteenth-century land battles—may have been partly responsible for the move by literate members of many indigenous communities after about 1650 to record their own stories in their own way. It is surely no coincidence that títulos began appearing in considerable numbers as evidence in litigation around the start of the eighteenth century.[4] Yet a careful reading indicates that they do not actually address the Spanish court officials who eventually read translations of them. Instead, they are directed at the people of a particular town and their future descendants.[5] Authors even warn against letting Spaniards see the titles, a point I will return to subsequently.

That a considerable portion of the contents of títulos does not relate directly to territorial claims also supports the interpretation that they were usually directed toward an internal audience. A drive to portray the increasing size and strength—and the concomitant autonomy—of the altepetl may have been the real motivation.[6] Land grants were only one component of such a portrayal. Other equally important developments that come to light in titles include prehispanic migrations and multiple settlements that preceded the definitive location; threats to the town from other indigenous groups, such as Mexica imperialists, that were turned back; efforts by founding fathers and mothers to sustain the community by guiding settlement, construction, agriculture, or worship (the construction of native temples and later churches, the selection of patron saints, and mass baptisms); epidemics; the reorganization of town centers on grid patterns; the designation of barrios, or wards; the appointment of Spanish-style town councils populated with local indigenous leaders, including a *juez gobernador* (town governor) or an *alcalde* (high-ranking town council officer); the organization of tribute payments; and so on. Two-dimensional sketches may accompany these narratives, the two forms of expression, written and pictorial, each mutually reinforcing the authority of the other (fig. 5.2).

Not every title or version preserved in multiple copies has all this information. Some elaborate more extensively on prehispanic events, underlining the ancient roots of the community; others recall more of the religious history, usually rooted in local pride and identity; some dwell on various boundary surveys and related commemorative acts, bolstering ter-

FIGURE 5.2. *Títulos* of San Matías Cuixingo. Photograph of sample page courtesy of the Archivo General de la Nación, Mexico. See also *Catálogo de ilustraciones* 1979, vol. 5, photograph 2237.

ritorial claims. Groups of titles from the same region, made by or for neighboring towns, such as those known for Chalco (Lockhart 1991), share prominent details or even whole sections almost verbatim; see, for example, the similar arrangement of persons on the landscape in figures 5.3 and 5.4. The Xochimilcan título borrows from annals, a more traditional historical genre. As all these examples and more that have come to the fore are showing, their basic characteristics repeat, facilitating their identification collectively as a distinct genre.

The examples of the genre considered here in greatest detail are three sets of titles from the Valley of Toluca, representing the towns of San Bartolomé Capuluac (also known as Capulhuac), San Martín Ocoyacac (also known as Ocoyoacac), and San Juan Bautista Metepec. A title from Coatepec de las Bateas provides corroborative material. In addition, wherever

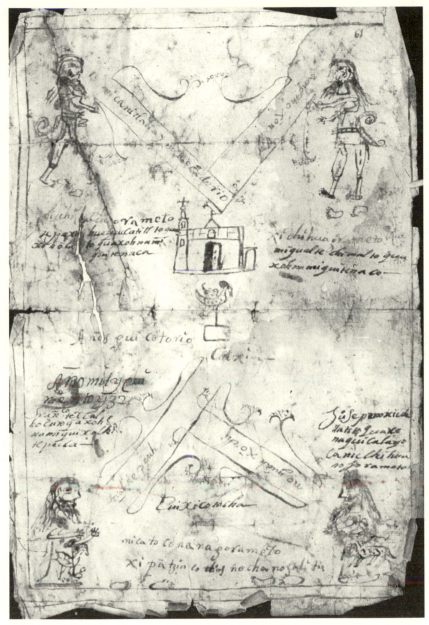

FIGURE 5.3. *Títulos* of San Matías Cuixingo. Photograph of sample page courtesy of the Archivo General de la Nación, Mexico. See also *Catálogo de ilustraciones* 1979, vol. 5, photograph 2236.

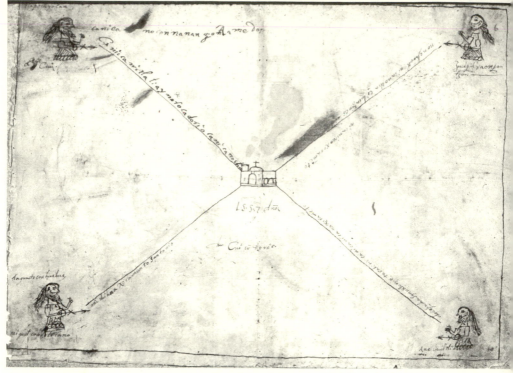

FIGURE 5.4. *Títulos* of Zoyatzingo. Photograph of sample page courtesy of the Archivo General de la Nación, Mexico. See also *Catálogo de ilustraciones* 1979, vol. 3, photograph 1176.

possible, I draw supporting information from the wider central Mexican region: from the four Chalco títulos examined by Lockhart (1991) plus three other Chalcan titles associated with San Andrés Mixquic, San Matías Cuixingo, and Los Reyes (near San Juan Temamatla) that I investigated in the national archives; from three heretofore unexplored Xochimilco-area títulos (which we might broadly associate with Chalco, too, for sharing the same basin)[7] associated with San Gregorio Acapulco (also known as Atlapulco), Asunción Milpa Alta, and Santa Marta; from one of the títulos of Huejotzingo; and from seven titles tied to Cuernavacan communities being studied by Robert Haskett (1987, 1990). The last include four from the regional capital itself plus one from Chapultepec, one from San Lorenzo Chiamilpa (also known as Chamilpa), and one from San Salvador

Ocotepec.[8] Where applicable, I draw additional comparisons from titles of western, southern, and southeastern Mesoamerica.

THE SWORD

The Spanish chronicler's formulaic depiction of "conquest" as a violent and prolonged contest little resembles references to European invasion and seizure of power in primordial titles. Lockhart (1991, 59) finds for Chalco that the "conquest proper hardly figures in the titles. It is merely signaled as 'the coming of Cortés' or 'the coming of the faith,' something taken as a cosmic event." The Chalcan Atlauhtla title, for example, refers only briefly to the surrender of the Mexican capital and some local fighting (Lockhart 1991, 54). The Chalco region sided with Cortés early in 1521 (Gerhard 1972, 103), which may account for the relative lack of discussion of armed conflict. The Cuernavaca and Toluca areas, on the other hand, resisted and met defeat in 1521, yet títulos from these regions similarly contain little information about battles. Poor memory alone cannot account for this, because the authors of various titles remember (or imagine) other prehispanic events in sometimes lengthy detail. Was it that battles of the Spanish campaign for imperial power occurred on fronts unobserved by títulos authors (or their ancestors), or were conflicts settled too quickly? The obvious deduction is that local repercussions of the Spanish invasion were not necessarily associated with the armed phase, nor was their impact linked only with the earliest post-Cortesian years.

The few references to the Spanish invasion in the Tolucan Capuluac titles, and they are oblique, include a simple statement that "Cortés came to win this new land" and one announcing that Mexico City had been refounded (AGN T 2860, exp. 1, cuad. 2, 68r). Nothing is said of the destructive forces or change of government that necessitated the rebuilding of the capital. On a more local level, the town founder named in the Metepec title claims to have aided in the subjugation of three barrios in his community, putting up five hundred pesos of his own money (Garibay K. 1949, 12), a considerable sum even if exaggerated for effect (a daily rural wage was one-eighth of a peso).[9] Like other caciques, he places himself in the critical role of empire builder.

One of the Xochimilco-area títulos, from Santa Marta, mentions ninety days of war in Santiago Tlatelolco in 1521. The reference seems to come from the annals of nearby San Gregorio Acapulco, which contain this and other battle information (McAfee and Barlow 1952, 105).[10] As with the Capuluac example, this is a reference to a distant front, apparently not a war endured by the earliest residents of Santa Marta but one that had a vague impact at home. It is surprising that Xochimilcan titles do not tell of fighting in the regional capital or of the dramatic burning of the city in 1521 (Prescott 1964, 531–36). The spectacular battles in the Cuernavaca region (Prescott 1964, 528–30) similarly escape notice in that area's known primordial titles.

The most notorious Spanish invader, Hernando Cortés, suffered a head injury and was taken captive temporarily just outside Xochimilco, but these records recall no such exciting details. He appears in most títulos as simply the marqués, or the Marqués del Valle, the title he used after forming his vast personal domain within a decade of capturing power. He is never described as a warrior, an unwelcome intruder, or a hated overlord, even though he personally led some of the battles and claimed significant portions of the Valley of Toluca, the Cuernavaca region, and, for a time, the Chalco area as his domain (Gerhard 1972, 94–95, 103, 330).

Oaxacan títulos offer somewhat longer accounts of armed conflict, which they associate with the coming of the Spaniards and their Nahua allies. Mixtec records recall welcoming Cortés but fighting against the Nahuas. The Nahuas who settled in Oaxaca remember battling the Mixtecs on behalf of both a Zapotec noblewoman and Cortés. When Cortés arrived on the scene, however, his supposed Nahua allies turned on the Spaniards, combating them valiantly until the Spaniards capitulated. We see the Nahuas, in a recurring pattern, painting themselves as conquerors or valiant warriors in their own right rather than as aides to the Spaniards. But despite the occasional conflict and rivalry with Spaniards, both Mixtec and Nahua titles of the Oaxaca area pragmatically underline their more general cooperation with the Europeans (Terraciano and Sousa 1992, 29–31, 46, 53).

The *Chronicle of Yaxkukul,* a Maya título studied by Matthew Restall, does not shy from "subjects such as death in battle," but it imparts no "sense of death and destruction" as major themes of the invasion (Restall 1991, 120). Memories of the Spanish takeover in Yaxkukul are records primarily of caciques' roles, not of the roles of Spaniards, although they include the principal Spanish invader, don Francisco Montejo, whose full title they respectfully and accurately reproduce. As in other accounts, alliance and cooperation with the invaders is the high note, with a corresponding elevation of status for members of the Pech cacique family who graciously received "Spanish officials and institutions (such as clergy and Christianity, encomendero and encomienda; oidor and congregación)" (Restall 1991, 114, 120).[11]

The way many primordial titles abbreviate the immediate period of the Spanish invasion and its subsequent events and place their own local families in prominent historical roles is reminiscent of the indigenous testimonies recorded secondhand in the sixteenth-century *relaciones geográficas* from New Spain. Rarely do these manuscripts, compiled mostly by provincial colonial administrators who relied upon native informants, provide any detail. Responding to a questionnaire that asked for information about who discovered and "conquered" the local province, by whose order, in what year, and so on (question no. 2), indigenous elders of the central Mexican highland towns frequently ignored the Spanish role in such events altogether, describing instead the activities of one or more caciques (and sometimes *cacicas,* their female equivalents)[12] who founded their communities in pre-Columbian times.[13] A cacique couple appears in figure 5.5.

The "mistake" in the relaciones geográficas behind the substitution of town founder (in the indigenous view) for conqueror (in the Spanish view) may be telling of the different mind-sets. It recalls and helps illuminate the Nahuatl term *tlalmaceuhqui* (literally, "land-deserver" or "land-achiever") that we find for town founder/conqueror in the primordial titles. If *tlalmaceuhqui* is a translation for conquistador, in the latter's meaning that comes from *ganar,* to take over/secure the land in a less violent way (Gibson 1980, 10), it may help clarify the intended sense behind the use of "conquest" in the *Relación anónima* from Querétaro. This manuscript speaks of an indigenous leader's conquering Chichimecs "in the proper way," which was peacefully (Gruzinski 1986a, 343).

When they did not respond in terms of indigenous "conquerors," informants of the relaciones geográficas would briefly mention that the famous Hernando Cortés, or the Marqués del Valle, had come and won Mexico. Sometimes, as in Teotenango, there is a memory of how one of Cortés's emissaries came to accept the town's allegiance, proffered peacefully (Acuña 1985–86, 2:277). A series of four accounts grouped together as the *Relación de Tequizistlan* (Acuña 1985–86, 2:211–51) reminds readers that everyone knows Cortés conquered Mexico and those wishing more

FIGURE 5.5. *Títulos* of Los Reyes (San Juan Temamatla). Photograph of sample page courtesy of the Archivo General de la Nación, Mexico. See also *Catálogo de ilustraciones* 1979, vol. 5, photograph 2306.

information should read a relación that was being prepared in Mexico City. From this, one would gather that the only "conquest" events of significance occurred in the capital.

Few are the examples of aggression on more distant fronts. In one account from Michoacán, no one could say—or perhaps felt like discussing— who it was that the marqués had sent to take over that province (Acuña 1985–86, 2:154).[14] It is highly doubtful that such communities had no recollection of or had heard no oral traditions about the Spanish invasion, which had occurred only two generations prior to the formation of the relaciones geográficas—especially in a place such as Michoacán where probably many could recall the sensational torture and execution of the Uacúsecha leader, the *cazonci*, discussed in chapter 3.[15] Other records, such as the primordial titles, testify to the longevity of community history. It was more a case of the Spanish defeat of the Aztec capital's simply not holding the same paramount significance for indigenous histories that European or creole histories accorded it. Perhaps, too, in the era of the relaciones, some indigenous informants found it prudent to respond in an abbreviated manner and censor their inclination to present their parents and grandparents as the true power figures.

The guardians of corporate memory in provincial towns, those who contributed the content of primordial titles, were equally uninterested in recounting or reluctant to recount the combat heroics of Cortés and his small armor-clad band of fortune hunters, if they had any knowledge of such activities. But titles recorders gave considerable attention to Cortés as the marqués, the powerful colonial administrator. Primordial titles regularly link the marqués to a string of other prominent Spanish officials, including the king, Carlos V, the first two Mexican viceroys, don Antonio de Mendoza and don Luis de Velasco, the younger viceroy Velasco, son of the first, and the first archbishop, don Juan de Zumarraga. The manuscripts treat all of them as influential leaders, not necessarily in their dealings with other Europeans but as figures who helped establish and strengthen the local indigenous community, its rank, its landholdings, its church, and its leadership—all of far greater importance than the men themselves, whose names often became confused. Most changes set in motion by the Spanish invasion and felt most notably at the local, altepetl level came with purported visits by these Spanish dignitaries or their representatives, some of whom circulated through the central areas possibly as early as the mid-1520s and more regularly by midcentury.[16]

Another somewhat mysterious recurring figure in the central Mexican títulos is a Spaniard, Pedro de Ahumada, who arrived in Mexico in 1550 (Lockhart 1991, 59) and may have served in both civil and ecclesiastical posts. His importance in the titles looms much larger than it does in general histories; in them he is known hardly at all, though perhaps he should be. "*Arsubizbuc* don Bero de omemadad," as he is called in the San Gregorio Acapulco título, was not really an archbishop but may have been an envoy of the archbishop (McAfee and Barlow 1952, 126). He appears as "Do Petro de Omada" in the Chalcan Tetelco title, as "Do P te Omemadad" in the same region's Zoyatzingo document (Lockhart 1991, 59), and as "*tlatohuani lisensiado* D PeDro De onmata" in the Cuixingo records (AGN T 2819, exp. 9, 55v). In the last, Ahumada acts in an official capacity, overseeing resettlement and other municipal rearrangements in 1559. François Chevalier (1963, 209) tells of a Pedro de Ahumada who reported to the high court in 1559 about indigenous leaders who were seizing community lands and selling them to Spaniards in the Mexico City region. This would fit with his activities reported for Cuixingo.

Possibly the same person, Pedro de Ahumada Sámano served in the 1550s as the governor for Cortés's estate, the Marquesado del Valle (Riley 1973, 91; Zavala 1984, 263), and was called simply "Señor Pedro de Ahumada" in a report about his activities in this capacity in the *Libro de las tasaciones* (1952, 582–84, 642). A few years later, "Señor pedro aomada" appears as a key expeditionary figure in the Nahuatl record of a sixteenth-century expedition against Zacatecs and Guachichiles in Nueva Galicia (Barlow and Smisor 1943, 9–10). His own account of this excursion, in Spanish, dates from 1562 (Barlow and Smisor 1943, Appendix). The Huejotzingo título has a campaign leader serving in an ecclesiastical function, with Gonzalo de Sandoval observing mass baptisms (TLAL, VEMC, file 24, item 3). Thus the sword and the cross are intermixed in the persons of these expedition heads and early administrators, who may have had a significance in the sixteenth-century indigenous world that has escaped modern researchers. Along with such high-level figures as the marqués and the king, they are later seen in a uniformly positive light for the support they lent to the local community.

CIVIL CONGREGATIONS

The importance of the "civil congregations" of the mid-sixteenth century is well known today, and in the *títulos* they are some of the more prominent occasions for visits by Spanish officials to indigenous communities. Many historians recognize *congregación* programs, an integral part of the consolidation of power, as disruptive forces. Their ostensible purpose was to condense dispersed populations following epidemics for better religious instruction and taxation. But critics see congregación programs as having resettled people against their will and sometimes as having contributed to the more rapid spread of disease (see, for example, de la Torre 1952; Gerhard 1972, 27). Although such appraisals seem just, it is instructive to note that the primordial titles do not put individual congregations in a wholly negative light.[17] Certainly, the titles recall considerable resistance to initial efforts to concentrate indigenous settlement, but their authors also appear satisfied, at least in retrospect, with the result: a stronger, more settled, more populous town.

According to the Ocoyacac title, several attempts were made to congregate people occupying the "hills and plains, woods and ravines, rocks, caves," and so on (AGN T 2998, exp. 3, 29r).[18] Another attempt involved the people of the neighboring communities of San Francisco Cuauhpanoayan and San Martín Obispo, who were settled together in exchange for a land concession from Viceroy Mendoza. In August 1556—a plausible date—the Ocoyacac title remembers a call to bring people in from outlying areas.[19] "Some came, others were afraid and did not want to come," but in the end, a successful survey of boundaries was celebrated with trumpet playing, the shooting of arrows, the presentation of flowers, neighbors embracing, and the sharing of a meal (AGN T 2998, exp. 3, 30r–v). There is a definite indigenous stamp on some of these salutory acts.

Whether or not the earliest congregación attempts in Ocoyacac failed is unclear; perhaps one simply built on its predecessors. Another call to the "ancients" to form a pueblo was made to the sound of a trumpet on February 19, 1564, again a plausible date, although its exactness is surprising. "They did not want to come," the title recounts, and war nearly broke out. But the animated men and women quieted down, exchanged flowers, and embraced when the boundaries were once more marked off for the new territory (AGN T 2998, exp. 3, 49v–50r).

The Metepec título also registers the theme of resistance ultimately overcome. In both this title and the one from Ocoyacac, there is little sense of the presence of any Spanish officials on the scene, let alone of their coercing people to abandon nonsedentary life. Instead, in Metepec it is a local man and woman (but apparently not a conjugal pair as in the Chalcan titles; see Lockhart 1991, 46) who convince their people to congregate. One says, "Let infidelity be rejected. Let God make us relinquish that which is not good. Let us be one" (Garibay K. 1949, 8). The other asks the people to give up living like deer and coyotes and to let God and the patron saint guide them (Garibay K. 1949, 10).

This precept was not simply one learned from the friars; it was a standard theme of ancient Mexican teachings meant to encourage people to lead a sedentary life.[20] But another motive is also possible. The male town founders, and indirectly their female counterparts, had something to gain by encouraging congregación and might therefore have remembered it more fondly than those whose lives were disrupted by resettlement. Larger, denser populations meant greater tribute assessments and a greater likelihood of the leaders' winning official colonial recognition as town governors. Local indigenous elites and Spanish colonial officials had a common interest in ensuring a smooth transition in the reorganizations that were taking place. Hence, in the Capuluac title we see Cortés and Viceroy Mendoza supervising the implementation of tribute payments, "first for God and then for the King in Castile" and finally for the indigenous juez gobernador of the local community, don Bartolomé Miguel (AGN T 2860, exp. 1, cuad. 2, 70r).

The Capuluac titles give a date of 1604 for this congregación, a date that jibes with the official record and corresponds to the second wave of population concentration in the late sixteenth and early seventeenth centuries.[21] The Capuluac titles also associate congregación with population growth rather than decline, perhaps because the town core became more populous despite the overall loss in smaller outlying settlements. An official came to issue house lots, the people designated four barrios and chose patron saints, and the land was measured and marked. All these events gave prestige to an altepetl and could help it gain status as a *cabecera* (head town) in the Spanish conceptualization of town hierarchy and its privileges (Gibson 1964, 33–57). The títulos of Santa Marta, for example, proudly illustrate various outlying settlements and their churches (fig. 5.6), and the

FIGURE 5.6. *Títulos* of Santa Marta. Photograph of sample page courtesy of the Archivo General de la Nación, Mexico. See also *Catálogo de ilustraciones* 1979, vol. 5, photograph 2303.

document from San Miguel Atllauhtla shows homage to Charles V of Spain (fig. 5.7)

THE CROSS

Although civil congregation, town council formation, and references to new tribute assessments are regular features in the municipal histories, religious changes set in motion by the arrival of the Spaniards are much more prominent. Spanish friars or priests are not much in evidence in the Chalco titles that Lockhart studied, but Christian themes certainly are (figs. 5.8, 5.9), especially in discussions of the local church, a "symbol of the town's existence and relative status" (Lockhart 1991, 62). Further study reveals that the church is a major feature of most central Mexican titles. Memories of original construction and worship in churches served as devices to show that community members were good Christians and therefore deserving of land (Gruzinski 1993, 116; Máynez, Blancas, and Morales 1995, 265; Roskamp n.d.). The Chiamilpa titles of Cuernavaca state outright that God gave its citizens their patrimonial land because they received the faith (AGN HJ, vol. 79, exp. 4). The Axayacatl título compilers say that land was granted to the town because the church was served (BNF-MM 102). Later construction and church repair provided a means to avoid *repartimiento* (labor drafts), which forcibly removed people from their communities. One suspects that a prehispanic cosmovision linked temples to the earth and to human agricultural activities, a view shared with the Christian world.

Friars do make occasional appearances in títulos, too. Although the phrases *ohualmohuicac yn tlaneltoquiliztli* and *oaçico yn tlaneltoquiliztli*, both meaning "the faith arrived," are benign formulas that appear in virtually all titles, we find the greatest Spanish intrusion and degree of coercion evidenced in references to various forms of forcible evangelism carried out by friars. Such references are particularly notable in the Valley of Toluca documents.[22]

The first priest to visit Capuluac came only once a month to say mass. But when this *clérigo* came, the town founder relates in the title, the people ran to hide.[23] Gradually, the town founder got them to listen to the priest (although at that time they "did not know the Castillian language") and encouraged them to accept baptism, which the priest supposedly

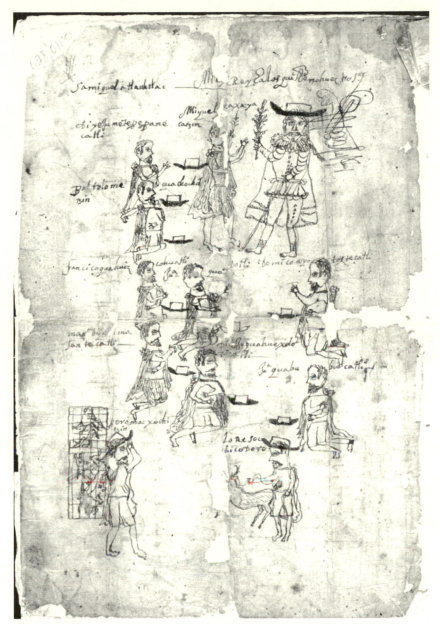

FIGURE 5.7. *Títulos* of San Miguel Atlauhtla. Photograph of sample page courtesy of the Archivo General de la Nación, Mexico. See also *Catálogo de ilustraciones* 1979, vol. 3, photograph 1544.

FIGURE 5.8. *Títulos* of Los Reyes (San Juan Temamatla). Photograph of sample page courtesy of the Archivo General de la Nación, Mexico. See also *Catálogo de ilustraciones* 1979, vol. 5, photograph 2304.

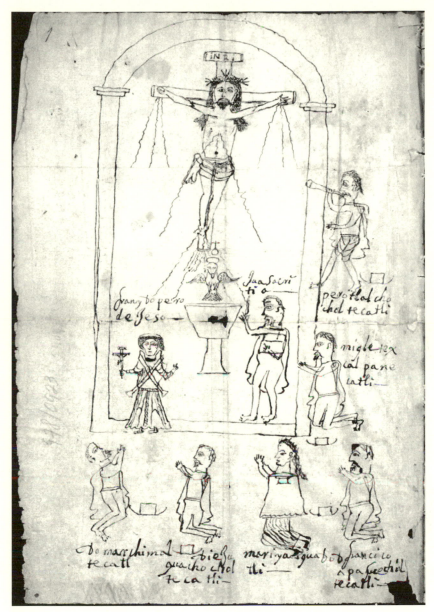

FIGURE 5.9. *Títulos* of San Martín Ocoyacac. Photograph of sample page courtesy of the Archivo General de la Nación, Mexico. See also *Catálogo de ilustraciones* 1979, vol. 5, photograph 2277.

initiated in 1539.[24] Still, they did not "believe properly," remembers the indigenous town founder, and so the priest had to come "to destroy that which they had been worshiping" (AGN T 2860, exp. 1, cuad. 2, 68v). On another occasion, the town founder's son aided the priest in "breaking up the gods" (70r).[25] Because much of this title is a record in the first person of statements supposedly made by the town founder and his descendants, it is not surprising that, given their roles as intermediaries assisting the ecclesiastics, they take for granted a Christian victory. Figure 5.10 illustrates church construction in Capuluac.

In the Metepec title, the "faith was installed," presumably at the urging of one local leader who claimed to have willingly aided the newcomers at the same time that a perhaps less compliant ruler "was expelled" (Garibay K. 1949, 7). Although this manuscript says nothing more of the former ruler, it affords some intriguing details of the evangelical campaign. The title relates that a Fray Bartolomé "is to go to conquer [the infidels], and they will really not desire it" (Garibay K. 1949, 10).[26] The town founder claims to have spent about a thousand pesos, another significant sum, to help build the first chapel and provide its adornments. On one occasion, when some people tried to remove the image of Santa Clara from their temple, he and others of "God's beloved" pursued the dissidents up a hillside, carrying ropes. "Howling like coyotes" during the chase, some of the fugitives fell down and succumbed to capture. One surrendered and promised to accept baptism. Finally, the victors returned Clara's image to the principal temple, and all supposedly rejoiced greatly (Garibay K. 1949, 10–11).

Stories about miracles and festivities punctuate these brief accounts of aggression and resistance. The Metepec title describes people as having been pleased by the religious instruction that introduced Latin grammar and other foreign languages to them (Garibay K. 1949, 7). On Friday, December 1, 1525, when three friars brought consecrated bread from Xalatlaco, the head town of the parish, to celebrate Holy Communion, there was supposedly "great happiness" (Garibay K. 1949, 7).[27] In general, the Metepec account is a string of remembrances (seemingly not in chronological order) of steady Spanish incursions and waning indigenous resistance, with ultimate victory falling to the intruders and with a swelling enthusiasm on the part of the new religious subjects. The title's authors

FIGURE 5.10. *Títulos* of San Bartolomé Capuluac. Photograph of sample page courtesy of the Archivo General de la Nación, Mexico. See also *Catálogo de ilustraciones* 1979, vol. 5, photograph 2251.

express pride in local chapels, in the communal labor behind their construction and maintenance, and in service to the patron saints. Some even make a concerted effort to leave a record of their own agency in inviting priests to their communities and taking other actions to establish a greater Christian presence.[28]

The *Códice Plancarte* places the decision-making power regarding the acceptance of Christianity with a prehispanic god of Uandaro, Michoacán. This god was dismayed by a light in the skies, probably a comet, and the indigenous priests tried to appease the deity by sacrificing many people and offering up a large number of human hearts. After a week of this, the god informed his believers (I presume this god was gendered male) that he no longer wanted to be their primary god because a new god (presumably the Christian one) would occupy that position. Although he asked that his people bury him (or his effigy) in a cave, room seems to have been left for his continued worship. Still, the patron saints John and Sebastian are the religious figures who occupy central positions toward the end of the manuscript (Roskamp 1998, 260).

Local people's role in selecting the patron saint of Milpa Alta dominates that community's primordial titles and is prominent in those of Capuluac. Chronology is again somewhat hazy. Indeed, Capuluac's first saint seems to have been chosen before any Spaniards had been on the scene. The patron of the earliest settlement of this town, a "stone saint"—presumably a prehispanic icon—was the object of pilgrimages made by different ethnic groups in the valley. The people of Coatepec de las Bateas may have similarly fashioned their own "saint's image" from stone without supervision or authorization, for the priest who came to say the first mass disapproved of it. He said to them, "This is not a saint, this is a stone; although you see it as a saint, it is not," and suggested that they go to Mexico City to get another image (Máynez, Blancas, and Morales 1995, 280–81).[29]

The Capuluac title reads that the worship of its "stone saint" occurred in the days when "we still do not really believe," when "in this land and its surroundings we do not yet believe [in Christianity]" (AGN T 2860, exp. 1, cuad. 2, 68r).[30] The authors exhibit possible confusion about what came before and after the arrival of the Spaniards, but they understand that there was a pre-Christian era experienced not only by their town but by the whole region. The Ocoyacac title, in a similar vein, incorporates a

Spanish term for "heathen" to describe the local inhabitants in the time before the faith arrived: *tigentilestlaca*, "we gentile people" (AGN T 2998, exp. 3, 18r, 28r, 29r).[31] It is intriguing that this foreign label, "gentile," which carries a certain negativity in the Spanish view (similar to that of "infidel," used in a manuscript mentioned earlier), had been embraced by the indigenous people. But perhaps they interpreted it less to mean non-Christian than to mean native to this land, or non-Spanish, imbuing it not so much with a religious significance as with an ethnic association. Was the use of *tigentilestlaca* representative of a dawning awareness of "Indianness" among people who also held a more immediate identification with their respective altepetl?

Interestingly, no longing is expressed in any of these titles for that earlier, pre-Christian time. No one hints that it was superior or something that should be recaptured. If anything, the títulos evince a sense of satisfaction that a misguided past has been overcome. Such sentiments are more forthcoming than, but not out of line with, the relatively favorable views we saw earlier in association with military conflict and civil congregations.

ANTI-SPANISH SENTIMENT

This is not to say that the period when many primordial titles were written down or recopied, probably the late seventeenth or early eighteenth century, was a carefree time. Grave problems accompanied the slow but hopeful regeneration of population that followed the devastating epidemics of the sixteenth century. The growth in the number of new families that needed fertile land, some of which had been usurped by Spaniards, was partially responsible for the formulation of these titles. The eighteenth-century relaciones geográficas of the Archbishopric of Mexico provide a glimpse into the evolving demographic situation.

The 1743 relación from Santa Clara Lerma, in the Toluca Valley, provides an instructive case study (Solano 1988, 1:129–43). Lerma was unusual in that it was a town founded in the early seventeenth century by and for Spaniards. The norm in this valley was for Spanish colonists either to maintain their principal houses in Mexico City, to live in the larger provincial cities and towns, such as Toluca, or to reside on their estates. But according to the relación, the town of Lerma had some forty to fifty Spanish families resident in 1743. The jurisdiction of Lerma also included four indigenous communities, and one of these towns, Santa María Tarasquillo, had another seven Spanish families living in it. The total indigenous population of the Lerma jurisdiction, including eighty families of "indios" in the Spanish town, came to 648 families. Somewhere between 121 and 133 families of mixed heritage (Spanish, African, and indigenous) also occupied the jurisdiction. Even at this late date, in the Spanish colony and in a part of the valley that had an unusually high concentration of Spanish settlement, the native population clearly dominated numerically. Still, the Spanish colonists and their offspring were multiplying and acquiring land, and some were taking up residence in indigenous communities.

Moving our focus to Tetzcoco (or Texcoco) (Solano 1988, 2:459–66), with its city and numerous indigenous pueblos, we see again how Spaniards were living among the locals. The city of Tetzcoco alone had the considerable number of 4,110 indigenous families, 560 mixed-heritage families, and 321 Spanish families in 1743. This relación is less precise in its listing of ethnic groupings in the nearby pueblos, usually lumping Spaniards and mestizos together and possibly omitting some of them. The resulting sums are therefore tentative, but still telling. Nonindigenous residents in the Tetzcoco-area pueblos and in the private estates interspersed among them amounted to 330 families, whereas indigenous families numbered 4,837.[32]

The mounting tension over precious resources that came with indigenous-Spanish (not to mention indigenous-indigenous) land competition surfaces in the primordial titles in the form of startling anti-Spanish remarks. Such remarks stand in striking contrast to the expression of generally favorable opinions of kings and viceroys.

The principal Spanish individuals who appear by name in these local historical narratives are colonial officials and high ecclesiastics who legitimate the town and bolster its claims. All the central Mexican títulos considered here treat these individuals alike. The titles never refer to their ethnicity and hardly even think of them as individuals. The texts sprinkle their legendary names about liberally while ignoring or confusing their first names and often their official Spanish titles. The títulos show them considerable respect nonetheless, referring to them as *tlahtoque*, rulers. The Mixquic document boasts that the viceroy was greeted with flowers and the playing of single-reed instruments called *chirimías* (AGN T 3032, exp. 3, 213–14r). The Capuluac title describes the younger viceroy don Luis de

Velasco as "cencan mahuiztililoni" (the truly honorable) (AGN T 2860, exp. 1, cuad. 2, 71v). The Reyes manuscript describes the elder Velasco, in an obviously mistaken but respectful manner, as "Rey noestro senior" (king our lord) (AGN T 3032, exp. 3, 277r).[33]

These titles reserve caution, fear, and anger for the generic Spanish individual who might penetrate the community's protective shield. For example, the Capuluac title defies any Spaniard—literally, *quixtiano,* "Christian," a Nahuatlization of the Spanish *cristiano*—ever "to alienate even a gourdful of maize or to plant half an almud of maize . . . and never can anyone sell land [to Spaniards]" (AGN T 2860, exp. 1, cuad. 2, 69r–v).[34] Later, it warns people not to make friends with Spaniards (*quixtiyanotin,* "Christians"), for they will try to take land (AGN T 2860, exp. 1, cuad. 2, 72r).[35] This warning comes in the midst of a discussion about a supposed outsider "who is not our relative, who is from another place; for he is really of another blood; he is a coyote."[36] This person of allegedly mixed Spanish and indigenous ancestry is said to have come from Mexico City and to have penetrated the local elite in the seventeenth century, gaining the title of *tlahtoani.* According to the título, the "big dog [*huey chichi*] ruined the town [*oquitlaco altepetl*]," and none of his descendants must ever be allowed to rule. These manuscripts regularly incorporate such examples of political factionalism between different elite lineages, which was a feature of everyday life in many pueblos.[37]

Primordial titles allowed their authors, while covering the political and religious history of the town, to establish age-old territorial claims both for the community and for prestigious families within it. Perhaps the documents were made partly for use in the courts, for they often turned up there, but they also informed and reminded the local inhabitants about crucial boundaries. For that reason they were guarded jealously. And if títulos were in part an attempt to replace lost land documents from earlier times, then their possessors probably wanted to be more careful with them the second time around. Leaders were reluctant to let anyone in the town show the títulos to outsiders, who might then be better prepared to counter their claims. Titles could serve as proof of ownership of land, even if they somehow fell into the hands of outsiders, whether indigenous, mestizo, or Spanish. It is this apparent frame of mind that we see in the Ocoyacac título's warning, "The Spaniards are already coming; do not show [this document] to them" (AGN T 2998, exp. 3, 47v). King Carlos V is said to have given possession of the land to Ocoyacac's townspeople, not to the Spaniards (*caxtiltecantli*, "people of Castile") (21r, 30r). These two remarks are nearly identical to the sentiment expressed in the título Charles Gibson (1964, 271) quotes: "Spaniards come to seize what we have justly won."

The Milpa Alta title, cautioning its citizens of that inevitable and undesirable march of the Spaniards, elaborates: "And you will all lose everything. The Spaniards will come, they will become your friends, *compadres* [religious co-parents], and in-laws, they will bring money, and with that, they will go taking away little by little all the lands that are found here" (AGN T 3032, exp. 3, 215r–v). The original Nahuatl of this portion is missing, but the Spanish captures the same flavor that Lockhart (1991) relates for the Chalco titles, a resistance to showing the papers to Spaniards and letting them usurp indigenous landholdings. The Zoyatzingo title also warns that the intruders are likely to worm their way into compadre relationships in order to get the land through purchase or gift. The Sula document describes them as tricky, deceitful people. Abundant examples of the same distrust of colonists color the lot of known primordial titles from central Mexico. Lockhart (1991, 62) suggests that although these documents reveal "an affirmative attitude . . . toward an overall Spanish-Christian framework, the same is not true when it comes to Spaniards as individuals."

In the collective memory of primordial titles, the supposed "conquest" is a cosmic event with only gradual repercussions, mainly religious changes, experienced in the first century of contact. After two or three centuries of Spanish occupation, coinciding with the written composition or recopying of these local histories, indigenous people were feeling the Spanish invaders' presence and threat profoundly, through the descendants of those invaders. The intruders were no longer conquerors per se (if they had ever been); they called themselves Christians and were nominally accepted as such. They or their predecessors came from a distant land called Caxtilan (Castile) or, more recently, Mexico City, and spoke a different language (*Caxtilan tlatoli*). But they were not mysterious. The titles raised the alarm only after the foreigners had made considerable inroads into indigenous towns. Apparently, enough Spaniards and mestizos had already formed associations or entered into compadre relationships with local indigenous people and had come to purchase or otherwise obtain corporate landholdings that a nervous portion of the community's leadership recognized a danger. In the titles, it is often the elders who warn future generations of the growing threat. It is interesting that the titles reveal a sense of urgency. It is only now that the Spaniards are coming, for it is now more than ever—in the seventeenth and eighteenth centuries—that colonists compete for space and threaten the autonomy of the recuperating indigenous community.

6

Supplanting the Metanarrative
TRANSCENDING CONQUEST

All history is thus: a radical selection from the immensely rich swirl of past human activity.

RICHARD PRICE, *FIRST-TIME: THE HISTORICAL VISION OF AN AFRO-AMERICAN PEOPLE*

After reviewing a broad range of provincial indigenous testimonies, textual and graphic, spanning nearly the entire period during which Mesoamerica fell to Spain and remained under Spanish rule, what conclusions can we reach about native views on these developments in their lives? Have we seen any evidence to sustain the interpretation that indigenous people perceived Europeans as radically different from themselves? That they were unable to cope with the newcomers' intrusion and with the maelstrom it supposedly triggered? Granted, Mesoamerican sources from the flashpoint of contact are few and secondhand, but the extant record furnishes only limited evidence to support such notions. The newcomers had strange faces and clothing, used odds means of traveling, and ate unusual foods. Their weapons were indeed impressive. They had special headgear, flags, and shields. But it was as people, as human power holders, that we find images of Spaniards woven fairly seamlessly into the tapestry of both momentous historical occasions and the routines of daily life—not usually as monsters or gods.

There is little doubt that *some* indigenous people of Mesoamerica viewed the Europeans who came ashore in the early sixteenth century as gods or godlike beings. But before we make too much of it, we need to consider whether it was a widespread impression and how long it lasted. Also, what did it mean in indigenous cultures to assign godlike characteristics to mortals? We should not conclude that this made them Christlike figures, objects of complete devotion and centuries-long worship. We should not assume that it was some naive folk who had no ability to size up accurately a foreign human being who gave shape to this sacred identity. Marvin Lunenfeld (1991, 268) reminds us: "The Inca rulers were themselves treated as gods—children of the sun—so it was not unreasonable to think the foreigners, although obviously in the form of men, could in some sense be divine. They too were called Viracochas." José Rabasa (1993, 110) writes in a similar vein: "Historical records tell us about the Indians and a taciturn Moctezuma who see the intruders as *teules*. The meaning of this term remains far from clear (what for instance is a 'god' in the Nahua pantheon?)" Luis Villoro (1992, 65) partially answers this question, saying that "according to the categories of the Aztecs, the gods were close to men and the distinction between the two was fluid."[1]

To illuminate this murky issue of possible divinity, it would be helpful to have more records from the contact period. Spanish sources on this subject are too self-serving to be of more than limited use in understanding the native frame of mind. We do learn from European accounts of events in the Caribbean that even if the first associations of divinity originated with native observers, it became convenient for invaders to manipulate and encourage this association, having interpreters tell new people they encountered in the region that the Europeans came from the heavens.[2] Perhaps they carried this island experience with them to the mainland and fostered its implantation there, too. Or perhaps news of the strangers' presence in the Caribbean spread to the mainland ahead of them, and that accounting included the possibility of divinity among the foreigners. It might also be that Mesoamerican peoples thought of it themselves, independently.

The fusion of prophecy with history in indigenous sources does not help to clarify much in this area, either. No known records prove that the prediction that the departing man-god Quetzalcoatl would return—an event that neatly coincided with Cortés's landing—was a prehispanic tradition. But indigenous people helped contribute to the myth's survival, regaining agency by saying, "We predicted this."[3] Ross Frank (1989, 201) writes that the Quetzalcoatl-Cortés myth took shape "during the 1530s and appeared fully formed by the 1570s and 1580s in the writings of the missionaries," but Cortés's *Second Letter* "provided the basic plot and text."[4]

An arrogant and confident Cortés supposedly laughed about how the Cempoalans "think us gods, or godlike beings" (Díaz del Castillo 1963, 117). He slyly sent "an old Basque musketeer with a very ugly face covered with scars, a huge beard, and one blind eye," not to mention a lame leg, to lead an expedition against some Mexica warriors outside Cempoala saying, "The people here think we are gods, or at least they have given us that name and reputation, and when they see your ugly face they'll certainly take you for one of their idols" (Díaz del Castillo 1963, 117). Whether this was true or simply Bernal Díaz del Castillo's idea of a good story (he says, "I tell his story here merely as a joke and to show Cortés's guile"), it is instructive that even this early in the game the Spaniards were qualifying the supposed indigenous belief in their divinity with phrases like "or godlike beings" and "at least they have given us that name and reputation." Still, they occasionally tried to nurture the fragile belief through trickery, whether by sending the unfortunate Basque to shock them or by burying their own dead so that the indigenous warriors "should not see that we were mortal" (Díaz del Castillo 1963, 150). Perhaps giving up on the myth's utility or making a gesture intended to gain the trust of new allies, Cortés made a turnaround in the Tlaxcalan campaign and told Xicotencatl's messengers "that we were men of flesh and blood like themselves, and not *Teules* but Christians" (Díaz del Castillo 1963, 162).

Many indigenous observers seem to have transcended the idea that the Spaniards were divine fairly quickly, regardless of its origin and continuing discursive manipulation on either side. Possibly a first step in rethinking the Europeans' sacredness involved questioning, as happened in the Andean arena no later than the 1550s, whether these were benevolent or malevolent gods ("dioses bienhechores" or "runaquiçacha que dice estragadores de gente"), and then whether they were gods at all or just "men like themselves" ("dioses u hombres como ellos") (Pease 1989, 184–85). In another record, possibly from 1534, some indigenous Peruvians were already equating "los christianos" with "los diablos," or devils (Pease 1989, 185n, 188). Through spies, Atalhualpa also supposedly found out that Pizarro and his followers were "men like ourselves" who could perform no miracles; when in need of water they could not produce rivers or fountains but had to carry water with them wherever they went (Pease 1989, 186).

In a speech attributed to Moctezuma by Cortés, with elaboration by Cortés's secretary, Francisco López de Gómara, the Aztec leader supposedly recounted how frightening the Spaniards were at first and how they "came from heaven," but he concluded, "Now I know you to be mortal men" (Frank 1989, 204). Although one is generally reluctant to trust the words that Spaniards put into Moctezuma's mouth, it is a reasonable possibility that he had indeed decided they were mortals. The thought had crossed people's minds before. Even prior to the Spaniards' meeting with Moctezuma, in the midst of the Tlaxcalan campaign, Bernal Díaz del Castillo (1963, 151) acknowledged that some Aztec messengers had been sent to study the foreigners and to determine "whether we were *Teules* as the Cempoalans asserted, and what things we ate." These messengers "had learned we were men of flesh and blood, and ate poultry, dogs, bread, and fruit when we had them." According to Díaz del Castillo (1963, 162), the Tlaxcalans believed that deities would not be interested in eating food, but desirous only of obtaining *copal* (native incense) and "parrots' feathers" for a sacrificial ceremony. Surely doubts about the intruders' divinity were already dawning as native observers scrutinized the invaders' tellingly mortal quotidian activities from the moment of their first arrival by ship. Indigenous women who had to serve them as slave mistresses—starting with the twenty they obtained in Tabasco (Díaz del Castillo 1963, 80)—surely achieved considerable intimacy with their personal habits, which may have borne little similarity to the behavior of indigenous deities. Unquestionably by mid-century, in the Sahaguntine corpus, the mocking of the Spaniards and the likening of their behavior, at times, to that of monkeys and pigs does not bring to mind sacredness; it makes them into "savages and *popolcas* (those who cannot speak Nahuatl)," says José Rabasa (1993, 111). As Ross Hassig (1994, 144) wryly comments, it was owing to "harsh experience" that perceptions of Spaniards' supernatural and invincible powers ceased.

THE *OTHER* OTHER?

When indigenous observers discounted the divinity of Spaniards, did they nevertheless continue to think of them in a way reminiscent of Europeans' "othering" of native Americans? If they did not think of the newcomers as sacred for long, did they develop new frameworks for explaining or under-standing the nature of these strangers and their culture(s)? Did they categorize them as clearly different from and unassimilable to their own culture(s), as a group requiring unique treatment? Did they stereotype them and distance them from the self, creating prolonged communication difficulties and social problems? What nouns did they employ to describe the newcomers? Were Spaniards strangers, outsiders, visitors, guests, friends, intruders, invaders, traders, explorers, conquerors, enemies, lords, or something else for which we have no neat Spanish or English transla-tions? What adjectives did they apply: welcomed, unwanted, hateful, admirable, feared, repugnant, heartless, haughty, ignorant, confused, vio-lent, greedy, rapacious, reliable, smart, powerful? Or again, do we lack equivalents in modern European languages for translating indigenous ways of viewing Europeans? To complicate the question further, how did all this vary from one indigenous culture to another and over time?

Jean Franco (1992, 177) sees a defining link between "Europe's 'oth-ering' of the rest of the world," its imperial expansion, and the discourse associated with that expansion. All too often, indigenous-authored mate-rial has been seen as peripheral to European colonial discourse, whether unwittingly contributing to the othering process or resisting it.[5] As Franco recognizes, such a perception leads to an entirely unsatisfactory way of assessing the full value of native texts. Indeed, applying the European con-ception of an "other" in reverse seems less fruitful than letting categories from native American experiences emerge from ethnohistorical records.[6]

To say that indigenous groups were ethnocentric in their views of the newcomers can also be limiting. James Axtell (1988, 127) argues, "As mem-bers of cultures, all people are ethnocentric. Our task is to discover the particular configuration of ideas and values that makes each culture dis-tinctive." So what were indigenous Mesoamericans' mental images of Euro-peans and the new polity and society taking shape around them? Which values guided how these images were shaped? Further, if we can possibly identify it, how did their mental images affect indigenous people's behav-ior toward the newcomers and the new milieu?

These are questions deserving of a larger investigation. Undeniably, native recorders of historical material recognized clear differences between themselves and the multifaceted foreigners. In a reading by Georges Bau-dot (1996, 50), the *Florentine Codex* presents Spaniards as monstrous, inhuman beings against whom magical defense mechanisms were ineffective. But was this perspective widespread or lasting? Did indigenous observers ever develop ethnic stereotypes for the invaders as a group? If so, they did so only after prolonged contact. In the pattern of imaging that emerges in chapter 1, we can see a differentiated treatment for various social types. Spaniards do not appear uniformly as unwelcome invaders. They do not, as a group, become hated overlords extracting unbearable taxes and labor. Some were soldiers, some were functionaries, some were ecclesiastics. Their diverse props helped identify them.[7] Many rode horses and carried flags. Some had armor; some had tables, pens, and parchment; some carried crosses or baptismal fonts; some directed labor and collected tribute. A few squared off in battle against indigenous opponents, ordered dogs to attack prisoners, or stood holding bloody, decapitated heads in hand—vivid reminders of deadly serious conflict and struggles for power. But images from late pictorials, such as the so-called Techialoyan codices, capture the Spanish conquerors simply standing benignly in their armor, lances pointed toward the heavens (*Handbook of Middle American Indians* 1975, vol. 14, fig. 85).

As indigenous author-painters recorded the portraits and activities of the new power holders, they were simultaneously inscribing their behavior with a familiar set of cultural constructs. This practice emerges in all kinds of pictorials, but it may be that annals demonstrate the smoothest incorporation of the foreign. Elizabeth Boone (1994b, 67–68) writes, for example: "All the Aztec pictorial annals, except the Codex Mendoza, include the Spanish invasion and conquest of Mexico and then continue with the colonial story. They simply incorporate new rulers and persons of note (such as Cortés and the first bishop, Juan de Zumárraga) and new events (such as the great diseases) along with the traditional events." Entries for the period of the conquest (as Europeans defined it) scarcely skip a beat. Boone finds that the trauma and destruction one might expect are not obvious in the annals.

One recurring assessment among scholars of indigenous views of Europeans across the hemisphere has to do with the way indigenous people endeavored to incorporate the newcomers into their understanding of the existing world.[8] Luis Villoro (1992, 67) asserts that "the initial attitude of the Aztecs was to invite the other to occupy a privileged place in their own world," and that they based their culture "on a desire for integration and harmony." Further, their "polytheism could allow for foreign gods and, as a consequence, for diverse cultures" (1992, 68). This openness might have reduced the length of time indigenous people saw the Spaniards as "others"—if in fact they ever did.

The paradigm of central Mexican histories was to think of the society's origins as involving successive waves of immigrants, each bringing a new god and settling in with the existing population without much initial conflict. As "father and grandfathers" remembered it, the first settlers in the Valley of Mexico came from Seven Caves and comprised seven successive groups. One group brought a goddess, Tonan Quilaztli ("Our Mother Quilaztli"), and other groups brought gods such as Ontontecuhtli ("Otomi Lord") and Huitzilopochtli. But once the population grew and became more sedentary, dividing up scarce resources such as land, "wars began." Peoples who did not cooperate were "conquered" (*pevallo*) and their tribute was increased. The most famous conquerors were the Mexica, the Acolhua, and the Tepaneca, "for they had conquered people in all parts of the world" (*onovian tepevaya çemanavac*) (*Primeros Memoriales*, 222–23).

INDIGENOUS SELF AS CONQUEROR

The epithet "vision of the vanquished," the title of Nathan Wachtel's 1977 book—however clever and resonant it seems on the surface—does not adequately encompass the many different perspectives coming from native sources.[9] Indigenous people's self-perceptions, at least as represented in their community histories, are regularly not those of vanquished, conquered, subordinated, overcome, or powerless people. It is not even clear that Spaniards on the scene would have uniformly seen them in this modern light. Although the conquerors bragged of their military victories and called their seizure of power a conquest, they did not consistently portray the Crown's new subjects as defeated persons. Native leaders were respected figures who deserved titles of nobility, sizable incomes from tribute, and service.[10] The leaders' daughters were worthy, if of sufficiently high social and economic position, to become Spaniards' wives. In the idealized official view, at least, average citizens were hardworking individuals who had to produce revenue for encomenderos (including members of the Moctezuma family) and the Crown, but they also had a right to work in their own economic enterprises or farm their own land, all protected, to some degree, by the colonial enterprise.

It seems to have been more common, primarily in the early years, for indigenous historical testimonies to lament the fall of their imperial or regional leaders and to agonize about losses at the local level. These sentiments also have a certain association with views coming from the demolished capital.[11] Among all the provincial sources surveyed here, it is principally in the Ajusco manuscript, orginating closest to the capital, that we find vivid descriptions of how the Spanish invasion wrought pain and suffering. It caused the loss of precious life and incurred hardship for the men and women who survived. It reduced the corporate territorial base upon which the surviving population would have to support itself. Yet even in this cry of anguish, we can see the indigenous people negotiating to preserve as much autonomy as possible and protect what resources they could.

As more manuscripts surface, we may find an ever stronger recurrence of the theme of indigenous people themselves in the role of conqueror.[12] Certainly, there is already much evidence that when looking back on early history, native people frequently thought first of the times before Europeans were on the scene—although they did not separate epochs the same way Europeans did, identifying them as, for instance, pre-Columbian or postconquest.[13] They recalled historic migrations, settlements, and conflict with other indigenous groups. When asked about the "conquest" of their community, they did not necessarily think of the Spanish seizure of power but sometimes provided a narrative of a town founding in what would have been the prehispanic era (again, never seen as such). The European presence or lack of it was not typically the pivotal point for native histories. If the authors of these histories recall the Spanish struggle for power, they often throw in what they had learned were key dates, such as 1519,[14] and mention some key figures, such as Cortés, but they quickly move the storyline forward to position themselves prominently as the principal actors on a semi-independent stage. Although these histories accord respect to the new Spanish power holders, their places in history seem often to stem not so much from the indigenous authors' desire to recall their authority for posterity as from their desire to mark moments when such people recognized the local indigenous leadership or the local land base.[15]

The Tlaxcalan tradition evinces perhaps an exaggerated enthusiasm for the Spanish conquest, presenting it somewhat more in line with the way the invaders themselves would have portrayed it but still giving generous helpings of agency to the indigenous participants. In the *Mapa de Cuauhtlantzinco*, Tepoztecatzin remembers carrying the Spaniards in his heart (Starr 1898, 19), but he has appropriated and possibly even subverted their evangelist narrative, making himself and his comrades the main protagonists. Rather than remembering the arrival and lasting presence of Spaniards, the *Mapa* caciques emphasize the latter's return to Spain, claiming that they have gone to tell Charles V of the caciques' wondrous deeds (Starr 1898, 18–20).

HYBRIDITY ISSUES

The *Mapa* perspective defies generalizations about indigenous views of Spanish colonialism as either resistant (see Seed 1995, 15) or "tragic and bitter" (Franco 1982, 40). Some might say, therefore, that the position taken in the *Mapa* is not an indigenous but a "hybrid" one. Such observers would identify colonial multiethnic and cultural constructions in the *Mapa* to explain its failure to "fit" an imagined indigenous mold. Although all cultures are of course hybrid in some sense, the point of hybridity studies is to examine the "ambivalence" of the "colonial aftermath" (Coombes 1994, 6). In describing Christian Saramakas of Suriname, for instance, Richard Price (1990, xiv) confesses that he first saw them as "being somewhere down the bumpy road leading to the hated but ambiguously alluring world of 'whitefolks.'" Plenty of observers have applied a "negative valuation" to the "marks of European missionization" on aboriginal traditions, such as the Mayan *Popol Vuh*, according to Dennis Tedlock (1994, 77). While some participants and observers alike, concerned with preserving racial or cultural purity, mourn hybridization, others find it a fertile ground for innovation and creativity. Rolena Adorno (1988, 12) recalls "new hybrid constructions that are greater than the sum of their parts and multicultural sources." Mexican nationalists have been known to trumpet the multicultural roots and unique *raza* ("race") of the modern nation—though some also regard cynically the subsistent indigenous populations of the modern day (see Rosaldo 1993, 241). Finally, some see hybridization as a kind of "counterconquest," a

144

vigorous remodeling by indigenous and African people of European cultural imports (see Fuentes 1992, 7).

In discursive analysis, hybridization provides a supreme challenge to definitions of identity. Homi Bhabha (quoted in Rabasa 1993, 110) writes about hybridization and the manipulation of the text, saying that "hybridity intervenes in the exercise of authority not merely to indicate the impossibility of its identity, but to represent the unpredictability of its presence." Hybridity can multiply and double back on itself in mind-boggling ways. Michael Taussig (quoted in Price 1990, xv) has identified a complex colonial process that has "bound Indian understandings of white understandings of Indians to white understandings of Indian understandings of whites." Similarly, Mary Louise Pratt (1993, 25) finds the "invaders' language appropriated by the invadee to address the invader; the invadee's interests expressed in discursive apparatuses adapted from the invader and redirected back at him."

In the context of colonial Mesoamerica, hybridity can result from "transculturation," which occurs when "members of subordinated or marginal groups [here read: indigenous peoples] select and invent from materials transmitted by a dominant or metropolitan culture [here read: Spanish colonial]" (Pratt 1993, 31). Seemingly all of the post-1521 pictorials and texts explored in this study, but especially the *Mapa de Cuauhtlantzinco*, supplant or borrow from and reshape fragments of the European "metanarrative" (cf. McEvilley 1992, 144). But in my view, they often do this to serve their own paramount and still essentially indigenous concerns of territoriality and community autonomy. This can involve the forging of a counternarrative at odds with Spanish colonial discourse (Franco 1992, 177). For example, Frank Salomon (1982, 31) finds that Andean writers were appropriating the "esoteric language of the victors" but using it to "reclaim in thought what had been lost in battle." José Rabasa's (1993, 110) reading of Sahagún's informants is similarly enlightening. He suggests that as they "adopt alphabetical writing and three-dimensional perspective, they transform those Western technologies by incorporating them to a native understanding of language and the world." We need to remember, too, that many of these manuscripts were recorded in indigenous languages, a political act in and of itself.

In some cases, even when manuscripts were written in Nahuatl or some other native language, there is considerable borrowing from Spanish perspectives, as in the *Mapa*. Yet even in these cases, the native or mestizo writers do not aim to take wholesale the identity of the foreigner and deny their own heritage. On the contrary, they are proudly enhancing their own identity (however multidimensional that might be), inscribing appropriated forms with new content for their own interested purposes while also reducing and submerging the Spaniards' roles. Whether conscious or not, their approach reflects what Amaryll Chanady (1995, 107) calls a "strategy of collective self-affirmation" and what Robert M. Hill (1989, 294) labels "a form of cultural resistance." It is reminiscent of the stance of Antonio D'Alfonso (quoted in Chanady, 1995, 106), a "neo-quebequois intellectual" who repudiates the melting-pot analysis. He writes, "I do not mix, I am an impure identity, but I am not hybrid."

The possible presence of hybridity in these manuscripts might call into question the entire framework of this volume by forcing us to ask, to what extent do the documents reflect indigenous viewpoints? Writing about the mestizo historians Diego Muñoz Camargo (1529–99), Juan Bautista Pomar (b. 1520s?), and Fernando de Alva Ixtililxochitl (1578–1648), Enrique Florescano (1994, 124) asserts that although their work was "based on old indigenous texts and oral traditions, [it] reveals a progressive distancing from the strictly indigenous and a very accentuated proclivity toward seeing the indigenous from the Spanish side." When the mestizo historians use terms such as "witchcraft . . . superstitions . . . idolatry, and other perversions" to describe native religious practices, as Muñoz Camargo does, Florescano (125) finds that they "thought and judged the Indians by the conquerors' values."[16]

Not knowing the precise authorship of most manuscripts consulted for this book, I cannot say for certain whether they were biological mestizos or just indigenous people influenced in various ways by the colonial context. Perhaps they were "impure," in D'Alfonso's sense of the term, but there is still something authentically indigenous about these manuscripts, even recognizing the group's internal heterogeneity and dynamism. They represent voices of the descendants of ancient inhabitants with primordial claims to the land and a strong sense of local collectivity and history.[17] When they respond to or comment on the increasing presence of powerful foreigners, they tend to reinforce a proud sense of self—a self that rarely acknowledges a condition of subjugation, a self that is internally diversified yet striving for unity of purpose, for survival and cultural preservation.

When the authors have a base in an indigenous community, this is especially the case. By emphasizing the corporate group and distinguishing it from outsiders, they underline what we now call indigenous, even if Christianized.[18]

It is tempting to equate anti-imperialist attitudes with indigenous ones or to expect indigenous people to have rejected Christianity in favor of their own legitimate spirituality. Clearly, modern indigenous perspectives tend to be anticolonial. A survey conducted by the American Indian Program at Cornell University found that the majority of indigenous people responding from South, Central, and North America considered the Columbian quincentenary (1492–1992) either as "500 years of native people's resistance to colonization or as an anniversary of a holocaust" (Axtell 1992, 251). But for individuals and communities who struggled to survive the colonial experience some centuries ago, such was not always the case. Fairly rare were the voices raised against European imperialism per se.[19] To generalize that an indigenous viewpoint was an anti-Spanish one is a risky projection of modern sentiments onto the past.

Undoubtedly, many—perhaps even most—native people found the Spanish invasion and occupation of their land repugnant. But there were some who welcomed the chance to forge new alliances and try to defeat old rivals. Were these people's opinions not indigenous? The Aztecs and Incas (or at least their upper echelons) were proud imperialists, and other empires had also drawn their territorial lines across the hemisphere prior to the sixteenth century, possibly bequeathing a conceptual legacy that esteemed geopolitical aggression.[20] It became natural for some to see European alliances as a means to strengthen their own positions. Like their neighbors who resisted foreign penetration—but following radically differing strategies—one of their principal goals was to preserve or enhance their local unit.

A scornful assessment might conclude that the position (and documentary record) of these people represented a betrayal of vital indigenous interests, or that it contributed, if sometimes inadvertently, to their people's subjugation, particularly when leaders chose a path of alliance in exchange for political office, reductions in tribute, and territorial recognition (see Stern 1982).[21] But lacking the conditions for forging a "pan-Indian" front, except on rare occasions, choices were limited, and individuals tried various means to ameliorate or at least negotiate that subjugation, often finding that they could simultaneously pursue their own individual aggrandizement along with community preservation.

THE WORN-OUT WELCOME

If they pursued or acquiesced to alliances with Spaniards in the sixteenth century and received some perquisites from them, by the seventeenth century, if not earlier, caciques were becoming more anxious about their slipping position in the colonial framework. From the colonizers' perspective, the usefulness of indigenous nobles as intermediaries was waning, and the nobles probably sensed this. Through increased mobility among the growing number of private estates, villagers were gaining familiarity with the Spanish language and other aspects of the colonizers' culture. As colonial administrators proliferated in the provinces, the need diminished for tribute collection to be directed through so many cacique mediators, who extracted their share.[22] Within caciques' own communities, their credibility may have been on the decline, too, as labor drafts and tax burdens increased for the survivors of epidemics, who sometimes waited years for new assessments of their towns' required production.[23] Caciques also increasingly thought of their traditional stake in corporate holdings as private, dispensable property. Growing ethnic diversity and political factionalism cast doubt on certain families' claims to hereditary power.

Mounting tribute burdens and competition over land threatened not only the indigenous leadership in a given town but the community as a whole, surely making everyone anxious. It was about this time that the official (or sometimes unofficial, self-appointed) bearers of community history began to awaken again to the developing threat from outsiders, particularly Spaniards, and to raise the alarm within their corporate units, hoping to shore up their own families' positions but also to protect the town as a whole. Revitalizing a tradition that spanned Mesoamerica, they wrote down oral traditions, translated or copied painted ones, and assembled and rewrote documentary fragments of town history, lacing their "primordial titles" with a strong dose of micropatriotism and a heightened awareness of the Spanish menace. Viceroys, archbishops, and other elite representatives of Spanish colonialism were hardly a part of it; rather, it was the Spanish settlers who increasingly occupied former indigenous landholdings and built homes in or near the pueblos who represented the peril. Only relatively recently penetrating the protected nuclei of the indigenous world, this ethnic group, in the view of the authors of the títulos, had already worn out its welcome.

The authors of these selective histories, heirs to the pre-Columbian "gatherers of the past" (Florescano 1994, 30), found little or no utility in the European conquest narrative. In their writings they transcended any memory of mass destruction and loss of life, seeing only distant transfers of power, if any at all, and trumpeting a reinforcement of local authority. Battles between their ancestors and foreign invaders happened on remote fronts or only briefly at home. They were far less significant memories than those which served to strengthen the local settlement, the recognition of the town council, the marking of territorial boundaries, and the construction of grand new temples, all of which enhanced the integrity and perceived autonomy of the indigenous community.

Notes

CHAPTER 1. *Rereading the Invasion*

1. One of the most detailed accounts is that by Bernal Díaz del Castillo (1963), but see Mignolo 1995 and Franco 1982, 40, for broader information about the literature. Although military technology, strategies, and tactics have been rejected by ethnohistorians as the principal explanations for Spanish seizures of power in Mexico and Peru, they were nevertheless important, as John Guilmartin (1991) shows for Peru. A recently re-released anthology of Spanish accounts from Mexico, in English, edited and translated by Patricia de Fuentes (1993), has a helpful foreword by Ross Hassig providing the perspective of recent scholarship. It should be noted that although Spaniards seized power from the Aztecs between 1519 and 1521, other areas took more time. In the Maya zone, large areas were finally seized by 1547, but some others bravely resisted for another 150 years or more (see Bricker 1981, 19).

2. Inga Clendinnen (1993, 13–14) provides a succinct outline of the major events of the Spanish seizure of power, dividing the process into two phases. The first phase commenced with the landing of the Cortés expedition near what is now Veracruz in 1519 and continued through the march toward the capital, the Spaniards battling along the way and winning over thousands of allies, especially in the province of Tlaxcala, where people were already enemies of the Aztecs. It encompassed the Spaniards' gaining access to the capital with relative ease and seizing the emperor, Moctezuma; ruling through him for six months; being distracted by the landing of a contingent sent by the governor of Cuba, who saw Cortés as an outlaw for rushing off without full permission to try to conquer Mexico; and facing difficulties in the capital while Cortés was on the coast, when fear of an uprising led to a massacre, under the direction of Pedro de Alvarado, of Nahuas during the festival of Toxcatl. A subsequent escalation of events led to Moctezuma's mysterious death and the Spaniards' mad dash from the capital in the dark of the night called "Noche Triste" in June 1520, with much loss of life on their side. The second phase involved Spanish recuperation and the expansion of alliances, the final siege between May and August 1521, and victory by the allied forces, European and (usually overlooked) indigenous. For the purposes of this

study, it is important also to acknowledge the massacre in Cholula, a joint Spanish and Tlaxcalan maneuver that followed the alliance between the two and preceded the massacre in Mexico City (Clendinnen 1993, 21).

3. The term *conquistador* and its English equivalent, *conqueror*, are used sparingly in this study owing to a reluctance to perpetuate the romantic image of invincibility and the idea of a thorough domination and subjugation of indigenous peoples implied in the concept of "conquest," which is similarly under reconsideration.

4. Accounts of the invasion from indigenous sources were only parts of a much larger corpus Sahagún compiled. On the suppression of Sahagún's work, an act intended mainly to stifle the indigenous religious content in it, see Franco 1982, 38. In another example of the censorship of native voices, suspicion exists that Powhatan's control over "the demeanor and content of the initial colonial conversation" in Virginia may have also led to the silencing of an account of it intended for publication in Europe in the seventeenth century (Hantman 1992, 75).

5. Julie Greer Johnson (1993, 5) discusses the early presentation of alternatives to Spain's mythological and utopian view of its colonial project, noting how some opposition writers of that period saw "the solemnity and sanctity of the image of the New World that the colonizer projected to be an elaborate façade and an intolerable deception." Counternarratives came from both inside the power-holding group and outside it.

6. David E. Stannard (1992, xii) uses the terms *holocaust* and *genocide* to speak of the deaths because he believes the destruction "was neither inadvertent nor inevitable." He emphasizes "the more virulent examples of this deliberate racist purge." Stannard's study spans all of the Americas and five centuries. Although there were truly horrible examples such as those he reproduces, I would not favor using the term genocide to describe the Spanish colonization project as a whole. Most atrocities were limited to entradas of the central areas and frontiers or to the behavior of isolated individuals who might not be representative of most settlers (who came in the wake of the conquest expeditions). Still, settlement was not a benign or justifiable act, and while I wish to caution readers of the seductive but inaccurate nature of the black legend, I do not wish to "exonerate . . . [the Europeans of] any moral blame" (Stannard 1992, xii, quoting Alexander Saxton) for the outcome of the imperialist design and the all-too-often racist character of the colonization project.

7. Frances F. Berdan (1993, 179) cites the many reassessments of these statistics and the methods that produced them. One major consideration is the creation of the ethnic and racial category mestizo, or person of mixed Spanish and indigenous heritage, which took in some of the population that otherwise would have fallen into the "Indian" category.

8. Carlos Fuentes (1992, 12) recognizes the importance of the legal protection, however insufficient, extended to indigenous agrarian communities in the viceregal period, communities that "had more rights over their water, forests, and land during the colonial regime than during their independent regime." Robert M.

Hill (1989, 295), who has studied the land struggles of the Cakchiquel Mayas, similarly concludes that they "were at least able to fight a spirited and largely successful holding action, until the 'liberal' reforms of the land laws in the later nineteenth century drastically changed the rules of the game." Patricia Seed (1995, 86–87) tells us of the Islamic roots of Spanish colonial protectionism.

9. This is reminiscent of Mayan records, some of which are especially notable for their graphic association of the Spaniards' arrival and the spread of disease (see Bricker 1981, 15).

10. I say males because they were in the majority, but indigenous women scribes and historians are also known to have existed and deserve further research. The *Códice Telleriano-Remensis* (1995, pl. 3), for example, shows a woman, glossed "la pintora" (the painter), at work. Another image of a woman putting quill or paintbrush to paper can be found in the Manuscrit Mexicain 385 of the Bibliotheque Nationale in Paris. The Otomí *Relación anónima* of the founding of Querétaro mentions a doña Juana Malinzi as intepreter, notary, and scribe (Gruzinski 1986a, 348). Finally, an unpublished colonial Mexican pictorial, the Codex Cardona, in a private collection, includes a portrait of a doña (María) Bartola (also mentioned in the writings of Ixtlilxochitl), who wrote a now lost chronicle of the Spaniards' siege of Tenochtitlan (Libro C, p. 39).

11. Nathan Wachtel (1977) wrote another pioneering work with a focus on indigenous Peruvians' perspectives, 1530–70. James Axtell (1988) also cites two articles from the 1970s that launched this new approach in the ethnohistory of colonial North America (so-called despite the usual exclusion of New Spain, with the exception of the far northern regions).

12. The quincentenary literature is vast. The bibliography at the end of this book cites a great many of these works. For some of the varying indigenous perspectives expressed in relatively recent times, see the special editions of *Northeast Indian Quarterly* (Fall 1990) and *Latin American Perspectives* (Summer 1992).

13. Franco (1992, 176) astutely describes discourse as being "a practice," one "that is formed by and attempts to regulate social action." Colonial discourse, she points out, is "the study of Europe's 'othering' of the rest of the world," and documents of "discovery and conquest" have contributed significantly to the creation of "subject" peoples.

14. A recent study by Matthew Restall, *Maya Conquistador* (1998), provides another excellent example of the translation of indigenous texts combined with analysis of the relatively neglected experiences in the Yucatán Peninsula, a southern component of the colonial Mesoamerican experience.

15. I try to avoid the historically pejorative cultural and geographical misnomer "Indian" and favor the use of "indigenous," another accepted translation of the term *indígena*, which is the preferred term in Spanish-language texts today. I use "native" as a synonym for indigenous and as a translation of *natural*, common in manuscripts of the viceregal era, although with some reluctance stemming from the negative connotation associated with more modern, racist uses of the term

"natives." All externally applied labels have the potential to offend some readers. Let me assure this audience that my intention is to employ terms of respect, neutrality, or greater accuracy whenever possible. To call the Spaniards "invaders," while a definite departure from earlier labels such as "adventurers" and "conquerors," is not intended as a slur but as a more appropriate descriptor. Yet this term does not serve as an adequate translation of the most common indigenous labels for Spaniards—Castilians or Christians.

16. Ignored here is the African contingent, another grouping that disguises internal variations. Africans who had spent time in the Iberian world, for instance, held vastly different perspectives from those who came directly to the Americas from their homeland. For colonial Mexico, some historians place Africans in the Spanish world, especially when seeking to delineate indigenous perspectives (see Lockhart and Schwartz 1983, 130).

17. See Lockhart and Schwartz 1983, 130, on the separation of these worlds. I wonder if the portraits of colonial *kurakakuna*, which Tom Cummins (1991, 224) describes as capturing a "fictive," "other," and "Spanish" identity, might better be examined as representing another line of evolving indigenous identities.

18. An example of extraordinary continuity in domestic technology is the persistence of the *metate* (maize grinding stone) from the Formative period through the present in some communities, a span of millennia (Yamamoto 1996, 54). But one hesitates to make a list of material or outward traits, for it is thoughts and beliefs that probably best unify the Mesoamerican cultural entity, as Gary Gossen (1994, 1) points out. Houses and clothing can take on radically new appearances, for instance, while the inhabitant's way of thinking remains less changed. Gossen (1994, 5–8) identifies five "symbolic clusters" in Mesoamerican thought that have persisted over considerable time and space.

19. Although the Spanish seizure of power and concerted efforts to reshape indigenous life definitely had major and lasting effects, I believe it goes too far to say that "within a few short decades, most of what comprised the Indian world was gone, swept away by disease, war, religious zealotry, and Spanish political and economic control" (Hassig 1994, 158). It comes down to a difference between "some" and "most" in an arena that is difficult to measure in any precise and objective way. Both approaches can actually serve similar ends. An emphasis on loss can facilitate a denunciation of the offense or the seizure of power, whereas an emphasis on retention can validate the defense or the resistance. Searching for balance, Frances Berdan opted for the title "trauma and transition" for her study of sixteenth-century central Mexico. But in her concluding remarks, after providing considerable evidence, she emphasizes "impressive persistence" (1993, 191).

20. As Gilbert Larochelle (1992, 27) has said, determining the certain identity of an image is implausible, for "an image comes from the constant exchange between a corpus which already exists a priori and the sum of approximate perceptions." He also paraphrases Paul Eluard, asserting that "the image has always been an issue of what remains to be seen, rather than what has already been seen,

an attempt to conceive more than has been perceived, to unite such notions in the mind despite their diversity" (LaRochelle 1992, 28).

21. Linda King (1994, 3) writes, "There are over 6 million Indians in Mexico, constituting 58 different ethnic groups. Their particular will to survive is witnessed by their sheer numbers and by the fact that their identification rests more than anything else on the fact that they do not speak or write the dominant language as their mother tongue."

22. Michel Foucault recognized power not only in the content of discourse but in the very ability to express oneself in society (see King 1994, 8). Robert M. Hill's (1989) analysis of the social uses of writing in Mesoamerica seems to support this assessment.

23. Anne McClintock (1994, 257) succinctly defines colonization as "direct territorial appropriation of another geopolitical entity, combined with forthright exploitation of its resources and labour, and systematic interference in the capacity of the appropriated culture (itself not necessarily a homogenous entity) to organise its dispensations of power." Postcolonialist approaches, while rejecting modernist historical tropes such as the "linear, progressivist model of historical development," do not necessarily reject historicism itself.

24. In his appropriately titled article "Caliban's Own Voice: American Indian Views of the Other in Colonial Virginia," Jeffrey Hantman (1992, 7) quotes Rob Nixon's explanation of the political agenda behind the popularity of revisionist versions of Shakespeare's *The Tempest:* "Once alienated people could generate a hearing for their counterhegemonic endeavors." The irony behind many postcolonial and ethnohistorical studies by nonindigenous scholars—not excluding the present one, which aims to capture indigenous voices—is that as much as we endeavor to represent other cultures fairly and to overcome the "them/us" paradigm, we are still often speaking primarily to ourselves about ourselves (see Pearce 1953, 232). We are writing cautionary tales about the legacy of imperialism and striving to find ways to build more equitable and harmonious multicultural societies (see Chanady 1995, 93). But if we try to avoid submerging the "heterogeneity" of the component parts of indigenous testimonies, and if we strive for "solidarity" over "charity or condescension," then we can study such testimonies as an act in "service of the people," according to John Beverley (1992, 9, 18; my translations).

25. S. L. Cline's (1993, 3) recent edition of *The Book of Tributes* from Morelos has brought to light one of the earliest "full-length local-level alphabetic text[s] in Nahuatl" that we have available for study today. It dates from the mid-1530s or early 1540s.

26. See also Nicolau d'Olwer and Cline 1973; Edmonson 1974; Nicolau d'Olwer 1987; Klor de Alva, Nicholson, and Quiñones Keber 1988.

27. Hans Roskamp (1998, 12–13) cautions us that the *Relación de Michoacán* does not necessarily contain general "P'urhépecha" (let alone "Tarascan") cultural perspectives but represents the particular views of the people of the region around Lake Pátzcuaro.

28. For example, in the early sixteenth century the Dominican friar Antonio de Montesinos chastised the Spanish colonists in the Caribbean for their cruelty toward the local people, saying that they were commiting mortal sin. They paid him little heed, but he kept trying (Hanke 1965, 17–18), as did some other ecclesiastics who were concerned about the morality of the situation. Bartolomé de Las Casas was the most critical, but there were others. Tzvetan Todorov (1987, 218) writes that fray Diego de Durán "misses no opportunity to condemn those who preach the faith sword in hand; his position here is not very different from that of Las Casas, another Dominican, even if his expressions are less virulent." Todorov (1987, 136–38) provides other examples of ecclesiastics' criticisms, such as those of Motolinia and Vasco de Quiroga, of diseases introduced, heavy taxation, slavery, and mine labor. Some of these men of relative conscience had considerable contact with indigenous communities, and rejecting their usual roles as agents of the invading power, they could take up the cause of the indigenous people. William B. Taylor (1993) found that in a sample of 142 rebellions in Mexican villages, 5 were led by parish priests. Of course indigenous petitioners did not depend upon the clergy to inspire their protests or rebellions, which were usually organized by native leaders.

29. Luis Villoro (1992, 64, 66, 68) similarly finds "extreme otherness" that could not be overcome, with the "annihilation of the great American cultures" the "inevitable result."

30. Susan Ramírez's 1996 book on sixteenth-century Peru, which borrows this image for its title, *The World Upside Down*, nevertheless shows, according to the jacket copy, "how indigenous people actively sought opportunities to defend the principles on which their community life depended." Julie Greer Johnson's (1993) use of the "upside down" image in her book title, *Satire in Colonial Spanish America: Turning the New World Upside Down*, neither implies victimization of indigenous people nor gives exaggerated agency to the colonizers. Rather, she shows how colonizers and Spanish hegemony were critiqued from within, through the use of satire.

31. James Axtell (1991, 17–21, 32) finds in indigenous responses to the Europeans a variety of efforts to reduce the differences between the two or to assimilate the Europeans, such as by sharing a smoke or sealing political and kinship alliances with them through gifts of women and children.

32. Roger Zapata (1992, 203) writes of the search to restore lost equilibrium. He also recognizes (205) how Guamán Poma's feelings varied from time to time as he "oscillated between collaborationism" and the "rejection of colonialism."

33. Chapter 2 is a revision of a paper given at the Third International Symposium on Codices and Documents about Mexico (*Códices y Documentos sobre México, Tercer Simposio,* Puebla, 1996), entitled "¿El otro otro? Interpretando imágenes y descripciones de españoles en los códices y textos indígenas." A brief methodological analysis with the same title and some of the same images has been published in Spanish by the Instituto Nacional de Antropología e Historia, Mexico, in a selected proceedings from the conference (Wood 2000).

34. Chapter 3 represents a revision of conference papers given at the 1992 meeting of the American Anthropological Association (San Francisco), entitled "A Critique of Conquest: The Primordial Title of Ajusco, Central New Spain," and at the Second International Symposium on Codices and Documents about Mexico (Taxco, 1994), entitled "The Ajusco Town Founding Document: Affinities with Documents of the Sixteenth Century" (now published as Wood 1997b).

35. Chapter 4 is a revision of a paper given at the 1994 meeting of the American Historical Association (San Francisco), entitled "Caciques' Influence over Community History: Negotiated Identities in the *Mapa de Cuauhtlantzinco* of the Tlaxcalan Tradition."

36. The manuscript may also provide insights into the possibly diverging meanings the English term *alliance* held for indigenous peoples. "Partnerships with native peoples" varied across the colonies, according to Patricia Seed (1995, 65), and even within a single European culture, such as the French, there could be different kinds of alliances with varying expectations.

37. Chapter 5 is a revised and expanded version of Wood 1991, which had two earlier renditions as papers given at the Forty-sixth International Congress of Americanists (Amsterdam, 1988) and the Eighth Meeting of Mexican and North American Historians (San Diego, 1990). I would like to express my appreciation to the editors of *Ethnohistory* for their willingness to have the article reproduced here with alterations.

Chapter 2. *Pictorial Images of Spaniards*

1. For a description of pre-Columbian Mesoamerican writing systems, see Boone 1994a.

2. James Axtell (1992, 101) finds that the Europeans' hair attracted even more attention than their skin color in indigenous communities of North America.

3. So impressed were some Mayas to see Spaniards eat custard apples that they originally labeled them "pond-apple foreigners" or "strangers who sucked custard apples" (see Bricker 1981, 25). Note how identity can become inherently linked to certain foods, just as it can merge with forms of dress, and so on.

4. Axtell (1991, 8) cites a reference to a ship as a "moving island."

5. The line drawings of this chapter aim to be precise reproductions. My assistant, Gabriela Quiñones, faithfully reproduces the various indigenous artists' facility, or sometimes a lack thereof, for either pre-Columbian or European techniques and styles. The one occasional addition she makes is to ground figures taken out of context.

6. Bernal Díaz del Castillo (1963, 224) tells us that Moctezuma "had a short black beard, well-shaped and thin." We can see this beard in his portrait on folio 69r of the *Codex Mendoza* (Berdan and Anawalt 1997, 143). Beards were rare although not unknown to Mesoamerican cultures, but Europeans' beards were thicker and came in a greater variety of shades. Frances Berdan and Patricia Rieff

Anawalt (1997, 223) suspect that the description of a beard that Sahagún quotes shows European biological influence: "chili-red, ruddy, it whitens, it becomes curly."

7. Elizabeth Hill Boone (1994a, 20) explains how the "semiasiographic systems" of Aztec codices "*are* texts." The term *semiasiographic,* taken from the scholars I. J. Gelb and Geoffrey Sampson, who study writing, contains the Greek word "semiasia," for "meaning" (Boone 1994a, 14, 15).

8. John B. Glass (1975a, 13–15) groups pictorials into two types: those made under "Spanish patronage" and those that fit the category "Native Colonial."

9. Some of these were probably copies or elaborations of earlier manuscripts. For example, the *Mapa de Chalchihuapan* that exists in the church archives of that community is dated 1808 (King 1994, 54).

10. I owe a considerable debt to Dumbarton Oaks and its then director of Pre-Columbian Studies, Elizabeth Hill Boone, for generously allowing me access to this collection for several months in 1995.

11. Glass (1975a, 7–9) explains the Spanish-language nomenclature and terminology associated with Mesoamerican pictorial manuscripts, including the usually amorphous labels *códice* (whether a screenfold, a roll, a strip, a large cloth or skin, a book, or an isolated page of varying size), *pintura, mapa* (not limited to cartography), and *lienzo* (associated with cloth).

12. A few Spanish women were on the scene during the campaign against the Aztecs, as Díaz del Castillo (1963, 302, 306, 407, 412) attests. We also know of at least one, María de Estrada, who rode into battle on horseback, invoking the name of Santiago. See *Relación de Tetela y Hueyapan* (2:271) in *Relaciones geográficas del siglo XVI: México* (Acuña 1985–86). A scene in the *Lienzo de Tlaxcala* (pl. 18) may show a Spanish woman on horseback fleeing Mexico City during what the invaders called Noche Triste, or Sad Night, when they suffered major losses (see López de Mariscal 1997, 136). Marvin Lunenfeld (1991, 271) recalls, from the *The Chronicles of Michoacán,* that "Castilian women were called *Cuchahecha,* which means ladies and goddesses." So we know that indigenous people were familiar enough with Spanish women to give them a label. But the codices hardly acknowledge Spanish women's presence in any capacity in the colony.

13. Blanca López de Mariscal (1997, 93ff.) provides examples of indigenous women in combat. Judging by indigenous texts and pictorials such as the *Codex Durán,* women warriors were in the minority. But this may require further investigation, because in the viceregal era, native women were very involved in localized rebellions (Taylor 1979).

14. The notorious invader Pedro de Alvarado gained the nickname Tonatiuh (Sun) among indigenous people across Mesoamerica because, according to Díaz del Castillo (1963, 187), to Moctezuma's emissaries he "looked like the sun," he was handsome, and he was a captain. The *Chilam Balam of Tizimin,* of the Yucatec Mayas, recalls Spaniards as the red-bearded "sons of the Sun" (Bricker 1981, 25, quoting Roys's translation).

15. Berdan and Anawalt (1997, 149) refer to the *maxtlatl* (loincloth) as "indispensable" for all Aztec men. I am unaware of any analyses of nudity.

16. The segmented body was a notable phenomenon in Mesoamerican art forms of various kinds and depicting a broad range of situations, none of them seemingly horrific or terroristic, according to the archaeologist Rosemary Joyce (personal communication, 1997).

17. In the *Anales de los Cakchiqueles* (1885, 189), the indigenous authors speak of these kinds of punishment by death as part of "varios hechos de violencia de los castellanos" (various acts of violence of the Castilians). Other executions appear in the *Lienzo de Analco* (Blom 1945, figs. 3 and 4), the *Códice Aubin* (Lehmann 1981, 270), and the *Lienzo de Aztactepec* (*Handbook of Middle American Indians* 1975, vol. 14, fig. 23).

18. Brotherston (1995, 35) explains well what is happening in this scene. There is a tragic history of the use of dogs in the campaigns. Despite a reluctance to fuel the black legend, Varner and Varner (1983, xiii) write: "Conquests inevitably involve evil; in that of the Indies, brutality expanded, sometimes into grotesque fiendishness, and contributing to certain of its most awesome aspects was the European dog."

19. Other alliances with graphic representation include, for example, that of the people of Tlatelolco in the war against the people of Zacatecas (see the *Códice de Tlatelolco*, from about 1565, reproduced in *Los códices de México* 1979, 44–45) and that of the Tlapanecas in the *Códice Azoyú I* (photograph LC-USZ9-21-7 in the collection of Mexican Indian Pictorial Documents, Archive of Hispanic Culture, Division of Prints and Photographs, Library of Congress, Washington, D.C. [hereafter LC/MIPD]).

20. The first indigenous martyrs were from Tlaxcala (Baumann 1987, 149). Max Harris (1992) sees "hidden transcripts of dissent" in the theater of the struggle for power in Tlaxcala in the sixteenth century, as we shall see in chapter 3.

21. James Lockhart (1991, 59) says that in the primordial titles, Cortés is "a symbol" and "a source of legitimacy." His presence is notable as a central figure in, for example, the *Mapa de Tonayan* (see photograph LC-USZ9-360 in LC/MIPD).

22. Cortés carries a lance in this image. The label "Marquez" refers to a title he obtained about a decade later, Marqués del Valle.

23. "Malinche," perhaps the best known form of her name today, is the Hispanicized form of Malintzin.

24. See, for example, the portraits of Cortés in the *Lienzo de Tlaxcala* (Reyes García 1993, 277–80), the *Mapa de San Pedro Tlacotepec* (Reyes García 1993, 296), the *Códice Durán* (Gruzinski 1992, 26), the *Códice de Huichapan* (the gloss reads, "don Martín cordes marques" [sic]; 1992, *lám.* 64), and the *Mapa de San Antonio Tepetlan*, published in *Handbook of Middle American Indians* 1975, vol. 14, fig. 59. In the *Pièce d'un Procès* (*Handbook of Middle American Indians* 1975, vol. 14, fig. 51), the "marqués" (Cortés?) appears behind a woman (doña Marina?) who is seated

on a curule chair (something extraordinary). Various images of doña Marina, or Malintzin, are reproduced also by Brotherston (1995, 33–44), with an interpretation about how these changed from the sixteenth through the eighteenth centuries and from different perspectives.

25. Malintzin is central in plates 45 and 51 of Book 12 of the *Florentine Codex*, for instance (see Lockhart 1993, 121, 125).

26. In litigation records in the archives, complaints are numerous against priests posted to the indigenous communities (see Haskett 1994; Taylor 1996, ch. 14). It would be valuable to make a more detailed investigation of the graphic images of priests who appear in the codices.

27. Not that indigenous people had no contact with bishops. We see in the *Tlaxcalan Actas* (Lockhart, Berdan, and Anderson 1986, 141), for instance, that the *regidor* (town councilor) of Ocotelulco went to Puebla for an audience with the bishop in 1550.

28. See, for example, the entry for 1526(?) in the *Tira de Tepechpan* (1944), the entry for 1532 in the *Códice Telleriano-Remensis* (Gruzinski 1992, 143), the arrival of the archbishop in 1554 in the *Códice Aubin* (Lehmann 1981, 263), and the entry for 1556 in BNP-MM40 (Lehmann 1981, 350). An archbishop makes a rare visit to a pueblo in the *Mapa de San Pedro Tlacotepec* (Reyes García 1993, 296).

29. Unpublished translation by Frances Krug; typescript in author's files.

30. Zumárraga's policies actually had a measurable impact on the indigenous world over time (see Baudot 1995).

31. Unpublished translation by Frances Krug in the author's files. *Diablos* (devils) is the approved term for pre-Columbian indigenous deities in the *Florentine Codex*. Its use, Lockhart (1993, 31) explains, was fairly broad among the Nahuas, resulting from their Christian religious instruction. We see another attestation in the *Annals of Quauhtitlan* (Lockhart 1993, 281). The *relaciones geográficas* regularly employ the term *demonios* (demons) to refer to pre-Columbian deities—probably an expression used by both the informants and the Spanish provincial administrators who wrote the reports.

32. They battle the gods and pray beneath a cross, for example, in the *Descripción de Tlaxcala* (Gruzinski 1992, 44–45), and they erect a cross in the *Lienzo de Tlaxcala* (Gruzinski 1992, 28) and in the *Códice de la entrada de los españoles en Tlaxcala* (Reyes García 1993, 287). A friar is standing next to a cross in the *Matrícula de Huejotzinco* (Prem 1974, 731v). Examples of the sacrament of baptism are found in the *Mapa de Cuauhtlantzinco* (Ojeda Díaz 1985), the *Códice Azcatitlan* (Robertson 1994, pl. 78), the *Lienzo de San Pedro Ixcatlan* (*Handbook of Middle American Indians* 1975, vol. 14, fig. 39), and the *Códice Telleriano-Remensis* (Smith 1968, 167). In documents from Tlaxcala, scenes of baptism are numerous (see Peñafiel 1909). For purposes of comparison, we find that in images woven into eighteenth-century wampum belts from what is now the United States, missionaries "invariably held or stood near crosses" (Axtell 1988, 136).

33. In the *Lienzo de Petlacala* (Oettinger and Horcasitas 1982, 51), the king wears eighteenth-century clothing. The crown, apparently recognized by the indigenous people as a symbol of ultimate power, appears at his feet. The crown is at the king's side in the scene from the *Mapa de Chalchihuapan* (Oettinger and Horcasitas 1982, 52). Charles V wears the crown and sits on a throne in the *Pintura de Doña María Antonia Maxixcatzin Caxtilanxochitl* (Reyes García 1993, 288). In the primordial titles of San Miguel Atlauhtla, in the Chalco region, James Lockhart (1991, 60) notes the importance of Charles V. Interestingly, a similar reverence for the king of Spain was preserved in Peru in the eighteenth century, in the time of the uprising of Tupac Amaru, whose followers purportedly hated all Spanish colonizers (Szeminski 1990, 169, 171).

34. See, for example, the *Lienzo de Tlaxcala* (*Los códices de Mexico* 1979, 48–49), in which these viceroys are accompanied by the president of the Real Audiencia (high court), don Sebastián Ramires de Fuenleal, and many other Spaniards. The first two viceroys, among others, appear also in the *Codex of 1576* (1893, 152, 153).

35. Primordial titles frequently exhibit some confusion about these figures. See Lockhart 1991, 59–60. In one case, at least, in the codices, an artist has don Martín Cortés confused with his father. See the *Códice de Huichapan* (1992, *lám.* 64).

36. Lockhart, Berdan, and Anderson (1986, 15) provide a detailed summary of the kinds of procedures the corregidor encouraged and supervised in the cabildo.

37. In contrast, the alcalde mayor of Tlapa appears as a beneficent man in the *Lienzo de Malinaltepec*, from the Sierra de Tlapa, eighteenth century (see Dehouve 1994, 126).

38. Standing human figures holding decapitated heads are a rather widespread theme in Mesoamerican art. They may not necessarily imply terror. The archaeologist Rosemary Joyce is currently trying to identify the significance of these images (personal communication, 1997).

39. There are various examples of encomenderos using force to demand services. In the *Códice Ríos* (*Antigüedades de México* 1964, 292 and *lám.* 136) we see a Spaniard obliging an indigenous man to participate in a labor draft for the construction an aqueduct in the region of Chapultepec. The laborer is tied up with a rope. In the annals of the Cakchiquels are various references to misery and affliction caused by the Castilians, probably encomenderos. See, for example, *The Annals of the Cakchiquels* 1885, 191–92.

40. For example, see *Códice Huapeán* (LC/MIPD photograph LC-USZ9-430-2).

41. For purposes of comparison, we find in what is now the United States that antler combs made by indigenous people typically bore images of Europeans on horseback (Axtell 1988, 137).

42. Anderson, Berdan, and Lockhart (1976, 44–45) also present the will of an indigenous noble of Tlaxcala in 1566, which mentions a horse, without saddle, that

was to be sold to pay for masses. Far from being Hispanicized, this man also bequeathed "a feathered cloak . . . with duck feathers," among other goods. The Cuernavaca gentleman, too, had "four feathered headdresses, three little shields used in dance ceremonies, three traditional indigenous drums of various sizes, and four parrots" (Haskett 1988, 44).

43. Men's clothing, for the most part, was already rather minimal, especially around the legs. Anawalt (1981, 211, 214) does highlight a few "limb-encasing" garments associated with warrior ceremonial costumes that the Aztecs and Tlaxcalans used in battle. But men would not have chosen Spanish garments in order to increase their mobility.

44. There were differences in the quality of clothing in pre-Columbian times between different social groups. In the *Relación de Zultepec* (Acuña 1985–86, 3:185) we see a remark that it was only the *principales*, or indigenous elites, of Michoacán who wore cotton clothing, whereas the average citizen went nude. After the Spanish invasion, distinctions continued. For instance, in the *Relación de Cempoala* of 1580 (Acuña 1985–86, 1:78), only members of the indigenous community who were "able" ("los que puedan") had adopted the use of shoes and hats.

45. Certainly not all indigenous people needed or delighted in the imported materials. Charles Gibson (1964, 124) cites a report of 1584 stating that some indigenous people had "fifteen or twenty pairs of shoes, bought from clergymen under compulsion and never worn."

46. Robert Haskett (1988, 46) provides examples of indigenous rulers who vigorously protected this privilege, cutting the hair of commoners who wanted to wear it long like Spaniards and confiscating outlawed clothing, especially in the eighteenth century.

47. The plumes in frames 66–68 of the *Florentine Codex*, for instance, are especially large, and the ones in frame 74 echo the feathers worn by the indigenous warrior in frame 73, directly above (Lockhart 1993, 135, 143). Berdan and Anawalt (1997, 208) discuss a feathered headdress in the *Codex Mendoza* that was associated with the declaration of war and represented "impending doom."

48. In paintings from the 1580s intended to symbolize the Inca dynasty, the Inca crown, or *maskha paycha* and *llawt'u*, appears in combination with feathers (Cummins 1991, 219).

49. In the Caribbean, the native king Guacanagarí reputedly placed his own crown on Columbus's head (Axtell 1991, 18), and in colonial French America Jacques Cartier received the "red hedgehog-skin band" one chief wore as a crown (Axtell 1991, 18–19). Both examples suggest a desire for political alliance on the part of the hosting dignitaries, not to mention a feeling that they were the approximate equals of the foreigners. If a great difference of status had been perceived, such actions might have insulted one party or the other.

50. For purposes of comparison, we find that in what is now the United States, eighteenth-century wampum belts displaying images of Europeans typically gave

them distinctive "frock coats and tall, wide-brimmed hats"; some had purple beards and white hearts, the latter apparently an indication of their guile (Axtell 1988, 136–37).

51. The *Título C'oyoi* of Guatemala refers to *quitem, quich'acat* ("their benches and their stools"), in a reference to the seats of authority for Quiche leaders (Carmack 1973, 320–21). Many scholars have noted this association between the Quiche ruler and his bench (*tem*) and pillow (*ch'akat*), or his mat (*pop*), in various sources including the Popol Vuh. A seat with a high feather canopy (*q'alibal*) also existed. Some scholars have equated such seats with "thrones," and several note their relationship with the jurisdiction—geographical and authoritative—of the ruler (Hendrickson 1989, 136). In the Suchitepec maps, according to Barbara Mundy (personal communication, 1997), there may be as many as four different indigenous seats, two with jaguar-skin coverings (one with a high back and one with a low back) and two reddish-brown seats (again with high and low backs).

52. The words *petlatl icpalli* (mat, throne) combined to form an ideograph representing power and rulership (Maxwell and Hanson 1992, 37).

53. In the Sochitepec maps (Barbara Mundy, personal communication, 1998), the only indigenous noble who occupies a curule chair is don Francisco Hernández, who may be the highest-status individual of the eleven who appear. He is also the only one who wears an elaborate spotted cloth (jaguar skin?). Some of the others occupy different kinds of indigenous seats, as noted earlier. Mundy suspects there may have been a hierarchical ranking of chair types.

54. Rosemary Joyce, who often finds in Mesoamerican art that males are standing or raised up while women are sitting or otherwise closer to the ground, prefers not to see this difference as subordination of women. She suggests a possible reading of women's association with the earth and men's association with the sun (personal communication, 1997).

55. In the *Lienzo de Malinaltepec,* from the modern state of Guerrero in the eighteenth century (Dehouve 1994, 126), the indigenous leaders occupy the table but the friar and alcalde mayor stand behind them, observing the meeting. A bishop and a friar write, sitting at a table, in the *Códice de Yanhuitlan* (1940, *lám.* 14), and a friar writes alone at another table (*lám.* 19). Documents (*tlacuilolli*) appearing alone or in the hands of Spaniards show us that writing was important for both European and indigenous cultures. See, for example, the *Códice Aubin* (Lehmann 1981, 266, 269), the *Histoire Mexicaine* (BNF-MM40, Lehmann 1981, 352), the *Códice Sierra* (1933, facsimiles 9, 14, 18, 22, 26, 28, 34, 41, 51, 57), and the *Fragmento Humboldt VI* from Berlin (Robertson 1994, fig. 68).

56. Writing served a similar function. Indigenous writers adjusted their technology, adopting ink and paper, and borrowed the new alphabet, but they continued to write in their own languages for centuries. Robert M. Hill (1989, 294) calls this act "a form of cultural resistance" for fending off the challenges of

Spaniards and for maintaining as much autonomy as possible within the colonial system.

CHAPTER 3. *A Cry from the Mountains*

1. On May 22, 1994, I visited the town's elaborate ceremony for passing on the custodianship of the land titles of San Miguel and Santo Tomás Ajusco from one public officer to another. It was called the Ceremonia de Cambio de Depositario de los Títulos de las Tierras de San Miguel y Santo Tomás Ajusco. A *lienzo* and other documents were on display in one of the classrooms of the secondary school. The Nahuatl original of the Ajusco conquest narrative was not among them, nor was the Spanish translation of 1710.

2. For more on the early eighteenth-century *composición* proceedings that affected so many central Mexican indigenous communities, see Wood 1984, 116–20. The Spanish translation made in 1710 was reproduced by officials in 1741; the latter can be found in AGN T, vol. 2676, file 4, 3v–6r. The original Nahuatl manuscript translated in 1710 was described at that time as consisting of four leaves. Marcelo Díaz de Salas and Luis Reyes García (1970) published a transcription made by Faustino Galicia Chimalpopoca in the nineteenth century of an incomplete Nahuatl version, presumably now lost. The Chimalpopoca version is in the National Museum of Anthropology in Mexico City, in the Archivo Histórico, Colección Antigua, vol. 254, folios 259r–260v. According to Díaz de Salas and Reyes (1970, 194), there also exists an 1848 copy of the Spanish translation of 1710. Unless otherwise indicated, all Spanish-language quotes herein come from the 1741 manuscript, all Nahuatl-language quotes come from Díaz de Salas and Reyes's (1970) transcription, and English translations are my own.

3. A scholar with the initials "F. H." (presumably Fernando Horcasitas) wrote a footnote to Díaz de Salas and Reyes' article (1970, 194) that reads: "La fecha y la procedencia de este valioso documento descubierto por Díaz Salas y Reyes son sugestivas de un códice Techialoyan perdido" ("The date and derivation of this valuable document discovered by Díaz Salas and Reyes are suggestive of a lost Techialoyan codex"). Perhaps León-Portilla followed this lead. Faustino Galicia Chimalpopoca, who made a transcription of the Ajusco narrative in Nahuatl, also made transcriptions of various Techialoyan codices. See, for instance, María Teresa Sepúlveda y Herrera's (1992, 30, 31) description of the following documents in Chimalpopoca's collection: 24c, 26e, 26f, and 27b. See also Sepúlveda y Herrera 1992, 39. Nicole Percheron, who has also published a transcription of Tecpanecatl's speech (1983, 33–34, 151–52) continues to raise the Techialoyan association. It should probably be noted that her appendix contains a typographical error, giving 1770 where it should read 1710, a date she nevertheless gives correctly in her text. The better we get to know Techialoyans, the more they stand out as a distinctive subset of the *títulos* (primordial titles) tradition, with their *amatl* paper, large hand, special orthography, unique pictorial style, and formulaic texts—in many

ways quite different from the Ajusco document. Techialoyans can have—but are less likely to have—lengthy candid texts reproducing detailed passages of local lore the way other títulos do. See Robertson 1975 and Wood 1998b.

4. For instance, the orthography of the Nahuatl copy made by Faustino Galicia Chimalpopoca contains an example of *ll* substituted for *y*, a post-1650 phenomenon. We also see *s* for *ç*. See Díaz de Salas and Reyes 1970, 208 (*semanahuac* for *cemanahuac*) and 210 (*llocque* for *yuhqui*), and Lockhart 1992, 336, 343, on the timing of these changes in colonial Nahuatl. Were these orthographic changes made by the transcriber, or were they in the "original" he copied from? The "original" in Nahuatl that was transcribed at an unknown date and translated in 1710 could have been a late colonial copy of something that had been originally recorded in the sixteenth century, then added to and recopied whenever new events had to be recorded or when the existing copy became too worn. Alternatively, it could have been an oral tradition from the sixteenth century that was first written down sometime in the seventeenth or eighteenth century. There is no way of knowing today which of these scenarios applies.

5. Most known examples of deliberate deception involved use of the Spanish language. See, for instance, Dyckerhoff 1979, Wood 1987, and Carrillo Cázares 1991. The Techialoyan manuscripts, written in Nahuatl, represent another group that some scholars find suspicious, whereas others acknowledge them to have some validity. See Wood 1998b.

6. Certainly, the sixteenth-century elements I explore here could have been familiar to a highly educated person who had studied early colonial manuscripts, and such a person could have crafted this Ajusco narrative to appear to date from the first years of the colony. Yet I have never seen such familiarity with early elements in suspect Nahuatl manuscripts from the eighteenth century, so I have serious doubts.

7. Percheron (1983, 33) drops the first *c* in this name, calling the man "Tepanecatl," apparently believing that a generic name was intended, a reflection of the ethnic heritage of the region, part of the former Tepanec empire. That is one possible interpretation. I lean toward preserving the *c*, however.

8. Lockhart (1992, 107, 134) discusses one from Tlaxcala and another from Cuauhtinchan. In the latter case, the title survived at least until the eighteenth century, with a *cacica* (noble indigenous woman) who was alive until 1704 being called "the Tecpanecatl" posthumously in 1737. Lockhart says this is "the latest instance known to me in which a preconquest lordly title is attributed to an individual" (1992, 135). If the Ajusco document was composed in the early eighteenth century, then its use of Tecpanecatl in this way would be similarly rare. In his early seventeenth-century account, Chimalpahin mentions a "Tecpanecatl teuhctli" in association with a division of Chimalhuacan in Chalco (see Schroeder 1991, 171). Tecpanecatl also evolved into a name used by caciques. A Tlaxcalan lord named Tecpanecatl accompanied Cortés to Cholula and fought with the Spaniards in Tenochtitlan (Gibson 1952, 205). His son, Francisco Tecpanecatl, is discussed later.

9. See Horn 1989, 164. In a personal communication (1992), Rebecca Horn also shared other examples of the name with a slightly different spelling, including Tequepanecal. These examples are equally ambiguous in terms of whether they represent names or titles.

10. Note the greater likelihood of finding baptismal names in Culhuacan in about 1580 than in the census of Cuernavaca around 1535–45 (Lockhart 1992, 120–21). Lockhart (1992, 119) suggests that virtually all the Nahuas of central Mexico had Spanish names as a result of baptism "well before 1550." Of course in this case, if Tecpanecatl is a title, then the absence of a given name is less significant.

11. These are (with unavoidable paleographical errors, because the Nahuatl fragment does not include the lists of names and we cannot verify them against the translation) Acaizacualtecatl, Mecatzin, Yxtlexochtzin, Cuauhotopotzin, Yxayatecpatl, Acamapitzin, Yxcoyotzin, Coyomecatsin, and Totolhuilacctsin.

12. The translation here reads, "Lo que hicieron y aún todavía lo están haciendo los blancos, gente de Castilla" (punctuation and spelling modernized). The Nahuatl is, "in tlein oquichiuhque ihuan zan quichiuhtoque in iztaque caxtillan tlaca" (Díaz de Salas and Reyes 1970, 208).

13. The detailed memory of the earliest saints' images in the titles of Coatepec de las Bateas, Toluca Valley, includes two references to their whiteness (Máynez, Blancas, and Morales 1995, 284–85, 288–89). This very considerable portion of the manuscript, which reveals the town founder's preoccupation with obtaining an increased Christian presence in the community, reads almost like a religious play from the sixteenth century, with frequent exhortations from the principal actor directed toward his reluctant flock.

14. The Nahuatl is "cenca iztac." Variations in phenotype may have been particularly noteworthy during the period of initial contact, upon the first meeting of people with conspicuous differences in skin color. It may have surged again during the Bourbon period, as is evidenced in the proliferation of labels devised by the white minority to describe the multiple, emerging, and often highly contrived social constructions for race mixtures such as those we see in Pedro Alonso O'Crouley's account of New Spain in 1774 (1972, 19 and preceding plates). The ruling minority was alarmed at the social mobility of racial others.

15. Another Guatemalan record with seemingly early roots, the *Chilam Balam of Tizimin*, refers to the Spaniards as "the sons of the Sun, the White men!" (Bricker 1981, 25, quoting Roys's translation).

16. The admiration the European perceived in the indigenous people's actions could have been a projection stemming from his own feelings of racial superiority.

17. In the Nahuatl, "yehuatl yancuic tocayotillo Marquez del Valle" (Díaz de Salas and Reyes 1970, 211).

18. This is not to say that I believe the foundation manuscript, as it existed when it was translated in 1710, had actually been written in 1531, but that some statements from that era may have been preserved through oral tradition or some fragment of a manuscript that was later incorporated into the town titles. As Inga

Clendinnen notes (1990, 105), "in Mexico there is a baffling hiatus in documentation for the first twenty years or so after the conquest." Perhaps it took some time for indigenous nobles to become so accustomed to writing their own language in the Roman alphabet that they would do so away from the watchful eyes of Catholic priests. Where the translation gives 1531, the partial Nahuatl transcription gives 1551, an error Díaz de Salas and Reyes (1970, 207–8, n. 39) attribute to Faustino Galicia Chimalpopoca. They suggest that the original Nahuatl long count for the date intended *cempoal* ("twenty") (1970, 20) where Galicia Chimalpopoca read *ompoal* ("forty") (1970, 40). They argue that early 1531 does ring true for some of the statements in the Ajusco document because that is approximately when Cortés took possession of the portion of the *marquesado* that encompassed the Coyoacan region. Also, by 1551, they argue, Cortés was already dead by four years—hardly the "recently named Marqués."

19. The Nahuatl is "aic moyolalia zan ican theocuitlatl in pepetlactehuillotl" (Díaz de Salas and Reyes 1970, 208). The translation reads, "Nunca se contentan solo con Escoria Divina y relumbrosos bidrios." The Nahua name for gold, translated literally, was godly excrement, an intriguing, visually evocative label.

20. See Craine and Reindorp (1970, ch. 27) for the relevant section of the *Relación de Michoacan*.

21. Quoted in Dussel 1995, 116.

22. Guamán Poma appropriately refers to silver as well as gold, because silver reigned in Peru by the time he wrote his chronicle in the early seventeenth century—although for him, gold hunger was still a vivid memory associated with the European takeover. In currently known late-colonial central Mexican histories from indigenous communities it is not a common memory.

23. The Nahuatl is, "Machiztitoc quename quixtililo inin cihuatzitzinhuan mahuiztique no ihuan in inichpochtzitzinhua" (Díaz de Salas and Reyes 1970, 208). The Spanish version of the passage quoted here reads, "Sabido es, de como les quitan sus Mugeres hermosas, y también sus Mugeres Niñas Doncellas." The document also mentions, "ihuan in ica mahuiltique in tecihuahuan in tlatoque" and "quineque iminca mahuiltizque in tocihuahua in toichpochhuan" (Díaz de Salas and Reyes 1970, 209–10). In the translation: "Nunca se contentan ... ni con burlarse de las Mejeres [sic]," and "quieren hacerles burla noestras mugeres tambien noestras Doncellas." The Nahuatl verb *ahuia* is at the root of the conjugations *mahuiltique* and *mahuiltizque*. Molina (1977 [1555–71], part 2, 9v) gives, for "Auia.tecan," "escarnecer de alguno o holgarse de su mal" (mock, ridicule, jeer, scoff, gibe, laugh at, or delight in another's misfortune). These translations seem to capture the essence of "hacer burla de," but the latter may also be a euphemism for rape. A *burlador* was a seducer, one who dishonored women and abandoned them, according to the *Diccionario de la Real Academia Española* and María Moliner's *Diccionario* (revealed to me in a personal communication from translator Amanda Powell.) It is certainly conceivable that rape was too delicate or shameful a matter to utter literally.

24. See, for example, Díaz del Castillo 1963, 330.

25. The reference to skin color may refer to cosmetic practices, yet it may also be relevant to the discussion of race difference recognition. Berdan and Anawalt (1997, 146) discuss a number of cosmetic applications that were yellow and note how women have a "pale yellow hue" to their skin in the ethnographic section of the *Codex Mendoza*.

26. In the Nahuatl, "in mahuiztique tlatohuanime altepepachoque cuauh-tlanahuatique" (Díaz de Salas and Reyes 1970, 208).

27. There is some question here about whether Moctezuma or Ixchocholli was meant. See Díaz de Salas and Reyes 1970, 209, n. 41.

28. In the Nahuatl, "in huey mahuiztic tlatoani Michhuacan cenca huey Calt-zontzi" (Díaz de Salas and Reyes 1970, 209). Roskamp (1998, 25) provides the *cazonci*'s name and ethnic identity.

29. That Franciscans might have somehow influenced the tone or content of this manuscript, a possibility hinted at earlier, is supported by the probable involve-ment of Fray Jerónimo de Alcalá in the compilation of the *Relación de Michoacán* (Warren 1985, 337) and by the participation of Franciscans in the earliest and best ethnographic materials. One of the Franciscans, a member of the legendary "First Twelve," Fray Martín de la Coruña, also known as Fray Martín de Jesús, testified in opposition to the activities of Nuño de Guzmán in Michoacán and even inter-vened personally at one point to stop a torture session (Baudot 1995, 414, 415, 424, 447). Georges Baudot (1995, 517) also discusses the controversy over what was perceived in royal corners as the Franciscans' overzealous utopian vision for indige-nous peoples.

30. In the Nahuatl, "mochin quexquich tecamahuiltiliztli" (Díaz de Salas and Reyes 1970, 209). The Spanish translation gives "todas cuantas burlas."

31. The Nahuatl is "ipampatica ca in tlatoque Azcapotzalco Mexico Tetzcoco Chalco onexicoittaloaya ihuan ipampa in onemictiloaya omimilo eztli no ihuan" (Díaz de Salas and Reyes 1970, 210). The translation reads, "La causa es porque los señores de Azcapotzalco, México, Tezcoco, y Chalco se veían con envidia y tam-bién porque se mataban, se derramó sangre los mismo."

32. In the Nahuatl, "ye otiquittaque oquixtlauhque occequintin tlatoque in tlein oquitlacoque ye huecau tlaca" (Díaz de Salas and Reyes 1970, 210). The trans-lation reads, "Ya vimos que pagaron otros señores la culpa que cometió la gente antigua."

33. If Franciscan friars had any influence in this narrative, it might not be a coin-cidence that they had numerous Tlaxcalan experiences (see Baudot 1995, 432, 449).

34. An exception to the rule may be found in the Xochimilco area titles; see Wood 1991, 181; Gruzinski 1993, 105–6.

35. The Nahuatl is "matiquimocenmacacan in caxtillan tlaca ic azo camo tech-mictizque" and "ma cacmo tlen titocalactican ic amo techmictizque" (Díaz de Salas

and Reyes 1970, 211–12). The translation reads, "Conviene que nos entreguemos a los hombres de Castilla" and "en nada nos metamos para que así no nos maten."

36. The Nahuatl is "tocolhuan . . . oquimoitalhuique ca hualazque occequintin huecatlaca techtlaocolmacacuihui techquixtiliquihue quimoaxcatizque . . . totlal" and "auh in axcan ye otiquittaque ohualquiz in ye huecauh tlatolli" (Díaz de Salas and Reyes 1970, 210). The translation reads, "Nuestros abuelos . . . dijeron que vendrían otros de lejos tierra a entristecernos, nos vendrían a quitar y hacerse dueños de . . . nuestra tierra" and "ya vimos cumplirse la antigua palabra."

37. Like the Ajusco manuscript, the *Codex Plancarte* was probably an accretive document (see note 53, this chapter), making it difficult to apply a date of origin. Also like the Ajusco document, it was translated in 1710. Given the Ajusco narrative's inclusion of themes from the conflicts in Michoacán, and the way both contain anguished views, in future investigations closer comparisons may be in order.

38. Werner Stenzel (1991, 108–9) also interprets prophecy after the fact as indigenous people's effort to give themselves more agency. He says their motive for referring to the Spaniards in this way was to "expresar conformidad de los vencidos con el acto del sometimiento" ("to express conformity among the vanquished with the act of submission"). Prophecies were not limited to Mesoamerica and the Andes. In what is now the United States, Axtell (1991, 7–8) finds examples of a foretelling about an invasion, for instance, by bearded men. One wonders whether there was any knowledge or memory of bearded Vikings from ancient settlements in what became Canada, at sites such as L'Anse aux Meadows (Fagan 1993).

39. The Nahuatl is "in yancuic theotl techhualiquilia in caxtillanhuaque" (Díaz de Salas and Reyes 1970, 211).

40. The Nahuatl is "matitocuatequicam" (Díaz de Salas and Reyes 1970, 211).

41. The Nahuatl is "ca in huel melahuac theotl ilhui motlallotoc" (Díaz de Salas and Reyes 1970, 212). For a discussion of the "solar Christ" in Nahuatl doctrinal texts of early colonial Mexico, see Burkhart 1988. Akin to this image in the Ajusco manuscript would be, among others, the examples Louise Burkhart relates from Sahagún's *Psalmodia* (1583) of Christ as a setting sun (Burkhart 1988, 247) and from his *Exercicio* (1574) of Christ as a rising sun (1988, 249).

42. The translation reads, "Y adoremos al nuebo Dios porque llo lo he calificado que es el mismo ha de ser que el noestro." The Nahuatl fragment does not include this portion of the original manuscript. Both the translation and the Nahuatl copy include an earlier reference to the "true and real God" (Tezcatlipoca?) who was being worshiped at the annual fiesta that brought on a massacre at the hands of the Spanish invaders (see Díaz de Salas and Reyes 1970, 197, 209).

43. Lockhart (1992, 417) says indigenous and Spanish elements in local traditions described in títulos are "so fully merged and integrated that there is no separating them."

44. In the Nahuatl, "yehuatl techpalehuiz inahuac in caxtilteca" (Díaz de Salas and Reyes 1970, 212).

45. The border survey includes not a single mention of the measurements of specific properties, which in Techialoyan codices are typically rendered in a number of *mecatl* (cord) lengths—another indicator that this manuscript is not of that group.

46. In the Nahuatl: "ihuan ic amo timictilozque macamo tiquiximatican mochi totlal" (Díaz de Salas and Reyes 1970, 212). The translation reads, "Y para que no nos maten combiene que lla no conoscamos todas noestras tierras."

47. Even most sixteenth-century cartographic histories idealize territorial limits (Mundy 1996, 115).

48. Díaz de Salas and Reyes (1970, 198, n. 15) link the reference to a probable *congregación* of pre-1550.

49. See Wood 1984 for the various methods employed to strengthen indigenous communities. See Wood 1990 on the "six hundred varas," which in areal measure were actually supposed to work out to 1,440,000 square varas, being measured 600 varas out in the four cardinal directions from the center of town and then squared off generously.

50. See Percheron 1983, 156 and front cover illustration. Also, see Percheron 1983, 151-52, for her transcription of Tecpanecatl's speech. Glancing at the illustrative style as well as the content of this manuscript, I immediately see affinities between it and the lienzos of San Bartolomé Coatepec (Harvey 1966) and Santa María Atlacomulco (Colín 1963, xvi–xviii and illustration), which may prove to have been made or copied by the same person or group. Another one worth investigating for links may be the "documento de título" of Coxtenco (now Huilotiapa?), a ward of San Cristóbal Texcalucan, which speaks of getting the six-hundred-vara allotment in 1621, a similarly confused measurement or date (Harvey 1993, 17).

51. Lockhart (1992, 416) recognizes a "process of accretion" in titles. He has also coined the description "accretive" and applied it to various cultural manifestations. This characteristic may reflect the dynamism between written and oral culture. Europeans tended to see the written text as fixed, but Mesoamericans may have viewed it as more fluid and dynamic, more reflective of oral culture, more responsive to different individual interpretations in varying social situations and with changing voices over time. Mesoamerican historical writing was more responsive to the vicissitudes of memory construction and remodeling, particularly as native population decline was compounded with a growing foreign presence, resulting in mounting crises in the seventeenth and eighteenth centuries. Serge Gruzinski (1986a, 349) makes some interesting points about writing systems, but his definitions fit European traditions better than indigenous ones. Further, he was exploring this topic at a time when we had less familiarity with indigenous texts than we do now; I doubt he would claim these days that indigenous people "never had the opportunity to create and draft whole texts themselves."

52. If some of the Ajusco narrative really dates from 1531, then the town was surely founded earlier than that, in pre-Columbian times. But perhaps in the view of the judge, the town was officially founded in 1531 because that was the year Spaniards seized power there.

53. Judges accepted one of Cuernavaca's primordial titles, called the "Municipal Codex," as valid in 1707 (see Haskett 1992, 9–10). We have also seen how composición officials cleared a Techialoyan codex from Tepezoyuca in 1696, 1715, and 1720 (Wood 1989, 258). In my view, although it is now impossible for an outsider to know the true locations of exact boundaries, all these kinds of indigenous land titles clearly included many sincere and legitimate land claims.

54. Gruzinski (1993, 104) holds a similar opinion. He describes the way the document "astonishes by the virulence with which it attacks the Spanish conquest. The tone has an unequaled harshness and despair."

55. In the Nahuatl, "in moxicoanime apizmique motocayotia cristianome," and "in temamauhtique caxtilteca" (Díaz de Salas and Reyes 1970, 209). The translation reads, "los envidiosos hambrientos que se nombran cristianos," and "los atemorisadores castellanos."

56. This passage reads, "zan yehuantin inincel quinequi tlatocatizque" (Díaz de Salas and Reyes 1970, 210). And in translation, "Solo ellos quieren mandar."

57. In the Nahuatl, "quineque ininxocpalco techpiezque" (Díaz de Salas and Reyes 1970, 210). The translation reads, "Quieren debajo de sus carcañales tenernos."

58. In the Nahuatl, "quinequi quimoaxcatizque in totlalhuan ihuan mochin quexquich totlatquiuh" (Díaz de Salas and Reyes 1970, 210). The translation reads, "Quieren hacerse dueños de nuestras tierras y todo cuanto es nuestra riqueza." This sentiment recalls a similar passage in Betanzos's 1551 chronicle of events in Peru: "I have seen that [the Spaniards] are fans of every thing that they see, and it seems fine to them to take it for themselves, such as women servants and golden and silver cups and good clothing" (quoted in Pease 1989, 187; my translation).

59. Gruzinski (1993, 104) suggests that by late in the viceregal period, the manuscript's "antiquity" accorded it a value for the community that outweighed its "embarrassing contents." I borrow the term "shameless invasion" from Domitila Chungara of Bolivia, who views what began in 1492 as "a shameless invasion that looted our wealth, that enslaved and raped our people." See the interview with her in *Latin American Perspectives* 19:3 (Summer 1992), 92.

60. Recent works by Roland Baumann (1987) and Max Harris (1990, 1992) relate examples of what they perceive as disguised transcripts of dissent in the colonial Tlaxcalan experience.

61. Another, similarly rare anti-imperialist statement I have come across in my own research was uttered in the midst of a heated controversy over water in the indigenous community of Apastla, near Zacualpan, in the 1780s (AGN Cr, 167, exp. 13): "al estanco, al estanquero, y al Rey habían de arruinar." Such sentiments might have been more common than we know, but few entered the written record.

CHAPTER 4. *A Proud Alliance*

1. The slides I shot of the copy at Tulane, with the assistance of Martha Barton Robertson, are not clear enough to make a good transcription for translating all the glosses and texts to English, and I have not yet arranged an extended viewing of the copy in the vault at the Museum of Natural History, University of Oregon. Therefore, remarks that follow are preliminary and are based on what I can read from my reproductions and what I can sufficiently verify in the translation published with Starr's photographs.

2. One or more copies of the *Mapa* were probably made during the priest's second visit to the pueblo in 1855.

3. Robert Haskett (1992, 12–13), who has surveyed hundreds of Nahuatl documents from the Cuernavaca region, has not seen *hasta* before 1731, a further attestation to its late adoption into the Nahuatl language.

4. Other examples from the *Mapa* include *totecullo* (our lord) in scene 6, *llehuatzin* ("he") in scene 16–17, and *ma lle mochihua* ("so be it") in scene 24.

5. The characters Alvarado and Cortés were major roles in a theatrical piece performed in Tlaxcala in the sixteenth century, *The Conquest of Jerusalem* (Baumann 1987, 142–43).

6. Díaz del Castillo took great interest in Tlaxcalan dramas. He recorded one of the plays performed in Tlaxcala in the sixteenth century, *The Conquest of Rhodes* (cited in Baumann 1987, 143). He also figured prominently as a character in plays performed there. Just as he went on to participate in the expedition into Guatemala, so did the Spaniards' Tlaxcalan allies, which led to the incorporation of that campaign into both the Spaniards' and the Indians' literary and historical accounts. Certain indigenous-language documents associated with Chalchihuapan, for instance, touch on the European invasion of Guatemala. Intriguingly, dramatic lore surrounding the intrusions into Mexico and Guatemala blend in dances performed even today in many towns in both nations (see Bricker 1981, 151).

7. Glosses and texts in the *Mapa* refer to Cortés as the Marqués del Valle (see, for example, scene 10: "Señor Dn fernando Cortes i marques del Balle"), a title he did not receive until 1529, making it unlikely that the manuscript draws from sources recorded at initial contact, even if such were not already exceedingly rare.

8. I suspect that Sarmiento received a Christian first name, too; its absence here supports the supposition that the manuscript was not contemporary with the four caciques. Other lords who play minor roles in the *Mapa* are Tlamacoxpili and Teopaxotzin, plus the lady Matlalcueyetzin, goddess of water and lord over the Tlaxcalan mountain that is now called Malinche or Malintzin (see Starr 1898, 12; Motolinia 1951, 316). After baptism, one of the caciques, Tepoztecatzin or Cacalotzin, bears the name don Jacinto Cortés, a reflection of don Hernando Cortés's supposedly having served as his godfather. Incidentally, an "Ant.o cortés [and] D. Yasinto" are two names that show up in a gloss on the *Mapa de Chalchihuapan* (Castro Morales 1969, 9).

9. A differing version of the story can be found in *Mexican Tales* (Goodspeed 1950, 166–69). This one speaks only of prehispanic events, but it also resonates with some features of the *Mapa*, such as a *teponaztli* drum and an *ocelotl* skin worn by Tepozteco. The drums played in the *Mapa* are reminiscent of the drums shown in plate 39 of the second volume of Fray Diego Durán's *Historia de las Indias de Nueva España e Islas de la Tierra Firme* (Garibay K. 1967). The battle scene in plate 62 is also remarkably like the battles depicted in the *Mapa*. Further efforts to compare these records may prove fruitful.

10. Evidence that such shortening could occur may be seen in the way the town of Totocuitlapilco, in the Toluca Valley, is often simply called "Toto" today. James Lockhart (1992, 118) also explains how Nahua names were sometimes apocopated.

11. The Sarmiento "surname" (with various Christian given names before it) appears various times in the decade of notarial records sampled by Cayetano Reyes García (1973, 31, 183, 206, 238–39, 246–47, 327, 352). One man named Joachín Teposteca appears in the same records (1973, 431–32), and we see Cacalot and Cacalotle (1973, 163 and 176), but no Cencamatl.

12. Starr believes Cacalotzin is the speaker, but the figure next to the gloss is identified as Tepoztecatzin. The original number for this gloss may have been 25, because it is to the left of scene 26. I am thankful to Don Dumond, director of the Museum of Natural History at the University of Oregon, for pointing this out to me.

13. It also seems curious that there is no tribute in this pictorial to St. John, the town's patron saint. Instead, the celebrated religious figure is the Virgen de los Remedios, of historical importance in the broader Cholula-Tlaxcala region. This is true, too, of the *Mapa de Chalchihuapan*, which venerates the same virgin and ignores its own *altepetl* patron, St. Bernard. See Castro Morales 1969. The "virgen conquistadora," as she is described in scene 18 of the *Mapa de Cuauhtlantzinco*, represents "an emblem of Tlaxcalan services and rewards," according to Charles Gibson. Her image was also "displayed on a table surrounded by painted mantles and floral decorations," much as it appears in the paintings of the *Mapa* (Gibson 1952, 35). Another unexplained place-name in the *Mapa* is that of Conchtlan, glossed on scene 32. This may refer to a town Starr says is mentioned several times in Diego Muñoz Camargo's *Historia de Tlaxcala* (Starr 1898, 21).

14. A pueblo with the name Santiago Xalitzintla appears in colonial records from San Andrés Calpa, 1722–1802. These are records of litigation between the owner of the ranchos called Totola and Zacatzingo and the indigenous pueblos of Santiago Xalitzintla, San Nicolás, and San Miguel de los Ranchos, over encroachments. See Méndez Martínez 1979, *ficha* 166. It would be worthwhile to check whether these litigation records contain any reference to primordial titles.

15. Cayetano Reyes García (1973, ix) notes that we have yet to determine the authenticity of the *mapas* of Cuauhtlantzinco and Chalchihuapan. I would argue that they are neither sixteenth-century records nor nineteenth-century fabrications

but were probably late viceregal-era renditions of an evolving pictorial and textual tradition that was shared across the region.

16. See Castro Morales 1969, 8, where, for example, we find *yehuatzin* written "llehuatzi." He credits Carlos Martínez Marín for the translations. I presume the latter also made the transcriptions.

17. See Dyckerhoff 1979; Wood 1987, 1989, 1997a, 1998b; Carrillo Cázares 1991.

18. The following excerpt, dated June 17, 1552, from the Nahuatl-language records of the municipal council of Tlaxcala, may be a reference to either the *Lienzo* or the *Descripción:* "A painting of Cortés's arrival in Tlaxcala and the war and conquest is to be prepared for presentation to the emperor; two regidores are to oversee the project and arrange for artists' supplies through the city majordomo and to choose the artists. At this point it is not decided whether the painting should be on cloth [*tilmatly*] or paper [*amatl*]" (Lockhart, Berdan, and Anderson 1986, 51). See also Martínez Marín (1989, 150), who makes a case for a date of 1551 for the *Lienzo*. His essay provides additional information about various other historical paintings in mural form in Tlaxcala that may have resulted from this municipal order of 1552 if, indeed, it does not refer to the *Lienzo*. The works of René Acuña (1984, 1985–86; Muñoz Camargo 1981) offer the most extensive discussion of Muñoz Camargo's *Historia* or *Descripción de Tlaxcala,* but see also Brotherston and Gallegos 1990 and Martínez 1990.

19. Glass's census (1975b, 214–16) lists eleven copies of the *Lienzo,* yet there were more. The codex contained in the manuscript in Glasgow represents another copy or version (Brotherston and Gallegos 1990, 129).

20. See Martínez Marín (1989, 154–57) on the mural painting tradition.

21. Indicative of regional naming patterns and serving as possibly legitimate local anchors for such manuscripts, Torres was a recurring cacique name in Cuauhtlantzinco at least as late as 1855, and Xicotencatl also appears in a list of dignitaries (see Starr 1898, 10).

22. See Lockhart's (1992, 15–28) discussion of the numerical principles of altepetl organization.

23. Starr (1898, 20) believes Cacalotzin is the cacique who became don Jacinto Cortés (who is inconsistently called "don"). Cacalotl means crow, which would support Starr's supposition. However, the name Tepoztecatzin appears as a gloss for the figures in both scenes 26 and 27.

24. Agustín Rivera (1993, 76) provides a detailed description of these coats of arms. César J. Meléndez Aguilar (1993, 282) reproduces the *Manta* in a line drawing. Rivera (1993, 77) supports a composition date for the *Manta* of "the second third of the sixteenth century."

25. Robert Stone and Yasmin Khan generously sent me slides of this manuscript in the Benson Collection at the University of Texas, Austin. They gave a paper, "García M8 Reviews the Conquest of Mexico," at a Columbia University–New York University conference on Hispanic literature in 1996.

26. See Dyckerhoff (1990, 51–52) for a discussion of Spanish-Indian land competition and problems with títulos in the Puebla region.

27. The *Codex of Cholula* similarly blurs the distinction between corporate and individual claims (see Simons 1967, 281).

28. See, for example, Gibson 1964, 259–67; Taylor 1972, 43–44; Lockhart 1992, 135; Wood 1998a. While such activities increased over time, there is evidence of them from the sixteenth century, as we see in François Chevalier's (1963, 209) reference to indigenous leaders seizing community lands and selling them to Spaniards in the vicinity of Mexico City in 1559. Haskett (1992) has explored the ways in which Cuernavacan cacique factionalism may have affected that region's many títulos. See also Dyckerhoff 1979; Wood 1989. On the corporate vision and its potential for internal variation, see Lockhart 1991, 41.

29. The *Codex of Cholula* refers to the Cholula massacre of 1519 as "treason" (*traición*) (Simons 1968, 293–94). But in line with what the *Mapa* might have had to say about it, this treason seems to have been committed by Moctezuma's warriors, who were waiting outside Cholula and who arranged with the people of Cholula to kill the Spaniards (Simons 1968, 295–96). Incidentally, San Bernardino Chalchihuapan appears on the *Codex of Cholula*, a further indication of a possible link in the lore shared by these manuscripts (Simons 1968, 314).

30. Gifts of gold also appear in the *Codex of Cholula* (see Simons 1968, 289).

31. These remarks from the *Mapa* were quoted from the back side of the manuscript by Don Dumond, director of the Museum of Natural History at the University of Oregon, in some notes that accompanied a 1992 exhibition of the pictorial.

32. Roland Baumann (1987, 147) also connects prehispanic historical record keeping with singing in the form of "national sagas," a loose translation for *melahuacuicatl*.

33. John Monaghan (1994, 88; and see Monaghan 1990) also finds that Mixtec codices may have functioned, "in Thompson's words, as 'prompt books' for songs and chants."

34. The source of this statement is Andrés Pérez de Ribas, quoted in Trexler (1982, 129). Trexler also offers other examples of *macehuales* participating in singing and dancing.

35. Mundy (1996, 111) supports the interpretation that pictorials were displayed for public viewing and that they often served to "remind community members of their shared history."

36. Harris's (1990, 65, citing Todorov) dismissal of indigenous language texts as representing merely "the Indian point of view as it was transcribed by European minds" goes too far. Plenty of native-language texts, such as títulos, were prepared away from the eyes of colonizers and for internal consumption. There is no evidence that Europeans had a direct hand in the contents of the texts of the *Mapa*, nor is there any evidence that the perspective of the *Mapa* was tailored simply to please colonial officials.

37. Diego Muñoz Camargo's (1892, 198–99) account of the caciques' response is even longer and more detailed. Further, in the seventeenth-century play *Colloquy of the Last Four Kings*, the Tlaxcalan lord Xicotencatl expresses concern about giving up a prehispanic deity: "I cannot see the reason why and yet if I do not, perhaps they will kill me. . . . There is no harder thing than to abandon one's old faith." See text in Castañeda 1936, 20.

38. There may have been other indigenous meanings, however. The Nahuas ("mexicanos" or "mexicaneros") of the Sierra del Nayar (Huichol country) had a sleeping ceremony that involved a healing function (see Preuss 1908).

39. This must have been Santa María Malacatepec, which is very near to San Juan Cuauhtlantzinco (Tichy 1979, map coordinates G5).

40. The serpent not only forms his throne but coils atop his head in the shape of a turban. Is the source of this symbol the imported folklore that pits Christians against Turks, the infidels of the old world? On the roles given the Turks in Tlaxcalan religious drama, see Harris 1990. Harris even makes reference (1990, 64) to "the high turban of a Moorish king" worn in a modern play in Huejotzinco.

41. See Wood 1991, 1998b; Lockhart 1991, 62. Anti-Spanish sentiment is also found in primordial titles, as noted earlier, although not directed at the church. See Wood 1991, 186–88, and chapter 5 in this volume.

42. Here I borrow the term *catolicidad* as Harris (1990) uses it. I would not go so far, however, as to embrace his anachronistic use of *indigenismo*. The Nahuatl documentary record from Tlaxcala—or anywhere else in early Mesoamerica, for that matter—rarely conveys a sense of indigenismo. Micropatriotism was the rule; the broad ethnic identity "Indian," as contrasted with Spaniard, only very gradually became a notable part of the indigenous consciousness (Lockhart 1991, 54; 1992, 114–16). If Tlaxcalans secretly pretended in their viceregal-era dramas to defeat the Spanish invaders, they would have done so as Tlaxcalans rather than as "Indians." Identification with the altepetl overshadowed any other solidarity. For example, the Huejotzincan letter to the king, mentioned earlier, typically takes great pains to differentiate between Huejotzincans and Tlaxcalans.

43. See, for example, the license granted to the indigenous governor of Tecamachalco in 1582 to "wear the clothing of a Spaniard and carry a dagger," in the Indios collection of the Archivo General de la Nación, vol. 2, no. 241.

44. Gruzinski (1992, 32) notes that not only were Tlaxcalans seeking privileges, they were warding off future threats to autonomy in their campaigns to get colonizers to remember the history of their alliance. Lest we paint the *Mapa* caciques as too naive, they probably acted much like the Tlaxcalan nobility, which was "aware of its position in a colonial universe" and able "to apply all possible pressure on the crown in order to win its case" (Gruzinski 1992, 40). In Gruzinski's study of the Otomí *Relación anónima* (1986a, 340–41), about the founding of Querétaro, we see another record possibly influenced by the Tlaxcalan tradition, transplanted to the north, in which the Spanish invasion is not mentioned. The indigenous protagonists refer to themselves as Catholics and play the role of con-

querors over the Chichimecs, in some ways emulating the Spanish but "without losing their own autonomy," says Gruzinski. The *Relación* also reads like a script, and the drama includes drums, trumpets, claims about being the first towns to receive Christianity, indigenous leaders preaching Christianity to the nonsedentary people, and a miraculous cross incident—themes that further seem to link it to Tlaxcalan regional lore.

45. See, for example, Sweet and Nash 1981.

46. A letter to the Spanish king written from Cholula in 1593, for example, speaks of the "principales" who "maltreat" the indigenous commoners, and for this reason they flee the region (Carrasco 1970, 182).

Chapter 5. *The Growing Threat*

1. Some titles seem to spring from literate individuals who sometimes possessed only an alleged community authority (Wood 1997, 224).

2. The remarkably similar contents of títulos and "First-Time" narratives of the Saramaka of Suriname may lead us to ponder whether such indigenous voices sang out across the hemisphere and the extent to which they chimed in with African Americans' voices. Richard Price (1983, 6–8) describes the "First-Time" narrative, a local history from a runaway slave community, as "the fountainhead of collective identity" and a "charter" for the "clan." He notes that these narratives contain genealogies and histories of political succession of clan leaders, migratory history intended to establish "land rights for posterity," and boundary surveys, among other elements that can also be identified in títulos. Price found the narratives to be cryptic, omitting all but snippets from larger stories (1983, 10) and often inserting "strings of names, serving a similarly rich mnemonic function" (8).

3. On the historicity of primordial titles, see Wood 1997a, 1998b.

4. This effort was not always in vain. The Cakchiquel, for instance, found considerable success in litigation by using their títulos and retaining Spanish legal counsel (Hill 1989, 295).

5. There are exceptions. For example, Matthew Restall (1991, 116) believes the *deslinde* (boundary survey) address in the chronicle of Yaxkukul (Maya) speaks to a non-native audience.

6. The altepetl was both unique and essential for the preservation of daily life and Nahua cultural forms, as Cayetano Reyes García argues (1995), and as many other scholars who are working with Nahuatl-language manuscripts are also finding.

7. Teresa Rojas Rabiela (1991, 64) mentions "la cuenca de Xochimilco-Chalco" in an essay in homage to Pedro Armillas.

8. Citations for the títulos of Toluca are the following (for abbreviations, please see the bibliography): AGN T 2860, exp. 1, sec. 2, 59r–80v (Capulhuac); AGN T 2998, exp. 3 (Ocoyoacac); Garibay K. 1949 (Metepec); and Máynez, Blancas, and Morales 1995 (Coatepec). The Metepec title was also consulted on microfilm in

the Byron McAfee Collection (UCLA/URL). More recently, the Colegio Mexiquense reissued a facsimile of the Garibay edition. Citations for títulos for other regions are AGN T 3032, exp. 3, 213r–216r (San Andrés Mixquic, Chalco); AGN T 2819, exp. 9, 40r–62r (San Matias Cuixingo, Chalco); AGN T 3032, exp. 3, 276r–277v (Los Reyes, near San Juan Temamatla, Chalco); McAfee and Barlow 1952 (San Gregorio Acapulco, Xochimilco); AGN T 3032, exp. 3, 207r–213r, 220r–227v (Asunción Milpa Alta, Xochimilco); AGN T 3032, exp. 3, 202r–206v, 317r–281v (Santa Marta, Xochimilco); TLAL, VEMC, exp. 24, item 3 (Huejotzingo); BNP, MM 102; BNP, MM 291/292; AGN HJ, legajo (bundle) 447, exp. 7, 1r–6v, and Barlow 1946 (four títulos from Cuernavaca); AGN HJ, vol. 48, pt. 2, exp. 9, sec. 3, 564–67v (Chapultepec, Cuernavaca); AGN HJ, vol. 79, exp. 4, 121r–125r (San Lorenzo Chiamilpa, Cuernavaca); and AGN HJ, legajo 447, exp. 81, 6r–8v (San Salvador Ocotepec, Cuernavaca). Robert Haskett recently concluded an expanded study that includes many more titles from the larger Cuernavaca region.

9. The figure of five hundred pesos is given in the Nahuatl as "macuili siento," or 5 × 100, showing the increasing influence of the decimal system, which gradually replaced the indigenous vigesimal method of counting. A similarly influenced presentation of five hundred as "macuilmacuilpoal," or 5 × (5 × 20), found in a Techialoyan manuscript (AGN T 180, exp. 3, 11r), represents perhaps an intermediate step between the two systems. Earlier, it might have read "centzontli ypan macuilpohualli," or 400 + (5 × 20). In the titles of Coatepec de las Bateas, the town founder refers in a similar way, but without giving a specific amount, to money he spent for the acquisition of a saint's image in Mexico City and for bringing a master mason for the construction of the church (Máynez, Blancas, and Morales 1995, 282–83).

10. The título of Acapulco (not the coastal resort) was published with the annals of the same town. The pairing of these two different types of documents is unusual but intriguing for what it might say about the authors' familiarity with different history genres.

11. Unlike many central Mexican titles, the Yaxkukul document uses the loanword *españoles*, meaning Spaniards ("Señor espaniolesob" and "espaniolesob"; Restall 1991, 120, 122). It also has *concixtador* (for conquistador, conqueror) and *conquista* (conquest) (Restall 1991, 126 n. 41). Tracing such loans can assist with periodization and evolving conceptualization. In his more recent book, Restall (1998) explores further the "Maya conquistadors" and their recontextualization of the calamity of "conquest." Charles Gibson (1980) made a fascinating study of the emergence of the terms *conquista, conquistar, conquistador*, and so on, and their evolving meaning in the sixteenth century in Spanish intellectual circles. As Gibson shows, Bartolomé de Las Casas had some discomfort with the terminology as well as its implications. What did not occur to Gibson was to explore the appropriateness of the term from indigenous perspectives, one of our present tasks.

12. In the *Relación de Yeytecomac*, for instance, the town founder is a male, but he brought a woman with him (Acuña 1985–86, 3:133–34). Women make their way

into primordial titles, too, with somewhat more frequency than in the *relaciones*. Men probably recorded all known titles and, perhaps a result, men still play most of the prominent roles in these town histories. But women do figure largely on occasion. Doña Ana Acaxochitl is a central character of the Metepec titles of the Toluca Valley (Garibay K. 1949). In the Nahua title from Oaxaca, the men summoned women and children to the site of a battle, and the conflict started only after they arrived (Terraciano and Sousa 1992, 46–47). The Axayacatl título of Cuernavaca mentions the presence of elder women (*illamatque*) (BNF MM 102, 3v), and the women of Mixquic (AGN T 3032, exp. 3, 213r) and Ocoyacac (AGN T 2998, exp. 3, 49v–50r) participated in a general way in early events. Apparently in pre-Columbian times, a supposedly Mexica woman and her daughter (who both had the Spanish last name García) led a contingent of potential settlers to Santiago Sula, Chalco, but the locals turned them away, according to the título from that town (Lockhart 1991, 49–51). In the Otomí *Relación anónima* from Querétaro, a Chichimec couple request baptism and Christian marriage ceremonies, and an indigenous woman acting as interpreter, notary, and scribe makes an appearance (Gruzinski 1986a, 343, 348).

13. Examples of relaciones with information about pre-Columbian town founders include those of Coatepec (Acuña 1985–86, 1:133), Chimalhuacan Atoyac (1:156–62), Chicoaloapan (1:170), Tepeapulco (2:171), Ocopetlayucan (2:82–83), Yeyetecomac (3:133–34), Hueypuchtla (3:142), Tezcatepec (3:146–47), and Tecpatepec (3:149–50). The king apparently directed questions 1–10 to Spanish towns and questions numbered 11 forward to indigenous communities, and some administrators followed these instructions (Mundy 1996, 61, and see the relaciones of Antequera, or Oaxaca, in Acuña 1984). Others, especially in the central highlands, applied all questions intended for Spanish communities to native towns, too.

14. Of course, the administrators who compiled this information did not have exemplary relationships with the indigenous communities (see Mundy 1996, 33–34). One, writing about the town under his charge, stated that the first conqueror or founder was not remembered and that all the "Indian elders" ("indios viejos") were dead and those who were alive did not remember. He added with disdain, "It is a town of little fame or renown, because it was never memorable" ("Es pueblo de poca memoria y nombradía, porq[ue] nunca fue memorable") (Acuña 1985–86, 2:97).

15. Descendants of the cazonci, trying to shore up their status in the colonial context, also preferred to emphasize the assistance Tzintzicha Tangaxoan had given the Spaniards (Roskamp 1998, 27). Confirming the sometimes detailed if still somewhat hazy memory of the Spanish incursion, several manuscripts from Michoacán try to pinpoint the date, given variously as July 20, 1521, July 21, 1522, and so on. Although various documents include paintings of Cortés, perhaps recognizing his superior authority, at least one pictorial recognizes Cristóbal de Olid as the expedition leader who entered the Uacúsecha capital (Roskamp 1998, 259–60).

16. Although personal visits of the highest dignitaries (below the kings) did occur very occasionally, primordial titles seem to exaggerate their frequency.

17. Furthermore, it should be noted that more *congregaciones* probably dissolved and more former sites were reoccupied than has often been recognized. See Wood 1984, chs. 2, 6.

18. This may be a formulaic way of saying "in the wilderness," for it echoes wording found by Lockhart (1991, 53 and n. 5) in the Zoyatzingo and Atlauhtla titles.

19. The Zoyatzingo congregación is said to have occurred in 1555 (Lockhart 1991, 62). James Lockhart (1991, 59) sees a clustering of similar dates in this decade for congregaciones mentioned in other títulos as well.

20. The Nahuas, proud descendants of the Toltecs, "are those who remained, those who could no longer migrate," according to the *Florentine Codex* (Sahagún 1950–82, Book 10, 170). The Otomí *Relación anónima* ironically captures the essence of the Nahua disdain for nonsedentary peoples (even though in this case the Otomís are using it to describe the Chichimecs): "They are fond of living in wild and remote places where no-one may see them. . . . they are of very low intelligence, very dirty in their dress and eating habits. . . . their language is barbaric" (quoted by Gruzinski 1986a, 350).

21. Other central Mexican títulos tell of congregaciones in this second wave, too. San Gregorio Acapulco's title, for example, mentions a congregación in 1603, another credible date (McAfee and Barlow 1952, 140–41).

22. Lienzos from Michoacán, for example, include portraits of Fray Angel de Valencia and Fray Martín de Jesús (Roskamp 1998, 260). Even more specific, the Yucatecan Annals of Oxkutzcab acknowledge the particular day in 1545 when six named friars launched Christianity in the local communities (Restall 1998, 81). One of the Cuernavacan titles gives so much information about the coming of the priests and religious changes that it would not be surprising to find that a *fiscal*, an indigenous assistant to a priest, had authored it (Haskett 1987).

23. Also, in the titles of Coatepec de las Bateas, the town founder predicts that the people will be frightened by the first mass (in the Nahuatl, "Auh in naxca ca quimonequiltia quimochihuilis in misa nan anmomauhtisque"; in the Spanish translation, "Y ahora como quiere hacerle la misa, luego se espantarán") (Máynez, Blancas, and Morales 1995, 280–81). Other, similar references to fear occur on pages 284–85 and 286–87.

24. The date is conceivable. Franciscans put down roots in Toluca possibly in the late 1520s but may not have established other parishes around the valley until the 1550s (Gerhard 1972, 176, 331). More research, however, could place these activities earlier in time. Several títulos date evangelization from the decades of the 1520s and 1530s. The Sula (Chalco region) document mentions that the "Catholic faith was in Mexico City already" before this town faced the selection of its patron saint (Lockhart 1991, 59), suggesting a time lag there, too.

25. In the Nahuatl, "oquimotlatlapannilico yn otictoteotiaya" and "onquitla-tlapannanto teonme."

26. In the Nahuatl, employing the Spanish loanword *conquistar*, "ca yehuatzin mohuicas quinmoconquistarhuis auh huel amo quinequisque."

27. The recollection of such an exact date here, as in most of the central Mexican títulos, is surprising. The year might also be early.

28. In the titles of Coatepec de las Bateas, the town founder, don Nicolás Miguel, plays a major role in seeing that the respectable saint's image is installed in a proper place of worship and that priests come to say mass (Máynez, Blancas, and Morales 1995, 272–91). In both Capulhuac and Coatepec, the town founders shared their first names with the patron saints, Bartolomé and Nicolás.

29. In the Nahuatl (somewhat problematical), "yni amo santo ynin tetla-masquitilia santo amo." In the Spanish translation, "Éste no es un santo, esto es una piedra."

30. In the Nahuatl, "Ayamo huel tintlanelTocan" and "Can Ayamo tintlanel-tocan Ypan ynin tlali ynhua nonhuiya cemananhuac."

31. This term and variations on it appear in many of the central Mexican títu-los. See, for example, AGN T 3032, exp. 3, 203v, 218r (Santa Marta) and 277r (Reyes Tlalaxayopanecan), or McAfee and Barlow 1952, 124–26 (San Gregorio Acapulco).

32. Ratios of Spaniards to indigenous people farther from the capital are even more striking. John Chance (1989, 39) tabulated the population of the Villa Alta district of Oaxaca for 1781, revealing a combined total of fewer than 300 Spaniards and mixed-heritage people as compared with 16,510 indigenous. Amos Megged (1996, 97) similarly found that the Spanish population in indigenous communities of the Chiapa province in 1611 was "significantly low." Of course, if they were seen by the local people as invaders, any number could be alarming.

33. Lockhart (1991, 60) gives examples of the way the Chalcan títulos confuse titles of office. Two of the Cuernavacan titles (BNF, MM 102, 3r; Barlow 1946, 215) and the Ocoyacac titles (AGN T 2998, exp. 3, 29v) also call the viceroy a king.

34. In the Nahuatl, "Ayc aqui oc ce quixtiano quiquixtiz manel ce xicanli tlaoli noço tlaco almo tlaoli quitocaz . . . Aic aquin quinamacaz tlalli."

35. In the Nahuatl, "Tla quemania quimocniuhtiz quixtiyanotin Nima nocuiliz y tlalli."

36. In the Nahuatl (somewhat puzzling), "Canmo totlacanmecayo oc cecni y ehua can huel oc oyez queni ce tlamantli y eztli quipie can coyotl."

37. See Haskett 1985, 140–47. He also discusses charges of nonindigenous ethnicity as a regular feature in election disputes for town council office (168–71).

Chapter 6. *Supplanting the Metanarrative*

1. Ross Frank (1989, 201) suggests that the ceremonial garb associated with divinity that the Aztecs gave the Spaniards would not have necessitated their conceptual equation of Cortés with a "supernatural being." When a Mexican warrior

put on a costume invoking the *teotl* Huitzilopochtli, he "represented the deity not in a supernatural or linguistic sense, but through a spiritual relationship and special power that the god conferred upon his impersonator."

2. See Columbus's writings in *New Iberian World* (1984, 2:43, 61).

3. In a similar but lesser-known example, the Itza of Yucatán predicted, in their histories, that their capital would be conquered during Katun 8 Ahau of their calendar, which began around 1695. The Spaniard Fray Andrés de Avendaño y Loyola took advantage of this and launched his mission to the Itza according to this time frame. In a sense, as Victoria Bricker (1981, 22–28) points out, the Itza therefore invited the Spaniards to come convert them, nullifying any logical application of the term "conquest." It might also be that Chief Powhatan's priests predicted (after the fact?) that a powerful nation would arise from Chesapeake Bay and "give end to his empier" (according to William Strachey, quoted in Hantman 1992, 76).

4. The similar association of the prophesied return of the Andean deity Viracocha (or Wiraqocha) with the arrival of the Spaniards in Peru dates from the 1550s (Pease 1989, 188). There, too, the Europeans deceitfully encouraged the indigenous people to see them as supernatural and as having come from the direction in which a native divinity figure once departed. And while some natives accepted this, others questioned it (Pease 1989, 189, 190). In the end, the term *Viracocha* applied to any Spaniard and had a negative connotation (1989, 191).

5. Franco (1992, 177) notices how the "native informant, translator, and mediator emerges on the boundaries of this discourse" of discovery and conquest.

6. Rolena Adorno (1988, 18) praises the work of Frank Salomon and Regina Harrison for letting such categories arise naturally from Andean materials and for not trying to impose European models. This is also a characteristic of James Lockhart's (1991) New Philology in Mesoamerican studies, which was a part of my training. Regarding the term *ethnographic history,* I find Richard Price's (1990, xiv) use of it in preference to *ethnohistory* appealing, because of its broader applicability—whether applied to "a modern industrial corporation or a nonliterate hill tribe." It is less condescending. Yet I am not sure how well sources written by the people under study fit the label *ethnographic.*

7. Labels for Europeans sometimes merged with labels for their props or their physical appearance and dress, as we saw, for example, in the P'urhépecha term *acacecha* ("people who wear caps and hats"), employed to mean Spaniards (Lunenfeld 1991, 270). Examples of technology's guiding identification of the little-known Europeans in North America are even more abundant. The Narrangansetts of Rhode Island called Europeans "coatmen" or "swordmen"; the Mohawks of New York called the Dutch "ironworkers" or "cloth makers"; the Hurons of southern Ontario called the French "Iron People"; the Pocumtucks called the French "Knive men"; and Virginians and other whites were called "Longknives" (Axtell 1991, 27).

8. The Powhatan, for example, quickly transformed the unknown into the known, according to Jeffrey L. Hantmann (1992, 79).

9. Wachtel (1977, 213) himself found "vanquished" unsatisfactory for indigenous views of changes in the Andes.

10. Tom Cummins (1991, 211) finds that the Spaniards saw the *kurakakuna*, or elite Andeans, "as a reasonable semblance of the colonists themselves." Ross Frank (1989, 188) notes how Europeans found Caribbean peoples to be vastly different from themselves but viewed Mexican society as "far closer to their own." Central-area sedentary peoples had a social and cultural organization that more closely approximated the European, facilitating foreign settlement and a smoother transfer of power with less disruption for these indigenous peoples than for semi- or nonsedentary peoples, who found the yoke of colonialism less tolerable or entirely unacceptable.

11. There are important exceptions that deserve further consideration, such as the Mayan accounts (see Bricker 1981, 13–52).

12. Marilyn Miller (1997, 48) reminds us how Diego Muñoz Camargo presented indigenous people as the "heroes" in his "'revisionist' history of American exploration," which represented a "new slant in 'discovery literature.'" His account makes Tlaxcalan leaders the key figures responsible for the Spaniards' having gained a secure foothold in the "New World."

13. Some did come to see a temporal break between the period when they had lived as "gentiles" or "infidels" and the period when they had come to live as "Christians," probably becoming accustomed to hearing of this chronological framework from the friars. See, for example, the Andean petition of 1562 quoted in Pratt 1993, 24. But the epochal division did not necessarily coincide with the shift in political control at the imperial level, and, as we see in central Mexican títulos, chronologies are not always linear.

14. When a Mayan history notes prominently, "The year 1519 arrived" (Bricker 1981, 25), it gives one pause, because this marks the landing of the Cortés expedition that ended up taking the Aztec capital, not the first European landing in the Maya zone (probably 1511). It is as though the native writers had been lectured by friars that 1519 was an obligatory date for histories covering that period.

15. The comings and goings of dignitaries in annals are an exception. This might be a feature of annals that writers adapted from prehispanic tradition; alternatively, it might reflect the influence of Spanish historians.

16. The issue of Muñoz Camargo's heterogenous perspective and voice has been a subject of continuing exploration (see Mignolo 1987; Miller 1997).

17. The Bering land bridge theory still enjoys large numbers of advocates despite growing support for dates at the Monte Verde archaeological site in Chile that would push waves of migration back much earlier than once thought (see "New Portrait Emerges of First Americans: Chilean Site Challenges Colonization Theories," *Christian Science Monitor*, February 12, 1997, 3; and "Old Habitation in a New World: Evidence of Human Life in Chile Dates Back 12,500 Years," *Los Angeles Times*, February 18, 1997, B6).

18. When they live in the cosmopolitan metropolis, Mexico City, possibly spending long hours with ecclesiastic scholars, producing historical works of an increasingly European nature and less obviously rooted in a native community (such as some of the annals), then perhaps this is less the case. But it is not necessarily so. The Nahua annalist Chimalpahin (1579–1660), for instance, was preoccupied with indigenous society and closely identified with it, associating in Mexico City not only with friars by also with indigenous intellectuals (Schroeder 1991, ch. 1). Regarding rural communities, I find both autonomy and corporation to be features that were internally pushed, even exaggerated when necessary, in the struggle for survival, agreeing with revisionist views of the "closed corporate community" (which even Eric Wolf, who coined the term, found inaccurate; Wolf 1957). I also use with caution the "folk-urban continuum" of Robert Redfield (1941), because there could be close-knit indigenous communities within larger and more heterogenous urban entities, and individuals in the countryside, such as muleteers and day laborers on estates, who had considerable contact with non-indigenous people. For a summary of Wolf's and Redfield's contributions to Mesoamerican studies, see Gossen 1994, 3. Eric Van Young also discusses the "allegiance to the natal village" and "primordial community loyalties" in "late colonial Mexico" in a compelling way (1996, 140–41; and see Van Young 1993).

19. See Ouweneel 1997, 75, for a list of indigenous colonial figures who envisioned that their own kings should preside over the *república de indios*.

20. Gary Gossen (1994, 1) notes how "Mesoamerica has evolved a peculiar identity, since at least 2000 B.C., as a region in which competing chiefdoms and, later, states were the name of the game."

21. The Nobel Peace Prize winner Rigoberta Menchú (Yáñez 1992) also calls for an objective, less romantic view of caciques who have defended their privileges and profited from the work of others, saying that they were crueler than Spanish colonizers and were driven by class interests over questions of race or ethnic solidarity. Even in the viceregal period in Mayan communities, caciques sometimes conflicted with their people and faced repudiation, seizure, and punishment for having cooperated with Spaniards (Bricker 1981, 21).

22. For instance, the municipal governor of Coyoacan in the mid-sixteenth century expected daily "three hens; two baskets of shelled maize; 400 cacao beans; 200 chiles; one piece of salt; tomatoes; gourd seeds; 10 (men to act as) guards; 8 (women to be) grinders of maize; 6 loads of wood; grass for horse fodder, five loads" (Anderson, Berdan, and Lockhart 1976, 151).

23. The anthology *Nuestro pesar, nuestra aflicción* (1996) contains Nahuatl accounts from about 1572 that include heartrending descriptions of the tribute and labor burdens of communities in Guatemala that surely echo similar sentiments from across Mesoamerica. In San Francisco, part of Zacualpan, Ciudad Vieja (Santiago de Guatemala), people told, for instance, how survivors of epidemics had to uphold the tribute obligations of the deceased, and how, if they failed, they faced incarceration and fines (*Nuestro pesar*, 1996, 33).

184

Bibliography

Archival Sources

Archivo General de la Nación, Mexico (AGN). Tierras (T), Criminal (Cr), and Hospital de Jesús (HJ) collections.

Bibliothèque Nationale de France (BNF). Fonds Mexicains. Manuscrit Mexicain (MM).

Library of Congress (LC). Division of Prints and Photographs, Archive of Hispanic Culture. Collection of Mexican Indian Pictorial Documents (MIPD).

Tulane University, Latin American Library (TLAL). Viceregal and Ecclesiastical Mexican Collection (VEMC).

Universidad de las Américas, Cholula, Mexico (UDLA). Library. Sala Porfirio Díaz. Barlow Collection (RBC).

University of California, Los Angeles (UCLA), University Research Library (URL). Special Collections. Byron McAfee Collection, Microfilm.

Published Sources

Acuña, René, ed. 1984. *Relaciones geográficas del siglo XVI: Antequera.* 2 vols. Mexico City: Universidad Autónoma de México, Instituto de Investigaciones Antropológicas.

___, ed. 1985–86. *Relaciones geográficas del siglo XVI: México.* 3 vols. Mexico City: Universidad Autónoma de México, Instituto de Investigaciones Antropológicas.

Adorno, Rolena. 1988. "Nuevas perspectivas en los estudios literarios coloniales hispanoamericanos." *Revista de Crítica Literaria Latinoamericana* 28:11–27.

___. 1989. "Arms, Letters, and the Native Historian in Early Colonial Mexico." In *1492–1992: Re/discovering Colonial Writing,* edited by René Jara and Nicholas Spadaccini, 201–24. Hispanic Issues 4. Minneapolis, Minn.: Prisma Institute.

___. 1990. "The Depiction of Self and Other in Colonial Peru." *Art Journal* 49:110–18.

Anales de Tlatelolco: Unos anales históricos de la nación mexicana y Códice de Tlatelolco. 1948. Edited by Heinrich Berlin-Newbartal and R. H. Barlow. Fuentes para la historia de México, 2. Mexico City: Antigua Librería Robredo.

Anawalt, Patricia R. 1981. *Indian Clothing before Cortes: MesoAmerican Costumes from the Codices*. Norman: University of Oklahoma Press.

Anderson, Arthur J. O., Frances Berdan, and James Lockhart, eds. 1976. *Beyond the Codices*. UCLA Latin American Studies Series, 27. Berkeley: University of California Press.

Anderson, Arthur J. O., and Charles E. Dibble, eds. 1975. *Florentine Codex: General History of the Things of New Spain, by Fray Bernardino de Sahagún*. Book 12, *The Conquest of Mexico*. Second edition, revised. Monographs of the School of American Research, no. 14, part 8. Santa Fe, N.M., and Salt Lake City: School of American Research and University of Utah Press.

Annals of the Cakchiquels. 1885. Edited by Daniel Garrison Brinton. Philadelphia.

Antigüedades de México basadas en la recopilación de Lord Kingsborough. 1964. Mexico City: Secretaría de Hacienda y Crédito Público.

Antigüedades mexicanas publicadas por la Junta Colombina de México en el cuarto centenario del descubrimiento de América: Homenaje a Cristóbal Colón. 1892. Mexico City: Oficina Tipográfica de la Secretaría de Fomento.

Axtell, James. 1988. *After Columbus: Essays in the Ethnohistory of Colonial North America*. Oxford: Oxford University Press.

———. 1991. *Imagining the Other: First Encounters in North America*. Washington, D.C.: American Historical Association.

———. 1992. *Beyond 1492: Encounters in Colonial North America*. Oxford: Oxford University Press.

Barker, Francis, Peter Hulme, and Margaret Iversen. 1994. "Introduction." In *Colonial Discourse/Postcolonial Theory*, edited by Francis Barker, Peter Hulme, and Margaret Iversen, 1–23. Manchester, England: Manchester University Press.

Barlow, Robert H. 1946. "Unos títulos de Cuernavaca." *Tlalocan* 2:213–22.

Barlow, Robert H., and George T. Smisor. 1943. *Nombre de Dios, Durango: Two Documents in Nahuatl Concerning Its Foundation*. Sacramento, Calif.: House of Tlaloc.

Baudot, Georges. 1995. *Utopia and History in Mexico: The First Chroniclers of Mexican Civilization (1520–1569)*. Translated by Bernard R. Ortiz de Montellano and Thelma Ortiz de Montellano. Niwot, Colo.: University Press of Colorado.

———. 1996. *México y los albores del discurso colonial*. Mexico City: Nueva Imagen.

Baumann, Roland. 1987. "Tlaxcalan Expression of Autonomy and Religious Drama in the Sixteenth Century." *Journal of Latin American Lore* 13:139–53.

Berdan, Frances F. 1993. "Trauma and Transition in Sixteenth-Century Central Mexico." In *The Meeting of Two Worlds: Europe and America, 1492–1650*, edited by Warwick Bray, 163–95. Oxford: Oxford University Press.

Berdan, Frances F., and Patricia Rieff Anawalt. 1997. *The Essential Codex Mendoza*. Berkeley: Unversity of California Press.

Beverley, John. 1992. "Introducción." In *La voz del otro: Testimonio, subalternidad y verdad narrativa*, edited by John Beverley and Hugo Achugar, 7–18. Lima: Latinoamericana Editores.

Bierhorst, John, ed. 1985. *Cantares Mexicanos: Songs of the Aztecs*. Stanford, Calif.: Stanford University Press.

Blom, Frans. 1945. "El lienzo de Analco, Oaxaca." *Cuadernos Americanos* 24:125–36.

Boban, Eugène. 1891. *Documents pour servir a l'histoire du Mexique*, vol. 1. Paris: E. Leroux.

Bonfil Batalla, Guillermo. 1987. *Mexico profundo: Una civilización negada*. Mexico City: Secretaría de Educación Pública and CIESAS.

Bonilla, Heraclio, comp. 1992. *Los conquistados: 1492 y la población indígena de las Américas*. Bogotá: Tercer Mundo Editores.

Boone, Elizabeth Hill. 1991. "Migration Histories as Ritual Performance." In *To Change Place: Aztec Ceremonial Landscapes*, edited by Davíd Carrasco, 121–51. Niwot, Colo.: University Press of Colorado.

___. 1994a. "Introduction: Writing and Recording Knowledge." In *Writing without Words: Alternative Literacies in Mesoamerica and the Andes*, edited by Elizabeth Hill Boone and Walter D. Mignolo, 3–26. Durham, N.C.: Duke University Press.

___. 1994b. "Aztec Pictorial Histories: Records without Words." In *Writing without Words: Alternative Literacies in Mesoamerica and the Andes*, edited by Elizabeth Hill Boone and Walter D. Mignolo, 50–76. Durham, N.C.: Duke University Press.

Boone, Elizabeth Hill, and Walter D. Mignolo, eds. 1994. *Writing without Words: Alternative Literacies in Mesoamerica and the Andes*. Durham, N.C.: Duke University Press.

Borah, Woodrow. 1984. "Some Problems of Sources." In *Explorations in Ethnohistory: Indians of Central Mexico in the Sixteenth Century*, edited by H. R. Harvey and Hanns J. Prem, 23–39. Albuquerque: University of New Mexico Press.

Borah, Woodrow, and Sherbourne F. Cook. 1963. *The Aboriginal Population of Central Mexico on the Eve of the Spanish Conquest*. Ibero-Americana, 45. Berkeley: University of California Press.

Bricker, Victoria Reifler. 1981. *The Indian Christ, the Indian King: The Historical Substrate of Maya Myth and Ritual*. Austin: University of Texas Press.

Brotherston, Gordon. 1979. *Image of the New World: The American Continent Portrayed in Native Texts*. Translations prepared in collaboration with Ed Dorn. London: Thames and Hudson.

___. 1995. *Painted Books from Mexico: Codices in UK Collections and the World They Represent*. London: British Museum Press.

Brotherston, Gordon, and Ana Gallegos. 1990. "El Lienzo de Tlaxcala y el Manuscrito de Glasgow (Hunter 242)." *Estudios de Cultura Náhuatl* 20:117–40.

Burkhart, Louise M. 1988. "The Solar Christ in Nahuatl Doctrinal Texts of Early Colonial Mexico." *Ethnohistory* 35:234–56.

___. 1989. *The Slippery Earth: Nahua-Christian Moral Dialogue in Sixteenth-Century Mexico*. Tucson: University of Arizona Press.

Carmack, Robert M. 1973. *Quichean Civilization: The Ethnohistoric, Ethnographic, and Archaeological Sources*. Berkeley: University of California Press.

Carrasco, Pedro, ed. 1970. "Carta al rey sobre la ciudad de Cholula en 1593." *Tlalocan* 6:176–92.

Carrillo Cázares, Alberto. 1991. "'Chiquisnaquis,' un indio escribano, artífice de 'títulos primordiales' (La Piedad, siglo XVIII)." *Relaciones* (Zamora, Michoacan) 48:187–210.

Castañeda, Carlos. 1936. "The First American Play." *Preliminary Studies of the Texas Catholic Historical Society* (Austin) 3.

Castro Morales, Efraín. 1969. *El Mapa de Chalchihuapan: Estudios y documentos de la región de Puebla-Tlaxcala*, vol. 1. Puebla: Colegio de Historia, Escuela de Filosofía y Letras de la Universidad Autónoma, Instituto Poblana de Antropología e Historia.

Catálogo de ilustraciones. 1979. 14 vols. Mexico City: Centro de Información Gráfica del Archivo General de la Nación.

Chanady, Amaryll. 1995. "Between the Plural 'Us' and the Excluded 'Other': Autochthons and Ethnic Groups in the Americas." *Diogenes* 170:93–108.

Chance, John K. 1989. *The Conquest of the Sierra: Spaniards and Indians in Colonial Oaxaca*. Norman: University of Oklahoma Press.

Chevalier, François. 1963. *Land and Society in Colonial Mexico: The Great Hacienda*. Translated by Alvin Eustis; edited by Lesley Byrd Simpson. Berkeley: University of California Press.

Clendinnen, Inga. 1987. *Ambivalent Conquests: Maya and Spaniard in Yucatan, 1517–1570*. Cambridge: Cambridge University Press.

———. 1990. "Ways to the Sacred: Reconstructng 'Religion' in Sixteenth-Century Mexico." *History and Anthropology* 5:105–41.

———. 1993. "'Fierce and Unnatural Cruelty': Cortés and the Conquest of Mexico." In *New World Encounters*, edited by Stephan Greenblatt, 12–47. Berkeley: University of California Press.

Cline, S. L., ed. 1993. *The Book of Tributes: Early Sixteenth-Century Nahuatl Censuses from Morelos*. Museo de Antropología e Historia, Archivo Histórico, Colección Antigua, vol. 549. Los Angeles: UCLA Latin American Center Publications.

Cline, S. L., and Miguel León-Portilla, eds. 1984. *The Testaments of Culhuacan*. Los Angeles: UCLA Latin American Center Publications.

Codex en Cruz. 1981. 2 vols. Edited by Charles Dibble. Salt Lake City: University of Utah Press.

Codex Telleriano-Remensis: Ritual, Divination, and History in a Pictorial Aztec Manuscript. 1995. Edited by Eloise Quinones-Keber. Austin: University of Texas Press.

Códice Aubin. 1981. [See: Lehmann, Walter.]

Códice de 1576. 1893. [See: *Histoire de la Nation Mexicaine*.]

Códice de Huichapan. 1992. Edited by Alfonso Caso; introduction by Óscar Reyes Retana M. Mexico City: Telecomunicaciones de México.

Códice de Tlatelolco. 1948. [See: *Anales de Tlatelolco*.]

Códice de Yanhuitlán. 1940. Edited by Wigberto Jiménez Moreno and Salvador Mateos Higuera. Mexico City: Museo Nacional, Secretaría de Educación Pública, Instituto Nacional de Antropología e Historia.

Códice de Xicotepec: Estudio e interpretación. 1995. Edited by Guy Stesser-Péan. Puebla: Gobierno del Estado de Puebla, Centro de Estudios Mexicanos y Centroamericanos, y Fondo de Cultura Económica.

Códice Kingsborough. 1992. [See: *Memorial de los indios de Tepetlaóztoc.*]

Códice Sierra: Traducción al español de su texto náhuatl y explicación de sus pinturas jeroglíficas. 1933. Edited by Nicolas León. Mexico City: Museo Nacional de Arqueología, Historia y Etnografía.

Códices de México, Los. 1979. Mexico City: Instituto Nacional de Antropología e Historia.

Colín, Mario. 1963. *Antecedentes agrarios del municipio de Atlacomulco, Estado de México: Documentos.* Mexico City: Departamento de Asuntos Agrarios y Colonización.

———. 1968. *Índice de documentos relativos a los pueblos del Estado de México: Ramo de Indios del Archivo General de la Nación.* Mexico City: Biblioteca Enciclopédica del Estado de México.

Coombes, Annie E. 1994. "The Recalcitrant Object: Culture Contact and the Question of Hybridity." In *Colonial Discourse/Postcolonial Theory*, edited by Francis Barker, Peter Hulme, and Margaret Iversen, 89–114. Manchester, England: Manchester University Press.

Cortés, Hernando. 1928. *Five Letters of Cortés to the Emperor.* Translated and with an introduction by J. Bayard Morris. New York: W. W. Norton.

Craine, Eugene R., and Reginald C. Reindorp, trans. and eds. 1970. *The Chronicles of Michoacán.* Norman: University of Oklahoma Press.

Cummins, Thomas B. F. 1991. "We Are the Other: Peruvian Portraits of Colonial *Kurakakuna.*" In *Transatlantic Encounters: Europeans and Andeans in the Sixteenth Century*, edited by Kenneth J. Andrien and Rolena Adorno, 203–31. Berkeley: University of California Press.

de la Torre, Ernesto. 1952. "Relación de la congregación del pueblo de Tianguistengo, Provincia de Meztitlan." *Boletín del Archivo General de la Nación* (Mexico), 23:147–83.

Dehouve, Daniele. 1994. *Entre el caimán y el jaguar: Los pueblos indios de Guerrero.* Mexico City: Centro de Investigaciones y Estudios Superiores en Antropología Social.

Díaz del Castillo, Bernal. 1963 [1580?]. *The Conquest of New Spain.* Translated with an introduction by J. M. Cohen. Harmondsworth, UK: Penguin Books.

———. 1976 [1580?]. *Historia verdadera de la conquista de la Nueva España.* Mexico City: Editorial Porrúa.

Díaz de Salas, Marcelo, and Luis Reyes García, eds. 1970. "Testimonio de la fundación de Santo Tomás Ajusco." *Tlalocan* 6:193–212.

Dussel, Enrique. 1995. *The Invention of the Americas: The Eclipse of "the Other" and the Myth of Modernity.* Translated by Michael D. Barber. New York: Continuum.

Dyckerhoff, Ursula. 1979. "Forged Village Documents from Huejotzingo and Calpan." *Actas of the International Congress of Americanists* 42(7):51–63. Paris.

———. 1990. "Colonial Indian Corporate Landholding: A Glimpse from the Valley of Puebla." In *The Indian Community of Colonial Mexico: Fifteen Essays on Land Tenure, Corporate Organizations, Ideology, and Village Politics,* edited by Arij Ouweneel and Simon Miller, 40–59. Amsterdam: Center for Latin American Research and Documentation.

Edmonson, Munro S. 1964. *Historia de las tierras altas Mayas según los documentos indígenas.* Mexico City: Universidad Nacional Autónoma de México.

———, ed. 1971. *Popol Vuh, English and Quiché. The Book of Counsel: The Popol Vuh of the Quiché Maya of Guatemala.* New Orleans: Middle American Research Institute, Tulane University.

———, ed. 1974. *Sixteenth-Century Mexico: The Work of Sahagún.* Albuquerque: University of New Mexico Press.

Fagan, Brian. 1993. "In the Footsteps of the Norse." *Archaeology* 46:14–16.

Farriss, Nancy M. 1987. "Remembering the Future, Anticipating the Past: History, Time, and Cosmology among the Maya of Yucatan." *Comparative Studies in Society and History* 29:566–93.

Florescano, Enrique. 1994. *Memory, Myth, and Time in Mexico: From the Aztecs to Independence.* Austin: University of Texas Press.

Foucault, Michel. 1972. *The Archaeology of Knowledge and the Discourse of Language.* New York: Pantheon.

Franco, Jean. 1982. "La cultura hispanoamericana en la época colonial." In *Historia de la literatura hispanoamericana,* vol. 1, *Época colonial,* coordinated by Luis Íñigo Madrigal, 35–53. Madrid: Cátedra.

———. 1992. "Remapping Culture." In *Americas: New Interpretive Essays,* edited by Alfred Stepan, 172–88. Oxford: Oxford University Press.

Frank, Ross. 1989. "The Codex Cortés: Inscribing the Conquest of Mexico." *Dispositio* 14(36–38):187–211.

Fuentes, Carlos. 1992. "Imagining America." *Diogenes* 160:5–19.

Fuentes, Patricia de, trans. and ed. 1993. *The Conquistadors: First-Person Accounts of the Conquest of Mexico.* Norman: University of Oklahoma Press.

Garibay K., Angel María, ed. 1949. *Códice de Metepec, Estado de México.* Mexico City: n.p.

———, ed. 1967. *Historia de las Indias de Nueva España e Islas de la Tierra Firme escrita por Fray Diego Durán, Dominico, en el siglo XVI,* 2. Mexico City: Editorial Porrúa.

Gerhard, Peter. 1972. *A Guide to the Historical Geography of New Spain.* Cambridge Latin American Studies, 14. Cambridge: Cambridge University Press.

Gibson, Charles. 1952. *Tlaxcala in the Sixteenth Century*. Stanford, Calif.: Stanford University Press.

___. 1964. *The Aztecs under Spanish Rule: A History of the Indians of the Valley of Mexico, 1519–1810*. Stanford, Calif.: Stanford University Press.

___. 1975. "A Census of Middle American Prose Manuscripts in the Native Historical Tradition." In *Handbook of Middle American Indians*, vol. 15, *Guide to Ethnohistorical Sources*, part 4, edited by Howard F. Cline, 311–21. Austin: University of Texas Press.

___. 1980. "Conquest and So-Called Conquest in Spain and Spanish America." *Terrae Incognitae* 12:1–19.

Gibson, Charles, and John B. Glass. 1975. "A Census of Middle American Prose Manuscripts in the Native Historical Tradition." In *Handbook of Middle American Indians*, vol. 15, *Guide to Ethnohistorical Sources*, part 4, edited by Howard F. Cline, 322–400. Austin: University of Texas Press.

Gillespie, Susan D. 1989. *The Aztec Kings: The Construction of Rulership in Mexica History*. Tucson: University of Arizona Press.

Gingerich, Willard. 1983. "Critical Models for the Study of Indigenous Literature: The Case of Nahuatl." In *Smoothing the Ground: Essays on Native American Oral Literature*, edited by Brian Swann, 112–25. Berkeley: University of California Press.

Glass, John B. 1975a. "A Survey of Native Middle American Pictorial Manuscripts." In *Handbook of Middle American Indians*, vol. 14, *Guide to Ethnohistorical Sources*, part 3, edited by Howard F. Cline, 3–80. Austin: University of Texas Press.

___. 1975b. "A Census of Native Middle American Pictorial Manuscripts." In collaboration with Donald Robertson. In *Handbook of Middle American Indians*, vol. 14, *Guide to Ethnohistorical Sources*, part 3, edited by Howard F. Cline, 81–252. Austin: University of Texas Press.

Goodspeed, Bernice. 1950. *Mexican Tales: A Compilation of Mexican Stories and Legends*. Mexico City: American Book and Print Co.

Gossen, Gary H. 1994. "Mesoamerican Ideas as a Foundation for Regional Synthesis." In *Symbol and Meaning beyond the Closed Community: Essays in Mesoamerican Ideas*, 1–8. Studies on Culture and Society, 1. Albany, N.Y.: Institute for Mesoamerican Studies, State University of New York at Albany.

Gruzinski, Serge. 1986a. "Mutilated Memory: Reconstruction of the Past and the Mechanisms of Memory among Seventeenth-Century Otomis." *History and Anthropology* 2(2):337–53.

___. 1986b. "Le Filet déchiré: Sociétés indigènes, occidentalisation et domination coloniale dans le Mexique central, XVIe–XVIIIe siècles." Ph.D. dissertation, University of Paris.

___. 1989. *Man-Gods in the Mexican Highlands, Sixteenth–Eighteenth Centuries*. Stanford, Calif.: Stanford University Press.

____. 1992. *Painting the Conquest: The Mexican Indians and the European Renaissance.* Paris: Flammarion.

____. 1993. *The Conquest of Mexico: The Incorporation of Indian Societies into the Western World, Sixteenth–Eighteenth Centuries.* Translated by Eileen Corrigan. Cambridge: Polity Press.

Gruzinski, Serge, and Nathan Wachtel, eds. 1996. *Le Nouveau Monde/Mondes Nouveaux: L'expérience américaine.* Actes du colloque organisé par le CERMACA (EHESS/CNRS) Paris, June 2–4, 1992. Paris: Éditions Recherche sur les Civilisations, Éditions de l'Ecole des Hautes Etudes en Sciences Sociales.

Guilmartin, John F., Jr. 1991. "The Cutting Edge: An Analysis of the Spanish Invasion and Overthrow of the Inca Empire, 1532–1539." In *Transatlantic Encounters: Europeans and Andeans in the Sixteenth Century,* edited by Kenneth J. Andrien and Rolena Adorno, 40–69. Berkeley: University of California Press.

Handbook of Middle American Indians. 1973–75. Vols. 12–15, *Guide to Ethnohistorical Sources,* edited by Howard F. Cline. Austin: University of Texas Press.

Hanke, Lewis. 1965. *The Spanish Struggle for Justice: The Conquest of America.* Boston: Little, Brown.

Hantman, Jeffrey L. 1992. "Caliban's Own Voice: American Indian Views of the Other in Colonial Virginia." *New Literary History* 23:69–81.

Harris, Max. 1990. "*Indigenismo y Catolicidad:* Folk Dramatizations of Evangelism and Conquest in Central Mexico." *Journal of the American Academy of Religion* 58:55–68.

____. 1992. "Disguised Reconciliations: Indigenous Voices in Early Franciscan Missionary Drama in Mexico." *Radical History Review* 53:13–25.

____. 1993. *The Dialogical Theatre: Dramatizations of the Conquest of Mexico and the Question of the Other.* New York: St. Martin's Press.

____. 1994. "The Arrival of the Europeans: Folk Dramatizations of Conquest and Conversion in New Mexico." *Comparative Drama* 28:141–65.

Harvey, H. R. 1966. "El Lienzo de San Bartolomé Coatepec." *Boletín del Instituto Nacional de Antropología e Historia* (Mexico City) 25:1–5.

____. 1986. "Techialoyan Codices: Seventeenth-Century Indian Land Titles in Central Mexico." In *Supplement to the Handbook of Middle American Indians,* vol. 4, *Ethnohistory,* edited by Ronald Spores, 153–64. Austin: University of Texas Press.

____, ed. 1993. *Códice Techialoyan de Huixquilucan (Estado de México).* Toluca: El Colegio Mexiquense and Gobierno del Estado de México.

Haskett, Robert. 1985. "A Social History of Indian Town Government in the Colonial Cuernavaca Jurisdiction, Mexico." Ph.D. dissertation, University of California, Los Angeles.

____. 1987. "Indian Town Government in Colonial Cuernavaca: Persistence, Adaptation, and Change." *Hispanic American Historical Review* 67(2):203–31.

____. 1988. "Living in Two Worlds: Cultural Continuity and Change among Cuernavaca's Colonial Indigenous Ruling Elite." *Ethnohistory* 35:34–59.

_____. 1990. "Indian Community Land and Municipal Income in Colonial Cuernavaca: An Investigation through Nahuatl Documents." In *The Indian Community of Colonial Mexico: Fifteen Essays on Land Tenure, Corporate Organizations, Ideology and Village Politics,* edited by Arij Ouweneel and Simon Miller, 130–41. Amsterdam: Center for Latin American Research and Documentation.

_____. 1992. "Visions of Municipal Glory Undimmed: The Nahuatl Town Histories of Colonial Cuernavaca." *Colonial Latin American Historical Review* 1:1–36.

_____. 1994. "'Not a Pastor but a Wolf': Indigenous-Clergy Relations in Early Cuernavaca and Taxco." *The Americas* 50:293–336.

_____. 1996. "Paper Shields: The Ideology of Coats of Arms in Colonial Mexican Primordial Titles." *Ethnohistory* 43:99–127.

Hassig, Ross. 1994. *Mexico and the Spanish Conquest.* London: Longman.

Hendrickson, Carol, 1989. "Twin Gods and Quiché Rulers: The Relation between Divine Power and Lordly Rule in the Popol Vuh." In *Word and Image in Maya Culture: Explorations in Language, Writing, and Representation,* edited by William F. Hanks and Don S. Rice, 127–39. Salt Lake City: University of Utah Press.

Hennessy, Alistair. 1993. "The Nature of the Conquest and the Conquistadors." In *The Meeting of Two Worlds: Europe and the Americas, 1492–1650,* edited by Warwick Bray, 5–36. Proceedings of the British Academy, 81. Oxford: Oxford University Press.

Hill, Jonathan D. 1988. "Introduction: Myth and History." In *Rethinking History and Myth: Indigenous South American Perspectives on the Past,* edited by Jonathan D. Hill, 1–17. Urbana: University of Illinois Press.

Hill, Robert M. 1989. "The Social Uses of Writing among the Colonial Cakchiquel Maya: Nativism, Resistance, and Innovation." In *Columbian Consequences,* vol. 3, *The Spanish Borderlands in Pan-American Perspective,* edited by David Hurst Thomas. Washington: Smithsonian Institution Press.

Histoire de la Nation Mexicaine. Depuis le départ d'Aztlan jusqu'à l'arrivée des Conquérants espagnols (et au de lá 1607). Reproduction du Codex de 1576, appartenant à la Collection de M. E. Eugène Goupil. 1893 [1576]. Edited by J. M. A. Aubin. Paris: E. Leroux.

Horn, Rebecca. 1989. "Postconquest Coyoacan: Aspects of Indigenous Sociopolitical and Economic Organization in Central Mexico, 1550–1650." Ph.D. dissertation, University of California, Los Angeles.

_____. 1997. *Postconquest Coyoacan: Nahua-Spanish Relations in Central Mexico, 1519–1650.* Stanford, Calif.: Stanford University Press.

Johnson, Julie Greer. 1993. *Satire in Colonial Spanish America: Turning the New World Upside Down.* Austin: University of Texas Press.

Karttunen, Frances. 1994. *Between Worlds: Interpreters, Guides, and Survivors.* New Brunswick, N.J.: Rutgers University Press.

_____. 1997. "Rethinking Malinche." In *Indian Women of Early Mexico,* edited by Susan Schroeder, Stephanie Wood, and Robert Haskett, 290–312. Norman: University of Oklahoma Press.

Kearney, Michael, and Stefano Varese. 1995. "Latin America's Indigenous Peoples: Changing Identities and Forms of Resistance." In *Capital, Power, and Inequality in Latin America*, edited by Sandor Halebsky and Richard L. Harris, 207–31. Boulder, Colo.: Westview Press.

King, Linda. 1994. *Roots of Identity: Language and Literacy in Mexico*. Stanford: Stanford University Press.

Klor de Alva, J. Jorge. 1991. "Religious Rationalization and the Conversions of the Nahuas: Social Organization and Colonial Epistemology." In *To Change Place: Aztec Ceremonial Landscapes*, edited by Davíd Carrasco, 233–45. Niwot, Colo.: University Press of Colorado.

Klor de Alva, J. Jorge, H. B. Nicholson, and Eloise Quiñones Keber. 1988. *The Work of Bernardino de Sahagún, Pioneer Ethnographer of Sixteenth-Century Aztec Mexico*. Albany and Austin: Institute for Mesoamerican Studies, State University of New York at Albany, and University of Texas Press.

Krippner-Martínez, James. 1990. "The Politics of Conquest: An Interpretation of the *Relación de Michoacan*." *The Americas* 47:177–97.

Larochelle, Gilbert. 1992. "Image and Representation of the Other: North America Views South America." *Diogenes* 157:23–40.

Las Casas, Bartolomé de. 1999 [1552]. *Brevísima relación de la destruición de las Indias*. Madrid: Editorial Castalia.

Lehmann, Walter. 1981. *Geschichte der Azteken: Codex Aubin und verwandte Dokumente: Aztekischer Text. Quellenwerke zur alten Geschichte Amerikas aufgezeichnet in den Sprachen der Eingeborenen*. Bd. 13. Berlin: Gebr. Mann.

Leibsohn, Dana. 1994. "Primers for Memory: Cartographic Histories and Nahua Identity." In *Writing without Words: Alternative Literacies in Mesoamerica and the Andes*, edited by Elizabeth Hill Boone and Walter D. Mignolo, 161–87. Durham, N.C.: Duke University Press.

León-Portilla, Miguel, ed. 1959. *Visión de los vencidos: Relaciones indígenas de la conquista*. Translated by Angel Ma. Garibay K. Mexico City: Universidad Nacional Autónoma de México.

———, ed. 1962. *The Broken Spears: The Aztec Account of the Conquest of Mexico*. Boston: Beacon Press.

———, ed. 1964. *El reverso de la conquista*. Mexico City: Editorial Joaquín Mortiz.

———. 1974. "Testimonios Nahuas sobre la conquista espiritual." *Estudios de Cultura Náhuatl* 11:11–36.

———, ed. 1992. *The Broken Spears: The Aztec Account of the Conquest of Mexico*. Expanded and revised edition. Boston: Beacon Press.

Lewis, Oscar. 1963. *Life in a Mexican Village: Tepoztlán Restudied*. Urbana: University of Illinois Press.

Libro de las tasaciones de pueblos de la Nueva España, siglo XVI. 1952. Prologue by Francisco González de Cossio. Mexico City: Archivo General de la Nación.

Lockhart, James. 1991. *Nahuas and Spaniards: Postconquest Central Mexican History and Philology*. Stanford and Los Angeles: Stanford University Press and UCLA Latin American Center Publications.

———. 1992. *The Nahuas after the Conquest: A Social and Cultural History of the Indians of Central Mexico*. Stanford, Calif.: Stanford University Press.

———. 1993. *We People Here: Nahuatl Accounts of the Conquest of Mexico*. Repertorium Columbianum, vol. 1. Berkeley: University of California Press.

Lockhart, James, Frances Berdan, and Arthur J. O. Anderson. 1986. *The Tlaxcalan Actas: A Compendium of the Records of the Cabildo of Tlaxcala (1545–1627)*. Salt Lake City: University of Utah Press.

Lockhart, James, and Enrique Otte. 1976. *Letters and People of the Spanish Indies: Sixteenth Century*. Cambridge: Cambridge University Press.

Lockhart, James, and Stuart B. Schwartz. 1983. *Early Latin America: A History of Colonial Spanish America and Brazil*. Cambridge Latin American Studies, 46. Cambridge: Cambridge University Press.

López de Mariscal, Blanca. 1997. *La figura femenina en los narradores testigos de la Conquista*. Mexico City: El Colegio de México.

López Sarrelangue, Delfina E. 1965. *La nobleza indígena de Pátzcuaro en la época virreinal*. Mexico City: Universidad Nacional Autónoma de México.

Lunenfeld, Marvin. 1991. *1492, Discovery, Invasion, Encounter: Sources and Interpretations*. Lexington, Mass.: D. C. Heath.

Mapa de Cuauhtlantzinco. 1898. [See: Starr, Frederick.]

Marcus, Joyce. 1992. *Mesoamerican Writing Systems: Propaganda, Myth, and History in Four Ancient Civilizations*. Princeton, N.J.: Princeton University Press.

Martínez, Andrea. 1990. "Las pinturas del Manuscrito de Tlaxcala." *Estudios de Cultura Náhuatl* 20:141–62.

Martínez Marín, Carlos. 1989. "La fuente original del *Lienzo de Tlaxcala*." In *Primer coloquio de documentos pictográficos de tradición náhuatl*, edited by Carlos Martínez Marín, 147–57. Mexico City: Universidad Nacional Autonóma de México.

Mason, Peter. 1990. *Deconstructing America: Representations of the Other*. London: Routledge.

Maxwell, Judith M., and Craig A. Hanson. 1992. *On the Manners of Speaking That the Old Ones Had: The Metaphors of Andrés de Olmos in the TULAL Manuscript, Arte para Aprender la Lengua Mexicana, 1547*. Salt Lake City: University of Utah Press.

Máynez, Pilar, Paciano Blancas, and Francisco Morales. 1995. "Título sobre la fundación de Coatepec de las Bateas." *Estudios de Cultura Náhuatl* 25:263–319.

McAfee, Byron, and Robert H. Barlow. 1952. "Anales de San Gregorio Acapulco." *Tlalocan* 3:103–41.

McClintock, Anne. 1994. "The Angel of Progress: Pitfalls of the Term 'Postcolonialism.'" In *Colonial Discourse, Postcolonial Theory*, edited by Francis Barker,

Peter Hulme, and Margaret Iversen, 253–66. New York: Manchester University Press.

Megged, Amos. 1996. *Exporting the Catholic Reformation: Local Religion in Early Colonial Mexico.* Leiden: E. J. Brill.

Meléndez Aguilar, César J. 1993. "Dibujos a línea de códices tlaxcaltecas." In *La escritura pictográfica en Tlaxcala: Dos mil años de experiencia mesoamericana,* edited by Luis Reyes García, 237–325. Tlaxcala: Universidad Autónoma de Tlaxcala y Centro de Investigaciones y Estudios Superiores en Antropología Social.

Memorial de los indios de Tepetlaóztoc o Códice Kingsborough ". . . a cuatrocientos cuarenta años. . ." 1992. Edited by Perla Valle P. Colección Científica. Mexico City: Instituto Nacional de Antropología e Historia.

Méndez Martínez, Enrique, ed. 1979. *Índice de documentos relativos a los pueblos del Estado de Puebla, Ramo Tierras del Archivo General de la Nación.* Colección Científica; Fuentes (Etnohistoria), 70. Mexico City: Instituto Nacional de Antropología e Historia.

Mignolo, Walter D. 1982. "Cartas, crónicas, y relaciones del descubrimiento y la conquista." In *Historia de la literatura hispanoamericana,* vol. 1, *Epoca colonial,* edited by Luis Iñigo Madrigal. Madrid: Cátedra.

———. 1987. "El mandato y la ofrenda: la descripción de la ciudad y provincia de Tlaxcala, de Diego Muñoz Camargo, y las relaciones de Indias." *Nueva Revista de Filología Hispánica* 35(2):450–79.

———. 1995. *The Darker Side of the Renaissance: Literacy, Territoriality, and Colonization.* Ann Arbor: University of Michigan Press.

Miller, Marilyn. 1997. "Covert *Mestizaje* and the Strategy of 'Passing' in Diego Muñoz Camargo's *Historia de Tlaxcala.*" *Colonial Latin American Review* 6:41–58.

Miranda, Francisco, ed. 1980. *La Relación de Michoacán.* Originally compiled by Fray Jerónimo de Alcalá. Morelia: FIMAX Publicistas Editores.

Molina, Fray Alonso de. 1977 [1555–71]. *Vocabulario en lengua castellana y mexicana y mexicana y castellana.* Preliminary study by Miguel León-Portilla. Second edition. Mexico City: Porrua.

Monaghan, John. 1990. "Verbal Performance and the Mixtec Codices." *Ancient Mesoamerica* 1:133–40.

———. 1994. "The Text in the Body, the Body in the Text: The Embodied Sign in Mixtec Writing." In *Writing without Words: Alternative Literacies in Mesoamerica and the Andes,* edited by Elizabeth Hill Boone and Walter D. Mignolo, 87–101. Durham, N.C.: Duke University Press.

Montiel, Edgar. 1992. "America—Europe: In the Mirror of Otherness." *Diogenes* 159:25–35.

Moreno de los Arcos, Roberto. 1991. "New Spain's Inquisition for Indians from the Sixteenth to the Nineteenth Century." In *Cultural Encounters: The Impact of the Inquisition in Spain and the New World,* edited by Mary Elizabeth Perry and Anne J. Cruz, 23–36. Berkeley: University of California Press.

Motolinia, Fr. Toribio de Benavente. 1951. *Historia de los indios de la Nueva España: Motolinía's History of the Indians of New Spain.* Edited by Francis Borgia Steck. Washington, D.C.: American Academy of Franciscan History.

Mundy, Barbara E. 1996. *The Mapping of New Spain: Indigenous Cartography and the Maps of the Relaciones Geográficas.* Chicago: University of Chicago Press.

Muñoz Camargo, Diego. 1892 [1576–95]. *Historia de Tlaxcala.* Edited by Alfredo Chavero. Mexico City: Secretaría de Fomento.

———. 1981 [1576–95]. *Descripción de la ciudad y provincia de Tlaxcala de las Indias y del mar océano para el buen gobierno y ennoblecimiento dellas.* Edited by René Acuña. Mexico City: Universidad Nacional Autónoma de México.

New Iberian World: A Documentary History of the Discovery and Settlement of Latin America to the Early Seventeenth Century. 1984. 5 vols. Edited by John H. Parry and Robert G. Keith. New York: Times Books.

Nicolau d'Olwer, Luis. 1987. *Fray Bernardino de Sahagun, 1499–1590.* Salt Lake City: University of Utah Press.

Nicolau d'Olwer, Luis, and Howard F. Cline. 1973. "Sahagún and His Works." In *Handbook of Middle American Indians,* vol. 13, *Guide to Ethnohistorical Sources,* part 2, edited by Howard F. Cline, 186–207. Austin: University of Texas Press.

Nuestro pesar, nuestra aflicción / tunetuliniliz, tucucuca: Memorias en lengua náhuatl enviadas a Felipe II por indígenas del Valle de Guatemala hacia 1572. 1996 [1572]. Paleography, translation, essays, and notes by Karen Dakin; introduction and historical notes by Christopher H. Lutz. Mexico City: Universidad Nacional Autónoma de México, Centro de Investigaciones Regionales de Mesoamérica, Instituto de Investigaciones Históricas, and Plumsock Mesoamerican Studies.

O'Crouley, Pedro Alonso. 1972 [1774]. *A Description of the Kingdom of New Spain.* Translated and edited by Seán Galvin. San Francisco: John Howell Books.

Oettinger, Marion, Jr., and Fernando Horcasitas. 1982. "The Lienzo of Petlacala: A Pictorial Document from Guerrero, Mexico." *Transactions* (American Philosophical Society) 72(7):1–67.

Ojeda Díaz, María de los Ángeles. 1985. *Catálogo de códices que se resguardan en la Sección de Testimonios Pictográficos (a partir de 1965).* Mexico City: Instituto Nacional de Antropología e Historia.

Ouweneel, Arij. 1997. "El pasado seguía vivo en Antonio Pérez: Envidias de estamentos de un indígena mexicano, 1757–1761." *Colonial Latin American Review* 6(1):71–96.

Pearce, Roy Harvey. 1953. *The Savages of America: A Study of the Indian and the Idea of Civilization.* Baltimore, Md.: Johns Hopkins University Press.

Pease G. Y., Franklin. 1989. "La conquista española y la percepción andina del otro." *Histórica* (Peru) 13:171–96.

Pellicer, Carlos, and Rafael Carrillo Azpeitia. 1985. *Mural Painting of the Mexican Revolution.* Mexico City: Fondo Editorial de la Plástica Mexicana.

Peñafiel, Antonio. 1909. *Ciudades coloniales y capitales de la república: Estado de Tlaxcala.* Mexico City: Secretaría de Fomento.

Pendergast, David M. 1993. "Worlds in Collision: The Maya/Spanish Encounter in Sixteenth- and Seventeenth-Century Belize." In *The Meeting of Two Worlds: Europe and the Americas, 1492–1650,* edited by Warwick Bray, 105–43. Proceedings of the British Academy, 81. Oxford: Oxford University Press.

Percheron, Nicole. 1983. *Problèmes agraires de L'Ajusco sept communautés agraires de banlieue de Mexico (XVIe–XXe siècles).* Etudes Mesoamericaines, 8. Mexico City: Centre D'Etudes Mexicaines et Centramericaines.

Pohl, John M. D. 1994a. "Mexican Codices, Maps, and Lienzos as Social Contracts." In *Writing without Words: Alternative Literacies in Mesoamerica and the Andes,* edited by Elizabeth Hill Boone and Walter D. Mignolo, 137–60. Durham, N.C.: Duke University Press.

____. 1994b. *The Politics of Symbolism in the Mixtec Codices.* Nashville: Tenn.: Vanderbilt University.

Pratt, Mary Louise. 1993. "Transculturation and Autoethnography: Peru 1615–1980." In *Colonial Discourse/Postcolonial Theory,* edited by Francis Barker, Peter Hulme, and Margaret Iversen, 24–46. Manchester, England: Manchester University Press.

Prem, Hanns J. 1974. *Matrícula de Huexotzinco (Ms. mex. 387 der Bibliothèque Nationale de Paris): Edition-Commentar-Hieroglyphenglossar.* Graz, Austria: Akademische Druck- u. Verlagsanstalt.

____. 1991. "Disease Outbreaks in Central Mexico during the Sixteenth Century." In *"Secret Judgments of God": Old World Disease in Colonial Spanish America,* edited by Noble David Cook and W. George Lovell, 20–48. Norman: University of Oklahoma Press.

Prescott, William H. 1964. *The History of the Conquest of Mexico.* New York: Bantam Books. (Originally published as *History of the Conquest of Mexico, with a Preliminary View of the Ancient Mexican Civilization, and the Life of the Conqueror, Hernando Cortez.* Philadelphia: J. P. Lippincott, 1843.)

Preuss, Konrad Theodor. 1908. "The Ceremony of Awakening (Wine Ceremony) of the Cora Indians." *Proceedings of the International Congress of Americanists, Sixteenth Session,* 489–512. Vienna: A. Hartleben's Verlag.

Price, Richard. 1983. *First-Time: The Historical Vision of an Afro-American People.* Baltimore, Md.: Johns Hopkins University Press.

____. 1990. *Alabi's World.* Baltimore, Md.: Johns Hopkins University Press.

Rabasa, José. 1993. *Inventing America: Spanish Historiography and the Formation of Eurocentrism.* Norman: University of Oklahoma Press.

Ramirez, Susan. 1996. *The World Upside Down: Cross-Cultural Contact and Conflict in Sixteenth-Century Peru.* Stanford, Calif.: Stanford University Press.

Ravicz, Marilyn Ekdahl. 1970. *Early Colonial Religious Drama in Mexico.* Washington, D.C.: Catholic University of America Press.

Redfield, Robert. 1941. *The Folk Culture of Yucatán.* Chicago: University of Chicago Press.

Restall, Matthew B. 1991. "Yaxkukul Revisited: Dating and Categorizing a Controversial Maya Land Document." *UCLA Historical Journal* 11:122–30.

———. 1998. *Maya Conquistador*. Boston: Beacon Press.

Reyes García, Cayetano. 1973. *Índice y extractos de los protocolos de la notaría de Cholula (1590–1600)*. Mexico City: Instituto Nacional de Antropología e Historia.

———. 1995. "El altepetl y la reproducción de la cultura Nahua en la época colonial." In *Tradición e identidad en la cultura mexicana*, with commentary by Ethelia Ruiz, 271–304. Zamora, Michoacan: El Colegio de Michoacan.

Reyes García, Luis, ed. 1993. *La escritura pictográfica en Tlaxcala: Dos mil años de experiencia mesoamericana*. Tlaxcala: Universidad Autónoma de Tlaxcala y Centro de Investigaciones y Estudios Superiores en Antropología Social.

Riley, G. Michael. 1973. *Fernando Cortes and the Marquesado in Morelos, 1522–1547*. Albuquerque: University of New Mexico Press.

Rivera, Agustín. 1993. "La manta de Tlaxcala o de Salamanca." In *La escritura pictográfica en Tlaxcala: Dos mil años de experiencia mesoamericana*, edited by Luis Reyes García, 75–77. Tlaxcala, Mexico: Universidad Autónoma de Tlaxcala y Centro de Investigaciones y Estudios Superiores en Antropología Social.

Rivera, Luis N. 1992. *A Violent Evangelism: The Political and Religious Conquest of the Americas*. Louisville, Ky.: Westminster/John Knox Press.

Robertson, Donald. 1959. *Mexican Manuscript Painting of the Early Colonial Period: The Metropolitan Schools*. New Haven, Conn.: Yale University Press.

———. 1975. "Techialoyan Manuscripts and Paintings, with a Catalog." In *Handbook of Middle American Indians*, vol. 14, *Guide to Ethnohistorical Sources*, part 3, edited by Howard F. Cline, 253–65. Austin: University of Texas Press.

———. 1994. *Mexican Manuscript Painting of the Early Colonial Period: The Metropolitan Schools*. Norman: University of Oklahoma Press.

Robertson, Donald, and Martha Barton Robertson. 1975. "Catalog of Techialoyan Manuscripts and Paintings." In *Handbook of Middle American Indians*, vol. 14, *Guide to Ethnohistorical Sources*, part 3, edited by Howard F. Cline, 265–80. Austin: University of Texas Press.

Rojas Rabiela, Teresa, ed. 1991. *Pedro Armillas: Vida y obra*. Mexico City: Centro de Investigaciones y Estudios Superiores en Antropología Social.

Romero de Terreros, Manuel. 1956. *Antiguas haciendas de México*. Mexico City: Editorial Patria.

Rosaldo, Renato. 1993. "Social Justice and the Crisis of National Communities." In *Colonial Discourse/Postcolonial Theory*, edited by Francis Barker, Peter Hulme, and Margaret Iversen, 239–52. Manchester, England: Manchester University Press.

Roskamp, Hans. 1998. *La historiografía indígena de Michoacán: El lienzo de Jucutacato y los títulos de Carapan*. Leiden: Research School CNWS, Leiden University.

____. n.d. "The Colonial Pictorial Land Titles from Carapan, Michoacan: Legitimation in Indigenous Society." Unpublished manuscript.

Sahagún, Fr. Bernardino de. 1950–1982 [n.d.]. *General History of the Things of New Spain: Florentine Codex.* 13 vols. Santa Fe, N.M., and Salt Lake City: School of American Research and University of Utah Press.

____. 1997 [n.d.]. *Primeros memoriales.* Paleography of Nahuatl te ct and English translation by Thelma D. Sullivan; completed and revised, with additions, by H. B. Nicholson et. al. Norman: University of Oklahoma Press.

Salomon, Frank. 1982. "Chronicles of the Impossible." In *From Oral to Written Expression: Native Andean Chronicles of the Early Colonial Period,* edited by Rolena Adorno, 9–39. Syracuse, N.Y.: Syracuse University Foreign and Comparative Studies Program.

Scholes, France V., and Ralph L. Roys. 1968. *The Maya Chontal Indians of Acalan-Tixchel: A Contribution to the History and Ethnography of the Yucatan Peninsula.* Norman: University of Oklahoma Press.

Schroeder, Susan. 1991. *Chimalpahin and the Kingdoms of Chalco.* Tucson: University of Arizona Press.

Scott, James C. 1985. *Weapons of the Weak: Everyday Forms of Peasant Resistance.* New Haven, Conn.: Yale University Press.

____. 1990. *Domination and the Arts of Resistance: Hidden Transcripts.* New Haven, Conn.: Yale University Press.

Seed, Patricia. 1995. *Ceremonies of Possession in Europe's Conquest of the New World, 1492–1640.* Cambridge: Cambridge University Press.

Sell, Barry David. 1992. "The Good Government of the Ancients: Some Colonial Attitudes about Precontact Nahua Society." *UCLA Historical Journal* 12:152–76.

Sepúlveda y Herrera, María Teresa, ed. 1992. *Catálogo de la Colección de Documentos Históricos de Faustino Galicia Chimalpopoca.* Mexico City: Instituto Nacional de Antropología e Historia.

Simons, Bente Bittmann. 1967. "The Codex of Cholula: A Preliminary Study." *Tlalocan* 5:267–88.

____. 1968. "The Codex of Cholula: A Preliminary Study (cont.)." *Tlalocan* 5:289–339.

Smith, Bradley. 1968. *Mexico: A History in Art.* Garden City, N.Y.: Doubleday.

Solano, Francisco de, ed. 1988. *Relaciones geográficas del Arzobispado de México, 1743.* 2 vols. Colección Tierra Nueva e Cielo Nuevo, 28. Madrid: Consejo Superior de Investigaciones Científicas.

Stannard, David E. 1992. *American Holocaust: Columbus and the Conquest of the New World.* Oxford: Oxford University Press.

Starr, Frederick. 1898. *The Mapa de Cuauhtlantzinco or Códice Campos.* Department of Anthropology, Bulletin 3. Chicago: University of Chicago Press.

Stern, Steve J. 1982. *Peru's Indian Peoples and the Challenge of Spanish Conquest: Huamanga to 1640.* Madison: University of Wisconsin Press.

Stenzel, Werner. 1991. *Quetzalcoatl de Tula: Mitogénesis de una leyenda postcortesiana*. San Nicolás de los Garza, Nuevo León, Mexico: Universidad Autónoma de Nuevo León, Facultad de Filosofía y Letras.

Sweet, David G., and Gary B. Nash, eds. 1981. *Struggle and Survival in Colonial America*. Berkeley: University of California Press.

Szeminski, Jan. 1990 "¿Por qué matar a los españoles? Nuevas perspectivas sobre la ideología andina de la insurrección en el siglo XVIII." In *Resistencia, rebelión, y conciencia campesina en los Andes: Siglos XVIII al XX*, edited by Steve J. Stern, 164–86. Historia Andina, 17. Lima: Instituto de Estudios Peruanos.

Taggart, James M. 1983. *Nahuat Myth and Social Structure*. Austin: University of Texas Press.

Taylor, William B. 1972. *Landlord and Peasant in Colonial Oaxaca*. Stanford, Calif.: Stanford University Press.

———. 1979. *Drinking, Homocide, and Rebellion in Colonial Mexican Villages*. Stanford, Calif.: Stanford University Press.

———. 1993. "Patterns and Variety in Mexican Village Uprisings." In *The Indians in Latin American History: Resistance, Resilience, and Acculturation*, edited by John E. Kicza, 109–40. Wilmington, Del.: Scholarly Resources.

———. 1996. *Magistrates of the Sacred: Priests and Parishioners in Eighteenth-Century Mexico*. Stanford, Calif.: Stanford University Press.

Tedlock, Dennis. 1994. "Creation in the Popul Vuh: A Hermeneutical Approach." In *Symbol and Meaning beyond the Closed Community: Essays in Mesoamerican Ideas*, 77–82. Studies on Culture and Society, 1. Albany: Institute for Mesoamerican Studies, State University of New York at Albany.

Terraciano, Kevin, and Lisa M. Sousa. 1992. "The 'Original Conquest' of Oaxaca: Mixtec and Nahua History and Myth." *UCLA Historical Journal* 12:29–90.

Tichy, Franz. 1979. "Pueblos, haciendas, y ranchos en el area de Puebla-Tlaxcala a fines del siglo XVIII: Aportación a la geografía histórica sobre los asentamientos del altiplano mexicano." In *Mesoamerica: Homenaje al doctor Paul Kirchhoff*, edited by Barbro Dahlgren, 159–64 and map. Mexico City: Instituto Nacional de Antropología e Historia.

Tira de Tepechpan. 1944. Mexico City: Librería Anticuaria G. M. Echaniz.

Título de Totonicapán. 1983. Edited by Robert M. Carmack and James L. Mondloch. Mexico City: Universidad Nacional Autónoma de México.

Todorov, Tzvetan. 1987. *The Conquest of America: The Question of the Other*. Translated from the French by Richard Howard. New York: Harper and Row.

———. 1990. "Los relatos de la conquista." In *Relatos aztecas de la conquista*, edited by Tzvetan Todorov, 449–79. Mexico City: Editorial Grijalbo.

Trexler, Richard C. 1982. "From the Mouths of Babes: Christianization by Children in Sixteenth-Century New Spain." In *Religious Organization and Religious Experience*, edited by J. Davis, 97–114. London: Academic Press.

Turner, Terence. 1988. "Commentary: Ethno-Ethnohistory: Myth and History in Native South American Representations of Contact with Western Society." In

Rethinking History and Myth: Indigenous South American Perspectives on the Past, edited by Jonathan D. Hill, 235–81. Urbana: University of Illinois Press.

Van Young, Eric. 1993. "Agrarian Rebellion and Defense of Community: Meaning and Collective Violence in Late Colonial and Independence-Era Mexico." *Journal of Social History* 27:245–69.

____. 1996. "Dreamscape with Figures and Fences: Cultural Contention and Discourse in the Late Colonial Mexican Countryside." In *Le Nouveau Monde/ Mondes Nouveaux: L'expérience américaine,* edited by Serge Gruzinski and Nathan Wachtel, 137–59. Actes du colloque organisé par le CERMACA (EHESS/CNRS) Paris, June 2–4, 1992. Paris: Editions Recherche sur les Civilisations, Editions de l'Ecole des Hautes Etudes en Sciences Sociales.

Varner, John Grier, and Jeannette Johnson Varner. 1983. *Dogs of the Conquest.* Norman: University of Oklahoma Press.

Vega Sosa, Constanza, ed. 1991. *Códice Azoyú I: El reino de Tlachinollan.* 2 vols. Mexico City: Fondo de Cultura Económica.

Villoro, Luis. 1992. "The Unacceptable Otherness." *Diogenes* 159:57–68.

Wachtel, Nathan. 1977. *The Vision of the Vanquished: The Spanish Conquest of Peru through Indian Eyes, 1530–1570.* Hassocks, England: Harvester Press.

Warren, J. Benedict. 1985. *The Conquest of Michoacán: The Spanish Domination of the Tarascan Kingdom in Western Mexico, 1521–1530.* Norman: University of Oklahoma Press.

Wolf, Eric. 1957. "Closed Corporate Peasant Communities in Mesoamerica and Central Java." *Southwestern Journal of Anthropology* 13:1–18.

Wood, Stephanie. 1984. "Corporate Adjustments in Colonial Mexican Indian Towns: Toluca Region, 1550–1810." Ph.D. dissertation, University of California, Los Angeles.

____. 1987. "Pedro Villafranca y Juana Gertrudis Navarrete: Falsificador de títulos y su viuda (Nueva España, siglo XVIII)." In *Lucha por la supervivencia en América colonial,* edited by David G. Sweet and Gary B. Nash, 472–85. Mexico City: Fondo de Cultura Económica.

____. 1989. "Don Diego García de Mendoza Moctezuma: A Techialoyan Mastermind?" *Estudios de Cultura Náhuatl* 19:245–68.

____. 1990. "The *Fundo Legal* or Lands *Por Razón de Pueblo:* New Evidence from Central New Spain." In *The Indian Community of New Spain: Fifteen Essays on Land Tenure, Corporate Organizations, Ideology, and Village Politics,* edited by Arij Ouweneel and Simon Miller, 117–29. Amsterdam: Center for Latin American Research and Documentation.

____. 1991. "The Cosmic Conquest: Late-Colonial Views of the Sword and Cross in Central Mexican *Títulos.*" *Ethnohistory* 38:176–95.

____. 1997a. "The Social vs. Legal Context of Nahua *Títulos.*" In *Native Traditions in the Postconquest World,* edited by Elizabeth Hill Boone and Tom Cummins, 201–31. Washington, D.C.: Dumbarton Oaks.

____. 1997b. "The Ajusco Town Founding Document: Affinities with Documents of the Sixteenth Century." In *Códices y documentos sobre México: Segundo simposio*, edited by Salvador Rueda Smithers, Constanza Vega Sosa, and Rodrigo Martínez Baracs, 333–48. Mexico City: Instituto Nacional de Antropología e Historia.

____. 1998a. "Testaments and *Títulos:* Conflict and Coincidence of Cacique and Community Interests in Central Mexico." In *Dead Giveaways: Indigenous Testaments of Colonial Mesoamerica and the Andes*, edited by Susan Kellogg and Matthew Restal, 85–111. Salt Lake City: University of Utah Press.

____. 1998b. "El problema de la historicidad de *Títulos* y los códices del grupo Techialoyan." In *De tlacuilos y escribanos: Estudios sobre documentos indígenas coloniales del centro de México*, edited by Xavier Noguez and Stephanie Wood, 167–221. Zinacantepec, Mexico: El Colegio Mexiquense and El Colegio de Michoacán.

____. 1998c. "Sexual Violation in the Conquest of the Americas." In *Sex and Sexuality in Early America*, edited by Merril D. Smith, 9–34. New York: New York University Press.

____. 2000. "¿ El *otro* otro? Interpretando imágenes y descripciones de españoles en los códices y textos indígenas." In *Códices y Documentos sobre México: Tercer Simposio Internacional*, edited by Constanza Vega Sosa. Mexico City: Instituto Nacional de Antropología e Historia, 165–96.

Yamamoto, Yoko Sugiura. 1996. "Tecnología de lo cotidiano." In *Temas mesoamericanos*, edited by Sonia Lombardo and Enrique Nalda, 51–70. Mexico City: Instituto Nacional de Antropología e Historia.

Yáñez, Aníbal, ed. 1992. "The Quincentenary: A Question of Class, Not Race. An Interview with Rigoberta Menchú." *Latin American Perspectives* 74(19):92–103.

Zapata, Roger A. 1992. "'Curacas' y 'Wamanis': La diléctica de la aceptación y rechazo del orden colonial en la 'Nueva corónica' de Guamán Poma." In *De conquistadores y conquistados: Realidad, justificación, representación*, edited by Karl Kohut, 203–11. Frankfurt am Main: Vervuert.

Zavala, Silvio. 1984. *Tributos y servicios personales de indios para Hernán Cortés y su familia: Extracto de documentos del siglo XVI*. Mexico City: Archivo General de la Nación.

Index

All references to illustrations are in italic type.

Acapulco (Atlapulco). *See* San Gregorio Acapulco (Atlapulco)

Accretive cultural manifestations, Lockhart's idea of, 170n.51

Adorno, Rolena, 105, 144, 182n.6

Ahumada, Pedro de, 120

Ajusco narrative, 20, 60–64, 143; executions in, 69–71; gold hunger in, 66–68, 77; invasion-era figures in, 64–66; official approval of, 74–76; prophecies in, 71–73; rape in, 68–69; territorial issues in, 73–74

Alcalá, Jerónimo de, 14, 168n.29

Alcaldes, 111

Alcaldes mayores, 43, *44,* 45, 161n.37, 163n.55

Alphabetical literacy, 14, 25, 145, 155n.25

Altepetl, 74, 111, 122, 177n.6

Alva Ixtlilxochitl, Fernando del, 105, 146

Alvarado, Pedro de, 53, 65, 80, 151n.2, 158n.14, 172n.5

Anawalt, Patricia Rieff, 158n.6, 162nn.43,47, 168n.25

Anderson, Arthur J. O., 161nn.36,42

Annals, 12, 23, 37–38, 112, 141, 178n.10, 183n.15; of Cakchiquels, 159n.17, 161n.39; of Oxkutzcab, 180n.22; of Quauhtitlan, 49, 160n.31; of Tlatelolco, 8, 51; of Tlaxcala, 38; Yucatecan, 180n.22

Anticolonialism, 147

Anti-imperialism, 76, 147, 171n.61

Anti-Spanish attitudes, 21, 59, 75, 76, 96, 99, 131–35, 147, 176n.41

Asunción Milpa Alta, *título* from, 114, 130, 134

Atlauhtla. *See* San Miguel Atlauhtla

Augustinians, 37

Axayacatl *título,* 124, 178–79n.12

Axayacatl Xicotencatl, 33

Axtell, James, 19, 65, 140, 156n.31, 157n.2, 169n.38

Aztecs, 3, 4, 8, 18, 53, 69, 72, 97, 137, 139, 141, 147

Bandelier, Adolph, 79, 85, 90

Baptism, 36, *36,* 39, 82, 88, *89,* 91, 97, 100, 104, 124, 160n.32

Battles and warfare, 26–30, *27, 28,* 33, 115–16, 142

Baudot, Georges, 37, 140, 168n.29

Baumann, Roland, 96, 97, 104, 171n.60, 175n.32

Berdan, Frances F., 13, 152n.7, 154n.19, 157n.6, 161nn.36,42, 162n.47, 168n.25

Bhabha, Homi, 145

Black legend, 4, 152n.6, 159n.18

Bonfil Batalla, Guillermo, 5–6

Bonilla, Heraclio, 7

Boone, Elizabeth Hill, 23, 97, 141, 158n.7